MISSED OPPORTUNITY

MISSED OPPORTUNITY

GORE, INCUMBENCY, AND TELEVISION IN ELECTION 2000

E. D. Dover

Westport, Connecticut
London

Library of Congress Cataloging-in-Publication Data

Dover, E. D.
    Missed opportunity : Gore, incumbency, and television in election 2000 /
E. D. Dover.
        p.   cm.
    Includes bibliographical references and index.
    ISBN 0–275–97638–6 (alk. paper)
        1. Presidents—United States—Election—2000.   2. Television and politics—
United States.   3. Political campaigns—United States.   I. Title.
    JK5262000.D68   2002
    324.973′0929—dc21   2001054585

British Library Cataloguing in Publication Data is available.

Library of Congress Catalog Card Number: 2001054585
ISBN 0–275–97638–6

First published in 2002

Praeger Publishers, 88 Post Road West, Westport, CT 06881
An imprint of Greenwood Publishing Group, Inc.
www.praeger.com

Printed in the United States of America

The paper used in this book complies with the
Permanent Paper Standard issued by the National
Information Standards Organization (Z39.48–1984).

10 9 8 7 6 5 4 3 2 1

TO MOLLY

1/2/03

CONTENTS

1

PRESIDENTIAL ELECTIONS IN THE TELEVISION AGE

In two previous books, *Presidential Elections in the Television Age: 1960–1992* and *The Presidential Election of 1996: Clinton's Incumbency and Television*, I advanced the perspective that the outcomes of modern national elections can be explained by the concept of mediated incumbency. The essential feature of this concept is that outcomes derive from an interplay of the political strength of incumbency and the manner in which news media, particularly television, interpret that strength and transmit it to their audiences. Modern elections are frequently depicted as candidate-centered campaigns. Here, solitary aspirants for office assume the primary responsibilities for advancing their own efforts. They must generate their own financing, develop their won followings, articulate their own messages, and sell themselves to an electorate as social tribunes who lack any attachments to partisan or governmental institutions. Not all candidates possess the same advantages when trying to fulfill these needs, however. Incumbents at all levels of the political order enjoy far greater success then their rivals in attaining the necessary resources for contesting and winning elections. The expansion in the size and scope of government over the past decades has provided incumbents with extensive institutional advantages not available to their political rivals. Incumbents have full-time political employment, opportunities for significant policy-making, access to financial resources, and professional and personal staffs that can enhance their prospects for longevity in office. These advantages lead to the modern electoral phenomenon that most incumbents both seek and attain reelection. The simultaneous increase in candidate-centered campaigns and the growth of efforts to limit the tenure in office of elected officials are not coincidences. Instead, they are a direct result of a political context where incumbency is the most significant of all electoral assets.

A second feature of modern political life is the rise of mediated communication, particularly television, as the primary form of political communication. Most voters have, at best, only an indirect association with governmental institutions and political actors. They can rarely observe the behavior of these by themselves but instead must rely upon mediated messages to acquire vital information and to ascribe meaning to that information. The existence of television in a context of active government and candidate-centered campaigns provides incumbents with some unusually powerful rhetorical opportunities with which to supplement the institutional advantages they derive from their public offices. It also provides some important opportunities for their rivals in the competition for power. Among the more politically significant components of television are the identification and reporting of news by large commercial organizations. Their product, televised news, is now the leading source of information for most voters about both the conduct of government and the promises made by candidates for public office. Televised news differs from political advertising in that incumbents and their rivals are unable to dictate its content. The content of televised news is the product of its creators, the reporters and producers referred to here as *television news media*. In addition, few observers would conclude that televised news is neutral in its effects. The visual imagery and verbal narratives that it comprises are significant components of the construction of meaning by individual members of viewing audiences. Many observers of American elections believe that voters cast their ballots while making retrospective evaluations of the immediate past. The meanings that voters derive or develop from mediated information can be critical to the evaluations they make of the performances and promises of the political actors who solicit their support. For these reasons, I have focused attention on the importance of mediated incumbency in the conduct and outcome of presidential elections.

Incumbency, mediated or not, is a far more significant factor in election outcomes today than it has been at any time in our national history. For example, in 1994, the Republicans recorded massive gains in Congress and attained majority control of the Senate and House of Representatives. Their takeover of the House was particularly impressive in the sense that it ended forty years of Democratic control of that chamber. The Republicans gained fifty-two seats from their partisan rivals that year. Overshadowed by this sweeping triumph was the fact that over 92 percent of the incumbents who ran for reelection to the House won despite this national partisan trend. The Republicans acquired over thirty of their new seats in districts where the incumbent Democrat did not seek another term. Democrats had retained control of the House for many years before 1994 because most of their members kept winning reelection; the Republicans have accomplished much the same since then. Incumbents have also dominated recent presidential elections, particularly nominations, although some incumbents have failed in their quests for second terms. In every election since 1956, the presidential party, that is, the one holding executive office, nominated the incumbent for another term regardless of how successful a president the incumbent might have been, or, if the incumbent had not been available, chose the vice president as its standard bearer. With this pattern in mind, I advanced the argument in my previous books that modern elections divide into three categories based on the strength of presidential incumbency: "elections with strong incumbents," "elections with weak incumbents," and "elections with surrogate incumbents." The first category consists of those tallies in which the incumbent wins; it includes 1956, 1964, 1972, 1984, and 1996. The second category contains the ones in which the incumbent loses, 1976, 1980, and 1992. The third, a major subject of this book, consists of elections when the presidential party nominates the vice president for the nation's highest office. This category composes four recent elections, 1976, 1980, 1988, and, most recently, 2000.

Incumbent presidents have been helped in their efforts at winning reelection by the institutional and rhetorical opportunities provided by the growth of government and the rise of television that did not exist until recently. Some presidents have used them well and have been rewarded with some of the most one-sided electoral victories in history; others have failed to grasp these new opportunities and have been swept from office. Incumbency has become so important as a factor in electoral outcomes that several political observers have developed mathematical models that predict the likelihood of success or failure by incumbent presidents at winning second terms. They have based these models on such factors as the condition of the national economy, the incumbent's standings in public opinion surveys, or the way the president may have fared in a number of political battles. I have discussed recurring patterns in the two categories of elections when incumbents seek new terms, strong and weak, and have shown that important differences relating to the performances of incumbents and the patterns employed by television news media in interpreting those performances exist between them. Strong and weak incumbents differ from one another on a variety of dimensions ranging from political accomplishments to communicative effectiveness. Television news media treat them differently as well. They structure their reporting in ways that often generate consensus behind strong incumbents and dissensus behind weak ones. In addition, they depict the campaigns for the nominations of the presidential and opposition parties in vastly different ways, depending on whether they perceive the incumbent as strong or weak. In those instances when they see the incumbent as strong, they illustrate him through imagery in which he appears to be governing the nation in a statesmanlike manner. When the incumbent appears weak, television news media focus on his problems and employ imagery in which he appears beleaguered and vulnerable. They also vary in their depictions of the incumbents' partisan opposition. In elections when a strong incumbent seeks reelection, television news media direct much of their attention toward divisive political conflicts and actors within the opposition party. They depict the leading contender from the nomination of the opposition party as a qualified alternative to the incumbent in those years when a weak incumbent seeks reelection.

The 2000 election, despite its many unusual features, was in a number of ways quite similar to the three earlier elections with surrogate incumbents. Beginning with Richard Nixon in 1960, we have seen the sitting vice president seek the highest office on four different occasions during the past four decades. Although Nixon, Hubert Humphrey in 1968, George Bush in 1988, and Al Gore may have met with varying degrees of success in their general election endeavors, all did win the nominations of their parties. The nomination of the vice president as the new leader of the presidential party when an incumbent retires has become so commonplace in American elections that most political observers believed Al Gore would be the 2000 Democratic nominee long before Bill Clinton had ever been inaugurated for his second term. This is a modern phenomenon, however. Before Nixon the last time when a vice president won a presidential nomination was 1836, when the Democrats advanced Martin van Buren as a successor to Andrew Jackson.

Every incumbent president who has sought reelection during the past half-century has either led his rival in national polls through most of the general election campaign or constantly trailed his rival during that same time. This is not true with the elections involving the four vice presidents, however. The vice presidents were all involved in competitive races with the outcomes often in doubt. The elections of 1960, 2000, and 1968 in that order have been the three closest elections of the past century. Each was decided by a popular vote difference of less than 1 percent. These three elections ended with the vice president's losing, however, and raise an important question. Is the vice presidency a double-edged sword in that it is a valuable stepping stone to a party nomination but a barrier to a general election victory? These elections were close enough that one may advance legitimate arguments about how chance happenings may have influenced the outcome, such as the vote count in Florida in 2000. Only one election with a surrogate incumbent resulted in a vice presidential triumph. The existence of one such election, 1988, and the closeness of the others suggest that one should not conclude that the vice presidency is necessarily a barrier to a general election victory. Instead, the electoral opportunities posed by the modern vice presidential office are ambiguous and worthy of consideration. We are certainly safe in assuming that other vice presidents in future decades will win the nominations of their party for president and then encounter some very uncertain prospects in their own general election bids. Elections with surrogate incumbents have occurred with such frequency in recent decades that one must now view them as recurring and integral components of the electoral process that are worthy of theoretical inquiry.

As suggested by the title, the central question to be answered in this book is to explain why Vice President Al Gore lost the election of 2000 rather than why his rival, Governor George W. Bush of Texas, won. Gore was the surrogate incumbent and occupied an office with unique institutional and rhetorical features that have become a central part of presidential elections and even the presidency itself. A study of the role played by mediated incumbency in elections when the president cannot succeed himself must necessarily focus on the words and deeds of the vice president rather than on those of his challenger. The central goal of my analysis is to determine what opportunities the vice presidential office raised for Gore and what dilemmas it posed for him. I also want to know how effectively Gore exploited these opportunities. The vice-presidential office and political context that Gore encountered also raised some unique dilemmas for his challenger George W. Bush. I also seek to determine the nature of those dilemmas and find out how well Bush confronted them. The vice presidency is an office of considerable importance in relation to presidential elections and will certainly remain so during coming years. The vice president has been the nominee of the presidential party in four of the past eleven elections. In addition, five other elections during this same time have included a former vice president as the nominee of one of the political parties. The incumbents Lyndon Johnson (1964), Richard Nixon (1972), Gerald Ford (1976), and George Bush (1992) were vice presidents when they assumed the nation's highest office; the opposition party nominees Richard Nixon (1968) and Walter Mondale (1984) were former vice presidents when they sought the presidency. In all, a sitting or former vice president has been the nominee of one of the major parties in nine of the past eleven presidential elections.

This chapter focuses attention on two matters, an introduction to the theme of mediated incumbency and a discussion of the historical and political reasons why the vice presidency has become an important institution in national elections. This discussion looks at the events that guided the creation of the vice presidency and other events that led to the decline of the office during much of the nineteenth century. The resurgence of the position as an office of some significance during the first half of the twentieth century follows. The chapter concludes with a review of the extensive development of the office during the past half-century as a major component of the contemporary presidency and includes a description of the partisan and electoral roles that have become so central to it.

The second chapter looks at previous elections with surrogate incumbents and general patterns of televised news coverage of election campaigns. There were several common features that distinguished these previous elections from others that have had actual incumbents. A review of these features is provided in ways that structure the expectations one would have about their recurrence in 2000. This chapter also focuses attention on the practices that television news media employ when reporting and interpreting the variety of events that occur in presidential elections. Particular emphasis is given to the extraordinary attention that news correspondents give to the electoral "horse race," that is, the battle for advantage they see occurring among the many candidates, and to the stereotypical roles they often assign to individual candidates, which depend on the way those candidates fit into the horse race.

The campaigns for the party nominations are the topics of the next two chapters. Chapter 3 looks at how these campaigns developed, often out of public sight, during 1999; Chapter 4 focuses attention on the highly public battles among the candidates in the caucuses and primaries of the first three months of 2000. These two chapters, and the two that follow, direct the reader's attention to the manner in which television news media illustrated the leading events of the campaign. The actions of the various candidates were available to most voters only through the mediated information provided by television. News media provided context and meaning for much of that information but did so in a manner that conformed to their perceptions of the campaigns' being horse races between stereotyped role playing combatants. These chapters describe the context and meaning that television news media ascribed to the campaigns and candidates. Chapter 3 begins in January 1999, when the numerous candidates for the party nominations started making their public announcements of intent; Chapter 4 ends on March 9, when the last remaining rivals of Gore and Bush concluded their failed efforts.

The eight-month general election campaign is discussed in Chapters 5 and 6. This phase of the campaign was long even by modern standards. Campaigns have become longer in recent decades as states have scheduled their primaries at earlier and earlier dates while finance laws have forced candidates to begin their fund-raising efforts about one year before an election. The rapid conclusion of the nomination campaigns within both parties by March 9 brought about an immediate focus on the general election even though Bush and Gore both lacked running mates and would not officially win their endorsements until August. The general election phase divided into four unequal parts. The first and longest of them encompasses the time between March and late July and includes the interim between the end of the primaries and the onset of the national conventions. This was when the candidates were attempting to reunite their partisans after the divisive primary battles. The second part, which was the shortest, includes convention-related events such as the selection of the running mates and the extensive television coverage of the quadrennial meetings that now render few important decisions. The events between March and August are discussed in Chapter 5.

The postconvention parts began on August 19 with the adjournment of the final national convention and extended through November 6, election eve. They divide about evenly into the predebate time of late August and the entire month of September and the debate period and its aftermath, all of October and the first week of November. The two candidates and their running mates spent the predebate time appealing to undecided voters in key states while the correspondents of network television illustrated them as combatants seeking advantages in the horse race that was the election campaign. The arrival of the debates in early October, three for the presidential and one for the vice-presidential candidates, changed the nature of the campaign. The candidates spent most of their time in practice sessions and in the debates themselves while television news media offered extensive analysis of the political effects of each candidate's verbal and visual performances. Finally, the last weeks of the campaign involved the candidates' rallying their faithful supporters to the polls in frantic get-out-the-vote drives while the broadcast networks kept count through tracking polls and colored maps of the likely Electoral College outcome. These features are discussed in Chapter 6.

The results and meaning of the election are reviewed in the final chapter, Chapter 7. The initial sections look at the results from two perspectives: statewide votes as cast in the Electoral College and voter preferences by identifiable group. The groups are based on such factors as income, sex, education, urbanization, ideology, and opinions on a variety of issues, including Clinton's performance as president and Clinton's personal behavior. The polling data used here are from the exit polls taken by the Voter News Service, a consortium financed by the television networks. Perhaps the most unusual feature of the election was the thirty-six day legal battle relating to the vote count in Florida. A summary of the major components of that controversy as they affected the election is provided here. The chapter concludes with a reconsideration of the three most significant recurring features of elections with surrogate incumbents that were initially discussed in Chapter 2. All three resurfaced in various ways in 2000. The chapter looks at how Bush and Gore both failed to master the dilemmas each faced that were unique to their positions of incumbent and challenger. It also explains how the election was a missed opportunity for Gore by showing how he failed to translate the advantages of incumbency into a victory in a year when the nation enjoyed peace abroad and prosperity at home.

A brief note about sources is in order. In focusing on the mediated aspect of this campaign, I have relied upon the daily telecasts of the three major networks, the American Broadcasting Company (ABC), the Columbia Broadcasting System (CBS), and the National Broadcasting Company (NBC), for most of data. There are other components of television news of course, including cable news, but I have chosen to use the three networks because of their long-time history of reporting about presidential election campaigns and the size of their viewing audiences. I have relied on polling data from the consortium of the Gallup Poll, Cable News Network (CNN) and *USA Today* in addition to the exit polls of the Election News Service. The Gallup organization has a long history of campaign polling and of measuring the performance of incumbents in office. This consortium also published more polls related to the election and did so over a longer period than any of the three networks.

EVOLUTION OF THE VICE PRESIDENCY

Origins and Early History

The vice presidency, as both a political office and a governmental institution, has evolved through four distinct eras, according to Michael Nelson, author of *A Heartbeat Away: Report of the Twentieth Century Task Force on the Vice Presidency*. The first of these is the founding period, which dates from the drafting of the Constitution in 1787 to the ratification of the Twelfth Amendment in 1804. The second includes the nineteenth century, that is, the years from 1804 to 1900, a time Nelson depicts as the nadir of the vice presidency, when the office enjoyed little respect or power. The first half of the twentieth century, beginning with the candidacy of Theodore Roosevelt in 1900 and proceeding to the ascension of Harry Truman as president in 1945, which was a time when the office grew in stature and importance, constitutes the third period. The fourth, the modern period, encompasses the years after 1945, when the vice presidency developed into a significant political and institutional office and emerged as a powerful stepping stone to a presidential nomination (Nelson 1988, 25). I discuss each of these in turn.

The vice presidential office originated in 1787 at the Constitutional Convention as part of the debate that created other national governmental institutions. It was not a matter that occupied a central part of the debate, however. Joel Goldstein, a leading scholar on the vice presidency, says the office was created for reasons that are, at best, obscure and, at worst, illogical. He identifies three reasons for its creation, including the pressing need of the framers to designate a presiding officer for the newly created Senate (Goldstein 1982, 4–6). With the Senate composed of two persons from each state, the ascension of one of a state's members to the presiding role would dilute the voting power of that state by half. Moreover, the framers did not wish to vest the tie-breaking power that accompanies the presiding role in a member of the Senate (Natoli 1985, 3). A vice president who was not an elected member of the Senate would fulfill the need for a presiding officer who could vote in instances of ties.

The second reason Goldstein identifies was to provide a constitutional means of succession to a vacant presidential office. Their language was obscure in the sense that it provided only that the powers and duties of the president would devolve on the vice president when the presidential office was vacant. It was unclear about whether the vice president would actually assume the office or simply serve until Congress could plan for a new election. The succession of a vice president to the presidency was not decided until 1841, when William Henry Harrison died after serving only one month of his term and John Tyler assumed office. Tyler proclaimed himself president and announced that he did not wish to be addressed as the "Acting President." The nation accepted his interpretation. Nelson adds that the vice-presidential office was also created to ensure that someone was well prepared to assume the presidency at a moment's notice and to prevent the Senate from having a stake in presidential vacancies (Nelson 1988, 5, 26–27).

Goldstein writes that the vice presidency was created in order to facilitate the election of a president. The framers opposed popular elections and proposed the indirect method of the Electoral College instead. They anticipated the problem that individual electors might face substantial pressures to vote for candidates from their own states. The framers responded by providing each elector with two votes and the stipulation that at least one had to be cast for a person who was not a resident of the elector's state. The person with the largest number of electoral votes, provided it constituted a majority of the total number of electors, would become president, and the person with the second highest number would become vice president. The requirement that the second-place finisher become vice president assured that each elector would take both votes seriously (Nelson 1988, 5).

Despite these ambiguous origins, the vice-presidential office had a promising beginning. The presidential election of 1789, the nation's first, ended exactly as the framers had anticipated. George Washington attained the votes of all sixty-nine electors and became president; John Adams finished in second place with thirty-four votes and became vice president. The remaining votes were cast for a wide variety of individuals whose support rarely extended beyond the boundaries of their own states or regions. Adams entered office with a history of a distinguished public career. He had served in the Massachusetts legislature between 1770 and 1774 and from 1774 to 1777 had been a member of the Continental Congress, in which he served on the Declaration of Independence drafting committee. In addition, he had held several important diplomatic positions between 1777 and 1787 in France, the Netherlands, and Great Britain. Adams was one of the negotiators for the treaty that ended the Revolutionary War and was the first American ambassador to Britain (DeGregorio 1993, 24–27).

As vice president, Adams took an active role in what was as yet a body without customs and traditions. He regularly presided over the chamber, guided the agenda, intervened in debate, and cast twenty-nine tie-breaking votes, a total that is still a record for vice presidents (Nelson 1988, 28). In contrast, Gore cast only four important tie-breaking votes during his first seven years in office, including one in favor of the initial Clinton budget in 1993 and one in 1999 supporting a new gun control law in the aftermath of a fatal school shooting in Littleton, Colorado. After two terms as Washington's vice president, Adams was elected president in the election of 1796. He failed to win a second term in 1800 and was succeeded by his own vice president, Thomas Jefferson.

Jefferson also entered the vice presidency with extensive qualifications of service in both state and national government. He served in the Virginia colonial legislature from 1769 to 1774 and the state legislature between 1776 and 1779, and he had been his state's governor for one term during 1779 to 1781. Nationally, he was the primary author of the Declaration of Independence, a member of the Continental Congress in 1783 and 1784, minister to France from 1785 to 1789, and Washington's secretary of state from 1790 to 1793 (DeGregorio 1993, 44–46).

There were problems with the vice presidency, however, and they quickly emerged during the Washington, Adams, and Jefferson presidencies. These problems eventually led to political and constitutional changes that ultimately reduced the office in stature and significantly weakened the quality of its occupants. Thomas Cronin, president of Whitman College and author of several books about presidential power, believes these problems derived from the fact that the office was a constitutional hybrid in that it appeared to be both legislative and executive in nature. The constitutional requirement that the vice president serve as the presiding officer of the Senate suggests a legislative emphasis, but this in undermined by the fact that the vice president is not an elected legislator and does not participate in senatorial debate. The election of the vice president in conjunction with the president and the constitutional requirement that the duties and powers of the presidential office devolve on him in cases of vacancies suggest instead that the office is executive. Unlike all other executives, however, the vice president is not subject to senatorial confirmation, has no constitutionally named executive responsibilities, and cannot be directed by the president (Cronin and Genovese 1998, 316–321).

Whereas the relationship between Washington and Adams was cordial, the relations between the next two presidents and vice presidents were not. The constitutional requirement that electors vote for two presidential candidates proved to be a serious defect after the retirement of Washington in 1796. Two political parties had developed and actively opposed one another for the presidency. Adams, the Federalist Party candidate, attained a slim majority of 71 of 138 electoral votes and became president. Several of Adams's supporters failed to vote for Thomas Pinckney, the other Federalist candidate, however; Pinckney garnered only 59 votes and finished third behind Jefferson, the candidate of the Democratic-Republicans. Jefferson, with 68 votes, thus became vice president. Despite this unusual outcome, Adams sought to involve Jefferson in a meaningful executive role. He asked him to serve as a member of a three-man delegation to France designed to calm a turbulent relationship that had developed between the two nations during some of the more violent phases of the French Revolution. Jefferson refused, arguing that a diplomatic role was improper for the vice president. He preferred to be free of attachments to the executive branch so he could criticize Adams from his legislative leadership position (Hatfield 1997, 21). Jefferson used this legislative position to develop his candidacy in 1800, when he once again opposed Adams.

Jefferson encountered vice-presidential problems of his own, however, some that the framers also had not foreseen. He attained seventy-three electoral votes in the tally of 1800 while limiting Adams to only sixty-five. To prevent repetition of the 1796 decision, both political parties exerted far more discipline on their electors this time and encouraged them to vote for both of their candidates. The Federalists anticipated a serious drawback with this approach, however, and planned to resolve it by designating an elector who would have the responsibility of casting one of his ballots for John Jay, who was not one of the party's candidates that year. Consequently, Charles C. Pinckney, brother of Thomas Pinckney and the Federalist candidate for vice president, attained sixty-four votes, one less than Adams. If Adams had been reelected, Pinckney would have replaced Jefferson as vice president. The Democratic-Republicans failed to anticipate this problem, however, as both of their candidates, Jefferson and Aaron Burr, received seventy-three votes. The tie forced the election into the House of Representatives, where each of the sixteen states held one vote. Burr refused to defer to Jefferson and attempted to win the presidency through this House vote. He did not succeed but did create considerable havoc while trying. The election was not resolved until the thirty-sixth ballot, when several Federalist congressmen who had been voting for Burr abstained. This gave Jefferson enough votes to assure the victory he thought he had won earlier.

Nelson believes Burr's nomination demonstrates that the parties had already started degrading the vice presidency into a device for ticket balancing (Nelson 1988, 29). Burr was from New York, a state that had cast its electoral vote for Adams in 1796. The Democratic-Republicans won control of the New York legislature in April 1800, thus allowing them the opportunity to choose the state's electors. Several states, including New York, required legislative choice of electors during the first decades of the nineteenth century. Burr's candidacy gave Jefferson the New York votes and greatly strengthened the Virginian's electoral chances.

The difficulties relating to the vice presidency that derived from the 1796 and 1800 elections encouraged Congress to initiate the Twelfth Amendment, which required separate ballots for president and vice president. This method transformed vice presidential nominees into partisan running mates of presidential candidates and eliminated the independence of the office. Steve Tally, author of *Bland Ambition*, a description of the individuals who have been vice president, states that the vice presidency soon became a second-rate office, to which only second-rate men aspired (Tally 1992, 35).

The running mate role, by itself, was not completely responsible for the decline of the vice presidency and for the low status of the office during the nineteenth century, but it was certainly a significant factor. A related and perhaps equally important cause derived from the practice of party leaders of selecting candidates for national office. The candidate-centered campaigns of the late twentieth century, in which solitary individuals seek the presidency by making personal appeals to voters through mass communication and voters directly choose partisan nominees through primary elections, did not exist in the nineteenth century. Party leaders chose their presidential nominees at national conventions while individual aspirants conformed to the political norms of the time and did not actively seek the office. Party leaders would supplement their choices by selecting the vice presidential nominees on the basis of electoral criteria, the geographical or factional balance such candidates could give the national ticket (Nelson 1988, 29).

This practice weakened the office because presidents had virtually no personal stake in the selection of their running mates. With little to gain by employing them in meaningful ways, presidents usually excluded vice presidents from their administrations. In order to justify, or perhaps rationalize, these exclusions, presidents often relied upon two constitutional arguments. They would claim the vice presidency was a legislative office, with the separation of powers doctrine's precluding vice presidents from executive responsibilities, and they would proclaim that the executive power, granted in Article II, was vested exclusively in the president (Goldstein 1982, 137–139). This practice did not change until Franklin D. Roosevelt insisted on selecting his own running mate during his third-term campaign of 1940 and, after finally accomplishing this, assigning executive responsibilities to him once in office. Roosevelt even hinted he would not accept the Democratic nomination unless the party honored his wishes. Roosevelt's success in this demand ended party leader choice of vice presidential nominees and contributed to the modern view that the vice presidency is an executive office (Cronin and Genovese 1998, 319).

The diminished status of vice presidents after the ratification of the Twelfth Amendment was not limited to their exclusion from the executive branch; their legislative importance also declined. The Senate eventually developed a variety of norms, traditions, and procedures in the decades following the Adams and Jefferson terms that excluded the vice president from any meaningful political activities. Moreover, the antebellum Senate featured a number of famous personalities, such as Henry Clay and Daniel Webster, whose presence often overshadowed that of the vice president. John C. Calhoun, in office between 1825 and 1832, was the last vice president who could appoint senators to standing committees (Nelson 1988, 30). It is perhaps ironic that Calhoun resigned as vice president in a dispute with Andrew Jackson, was then elected as a senator, and eventually became far more influential in this new role than he had been previously as vice president.

The list of nineteenth-century vice presidents is far from impressive. After Calhoun, none was nominated for a second term. Moreover, party leaders were so concerned with balancing their tickets for electoral purposes that they frequently failed to consider the health of nominees. Six vice presidents died in office during this century, compared to none during the twentieth century. Perhaps the strongest evidence of the mediocrity of nineteenth century vice presidents is that not one of the four who succeeded to the presidency as a result of a vacancy in that office received the nomination for president of his party in the next election. In contrast, all five vice presidents who succeeded to the vacant presidential office during the twentieth century were nominated for reelection. This lowly status of the vice presidency would soon change, however.

The Early Twentieth Century

The vice presidency increased moderately in importance during the first half of the twentieth century, although it remained essentially a legislative office. Nelson advances three reasons to account for this newfound status, including the nomination changes discussed previously. The office also grew in stature through the development of both the national news media and the new styles of campaigning that eventually dominated presidential elections. Growth in the readership of mass circulation magazines and creation of newspaper wire services contributed to the development of more nationally focused media. Magazines drew readers' attention to many of the same concerns, and wire services provided similarity in information in newspapers in all parts of the nation (Nelson 1988, 31).

A distinguishing feature of nineteenth-century presidential elections was that candidates were not expected to campaign for office, even after receiving a party nomination. Instead, they left the active campaigning to party organizations and elected officials. This practice changed with the nomination of William Jennings Bryan by the Democrats in 1896, however. Bryan traveled extensively that year, breaking old traditions, speaking at partisan rallies, and ushering in a new campaign style that was imitated by nearly all nominees of the twentieth century. Bryan's efforts even forced the Republican nominee, William McKinley, to campaign, although McKinley hardly attempted to imitate his Democratic rival. McKinley spoke from the front porch of his Ohio home to crowds of visitors who had traveled by rail to meet and hear him, while his campaign manager Mark Hanna raised much of the money needed for paying these fares from supportive corporate interests. Despite losing that year's election, Bryan won the Democratic nomination again in 1900 and engaged in yet another personal solicitation for votes. The Republicans countered Bryan by nominating Theodore Roosevelt, governor of New York, as McKinley's new running mate. Roosevelt easily matched Bryan's efforts by delivering 673 speeches in twenty-four states to approximately three million listeners (Nelson 1988, 31). With this, the vice presidency ceased to be a political office whose primary purpose was balancing a partisan ticket. Roosevelt enhanced the office and contributed to an increase in the quality of its future nominees. This active campaign role also helped vice presidents become more popular and better established with party activists (Nelson 1988, 43).

Despite these changes, the power and prestige of the vice presidency did not increase significantly during the first half of the twentieth century. Granted, presidents began assigning more responsibilities than campaigning to their vice presidents, but it was not until Richard Nixon held office during the 1950s that these changes actually had any meaningful institutional impact. Nonetheless, the seeds of an activist vice presidency were planted in the early twentieth century even though the position remained essentially hollow until Nixon (Goldstein 1982, 137).

Gradual changes were soon apparent, however. Thomas R. Marshall, governor of Indiana, became the first two-term vice president since Calhoun when he won reelection in 1916 on Woodrow Wilson's ticket. Wilson assigned Marshall the task of speaking at rallies on behalf of the sale of war bonds. In addition, Marshall presided over cabinet meetings during the seven months Wilson spent in Europe in 1919 (Hatfield 1997, 341–342). Warren G. Harding started the practice of inviting the vice president, Calvin Coolidge in this instance, to meet regularly with the cabinet (Nelson 1988, 32). After succeeding to office on Harding's death in 1923, Coolidge won his own term a year later with Charles Dawes as his running mate. Dawes had held high offices in three previous administrations, including a term as the initial director of the Bureau of the Budget, and had been awarded the Nobel Peace Prize for his restructuring of German war reparations. Charles Curtis and John Nance Garner, vice presidents under Herbert Hoover and Franklin D. Roosevelt, were serving as Senate majority leader and House speaker, respectively, when they were nominated by their party conventions (Nelson 1988, 32).

Garner was a transitional figure in the vice presidency whose time in office was a watershed in the evolution of the office (Hatfield 1997, 323). He had sought the Democratic presidential nomination in 1932 but ceased his efforts after the third convention ballot. With this, the Democrats united behind Roosevelt and then added Garner to the ticket. Garner's experiences as speaker helped him fulfill an important legislative liaison role in the Roosevelt administration in which he used his influence with individual members to advance the New Deal agenda. His influence declined substantially, however, during his second term, when he opposed several of Roosevelt's policies, because many congressmen realized he was no longer a member of the inner circle of presidential advisers. Garner was not interested in a third term in 1940. Mark Hatfield, former U.S. senator from Oregon and author of a book about the vice presidents, describes Garner as the last of the Washington-based vice presidents whose duties were primarily legislative, before "the coming age of telecommunications and travel enabled future vice presidents to assume higher profiles as representatives of their administrations, as wide-ranging campaigners, public spokesmen, and foreign emissaries" (Hatfield 1997, 323).

A far-reaching and significant change occurred in the relationship between the president and vice president in 1940 after Roosevelt demanded that the Democratic convention honor his choice of Henry Wallace, at the time secretary of agriculture, as his vice presidential running mate. With this, the vice presidency became more closely associated with the executive branch. Governance criteria outweighed electoral criteria in vice presidential choice. Competence to hold high executive office and personal loyalty to the president replaced political balance as the leading selection criteria for potential vice presidents (Nelson 1988, 33–34). Previous reliance on election criteria had discouraged vice presidential competence because many potential candidates realized they might be dropped from the ticket after only a single term. The prospect of being replaced forced many talented political leaders to reject the office (Nelson 1988, 43–44).

The greater quality of vice presidential nominees has encouraged both voters and media to display an intense interest in a presidential candidate's running mate choice, Nelson writes. The choice reveals the candidate's judgment since the vice president serves as insurance in the event of a future tragedy. A running mate of questionable competence can invite unfavorable press coverage of a presidential nominee and may well compromise that nominee's electoral prospects. Running mate searches are now designed to "yield a reasoned, responsible selection sensitive for the public desire for a worthy presidential successor" (Nelson 1988, 45). The enhanced role of the modern vice president is also apparent in the enactment of the Twenty-Fifth Amendment, which describes circumstances of presidential disability in which the vice president will serve as acting president. It also provides a means for filling a vice presidential vacancy without waiting until the next election, an event that was nearly four years away in the case of Truman (Nelson 1988, 3–4).

Presidential control of the selection process has increased the compatibility between presidents and their vice presidents and has encouraged presidents to use their vice presidents as administrative and partisan spokesmen, particularly with party activists. Presidents frequently strive to create public images as nonpartisan statesmen. They encounter a dilemma when they assume the role of party spokesman while seeking to preserve this statesmanlike imagery, however, and tend to resolve it by assigning the partisan role to the vice president (Goldstein 1982, 141–142).

After insisting on the right to choose his own vice president, Roosevelt appointed Wallace to an unprecedented number of executive responsibilities. At various times during the Second World War, Wallace chaired the Economic Defense Board, the Supply Priorities and Allocations Board, the War Productions Board, and the Board of Economic Warfare (Light 1984, 14). Roosevelt established the first of these, the Economic Defense Board, in July 1941 to purchase strategic materials for a future war; Roosevelt later created the other boards, to oversee the domestic economy, strategic imports, exports, shipping, and foreign exchange (Cronin and Genovese 1998, 322). Wallace was a forerunner of the modern vice president, Hatfield writes, in that he served as an executive assistant and international emissary for the president. Wallace took a particularly active role in foreign policy in that he was the first vice president to travel abroad and often served as the president's personal ambassador (Hatfield 1997, 399–403).

The personal relationship between Roosevelt and Wallace eventually soured, and Roosevelt sought a new running mate in 1944. The Democratic convention, with Roosevelt's encouragement, denied Wallace renomination and bestowed the vice presidential nomination on Harry S Truman. It is impossible to determine what role Truman might have played as vice president if Roosevelt had not died three months into his fourth term. It is likely he would have developed a role similar to that of Wallace, although he might very well have had a better personal relationship with Roosevelt. Truman's ascension to the presidency during the critical final stages of the Second World War and the need for strong presidential leadership in the emerging postwar world convinced many people of the importance of the vice presidency. They also helped set in motion a variety of events that increased the powers and prestige of the office and the political quality of its occupants.

DEVELOPMENT OF THE MODERN PRESIDENCY

To appreciate fully the expanded importance of the vice presidency's executive and political roles during the second half of the twentieth century, one must also be aware of the institutional and rhetorical development of the presidency that occurred during this same time. The vice presidency of today, and particularly its surrogate component, would be impossible without that presidential development. The surrogate component itself is a significant political artifact of the modern presidency and can be understood only in this light. I have discussed presidential development in a previous work and summarize those findings here. For a more extensive discussion, the reader should consult that work (Dover 1998, 9–29).

The primal events that led to the development of the modern presidency were the Depression and the Second World War. These events forced new issues onto the nation's political agenda, and Franklin D. Roosevelt's response to them transformed the conduct of government. People began to look to the national government and the presidency for solutions to many of their most pressing problems. With this, the presidency began to play a central role in a new political order (Goldstein 1982, 16–37). This new role developed both institutionally and rhetorically.

The Executive Office of the President (EOP) constitutes the institutional component of the modern presidency. It was created through Reorganization Act 1 in 1939 for the express purpose of providing the president with what the Brownlow Commission had described as "greatly needed staff assistance." Franklin D. Roosevelt had actually appointed the commission several years earlier in order to investigate presidential staff assistance and make this recommendation. The EOP began with a limited purpose of providing additional staff, but it eventually grew into a power organization or presidential secretariat, "a central staff that enables the Chief Executive to direct and supervise the work of the Executive Branch" (Barilleaux 1988, 17). It comprises eleven administrative divisions and employs more than twenty-two hundred people (Pfiffner 1994, 91–108). In contrast, Roosevelt's White House staff consisted of only thirty-seven persons before the creation of the EOP (Hart 1995, 6–37).

One of the most powerful components of the EOP is the Office of Management and Budget (OMB). Formed in 1921 as the Bureau of the Budget (BOB) and initially located within the Treasury Department, it became an integral part of the institutionalized presidency in 1939 when Roosevelt moved it to the EOP. The budget office gained power and prestige afterward and a new name in 1969, when Richard Nixon added managerial review of other governmental agencies to its purview. Today, the OMB assists the president in preparing and administering the federal budget, in developing legislative initiatives the president can submit directly to Congress, and in reviewing proposals advanced by federal agencies to determine whether they conform to the president's agenda (Hart 1995, 80–86).

The growth of the EOP was not the exclusive result of initiatives advanced by power-maximizing presidents such as Roosevelt: Congress willingly contributed to its development. Congress created two additional components of the EOP during the years immediately after the Second World War and by doing so expanded the president's staff and responsibilities even further. Congress created the Council of Economic Advisers (CEA) in 1946 to assist the president in preparing an annual report on the condition of the national economy. Congress also required the president to propose legislation he considered necessary to create a politically acceptable balance among growth, prices, and employment. The National Security Council (NSC), which Congress created the following year, comprised several leading governmental officials and served as a presidential advisory body on foreign and defense policies. The CEA was established by a Democratic congress in order to assist a Democratic president, Truman, whereas the NSC was created by a Republican Congress in order to constrain that same Democratic president. Regardless of congressional motives, these two components, in conjunction with the OMB, expanded presidential power and transformed the president into the government's manager, the nation's chief economic planner, and the dominant player in national security affairs (Cronin and Genovese 1998, 142–150).

This growth in the magnitude of institutional power has encouraged presidents to become far more individualistic and aggressive in their pursuit of policy and political goals. All too frequently, presidents have used their powers to circumvent the traditional functions of other governmental institutions and have tried to shift the blame to others when they have failed. Presidents have enhanced their power by constructing coalitions of affected interests and blocs of congressional supporters who have wanted a more active role of the president (Seligman and Covington 1989, 38). Presidents have developed prerogative powers that advance executive control of domestic policy-making through the OMB and the domination of foreign and defense matters through the NSC (Barilleaux, 1988, 14–17). They have personalized governmental policies by preempting departmental managerial roles (Milkis and Nelson 1994, 330–340); in addition, they have used the EOP as a means of placing significant policy-making beyond the reach of congressional oversight (Hart 1995, 234–241). Finally, modern presidents have employed budgetary powers to make Congress appear to be the driving force behind governmental attempts to reduce spending on popular programs (Fisher 1993, 189–204).

A second feature of presidential expansion has been the development of a rhetorical role increasingly linked to television. James Ceaser, author of a 1981 study that first raised this idea, describes a "rhetorical presidency," in which the president has a public relations role, which Ceaser attributes to three twentieth-century factors: the doctrine of presidential leadership, the modern presidential campaign, and the mass media (Ceaser 1981, 161). Presidents employ rhetoric as a method for creating active opinions by tapping into the public's feelings and articulating its wishes, then use those opinions in order to pressure Congress to support their policies, Ceaser writes. Presidential candidates use their campaigns as opportunities to demonstrate their capacity for personal leadership by inspiring the public through speeches that exhort and set forth grand and ennobling views, he adds. News reporters contribute to this role in that they see the president as more an individual tribune than an institutional leader and characterize his actions primarily as those of a solitary actor (Cronin 1980, 83). Mass media enhance this rhetorical role when they replace written messages with spoken words and when they depict presidents and candidates as delivering them in visible and dramatic performances (Ceaser et al. 1981, 164). Rhetoric can magnify presidential responsibility because it surrounds the president's power with mystique (Lowi 1985, 15). The president's ability to attract and motivate a television audience may actually be as important as his ability to employ his institutional powers (Neustadt 1990, 185).

The presidency is buffeted by two constitutions that constrain and shape its actions, Jeffrey Tulis, author of *The Rhetorical Presidency*, claims. One is the written Constitution, with its separation of powers and checks and balances structure; the second, which is rhetorical, is buttressed by the mass media and the primary elections that serve as the method by which we now choose our presidents (Tulis 1988, 17–18). Rhetorical power is a special case of executive power, Tulis adds, in that it justifies presidential actions and provides the people to whom it is addressed with the metaphors, categories, and concepts of political discourse they need to assess its use. Mass media also provide the contexts for the president's rhetorical role because presidential messages are filled with short one-sentence paragraphs designed to accommodate the interests of television news (Tulis 1988, 186–188, 203).

Whereas the origins of the modern presidency trace to the early twentieth century, much of the actual development of the office has taken place since the end of the Second World War. This time corresponds with Nelson's fourth period of vice presidential history, in which the vice presidential office has been transformed from one that was weak and quasi-legislative into one that has become an integral part of the contemporary presidency. It also involves the transformation of the occupant of that office from an obscure Throttle-bottom into the president's most important political surrogate and usual partisan successor.

The Vice Presidency since 1945

Truman's sudden ascension to the presidency—he had held office for less than three months—convinced people of the expanded importance of the vice presidency in a time of increased presidential power. Marie Natoli, a scholar of the contemporary vice presidency, says that the Truman succession marked the beginning of a new vice presidency and that all future occupants of the office "would be conscious of their responsibility to prepare for the smooth transfer of power and leadership should the need arise" (Natoli 1985, 135). Vice presidential nominees since Truman have been more qualified for the presidency than at any time in American history and frequently are more qualified for the nation's highest office than the presidents who selected them. Henry Cabot Lodge, Jr.; Lyndon Johnson; Walter Mondale; George Bush, Sr.; and Albert Gore, Jr., had more national governmental experience than their running mates, Richard Nixon, John F. Kennedy, Jimmy Carter, Ronald Reagan, and Bill Clinton. Moreover, Earl Warren, Estes Kefauver, Hubert Humphrey, Johnson, Mondale, Bush, and Gore had actively sought the presidency prior to their vice presidential nominations (Nelson 1988, 7). Nelson finds three reasons for this trend, including the public's increased concern for the competency of vice presidents. He also considers that greater reliance of presidential candidates on governance criteria than on electoral criteria in choosing their running mates and the increased visibility of the vice presidency during a period of pervasive national government and electronic communications important (Nelson 1988, 8). One can see evidence of this increased visibility in the fact that televised debates have regularly included vice-presidential candidates since 1976.

Nixon played a major role in developing the modern vice presidency. In a sense, he created the televised version of the office, which itself is a special case of the televised or rhetorical presidency. This televised role originated quite by accident: Nixon was forced to rely on it during the 1952 election campaign when a scandal about his personal finances nearly forced him off the Republican ticket. Nixon saved his threatened career when he reassured a national television audience of an estimated sixty million viewers, the largest number to watch a political event until the 1960 Kennedy-Nixon presidential debates, of his innocence of any wrongdoing. The public reaction to the "Checkers" speech, which was overwhelmingly favorable, encouraged Eisenhower to retain Nixon as his running mate (Hatfield 1997, 437).

Once in office, Nixon expanded the role of the vice president as none of his predecessors had. Nixon's importance did not derive from the power inherent in the office, for there was little of that, but from personal functions he served. His roles were primarily political in that he served as a party liaison, campaigner, and goodwill ambassador on behalf of Eisenhower. Eisenhower had little interest in political campaigning and left most of the more partisan tasks to Nixon. Despite this extensive partisan activity, Nixon helped bring about a substantial expansion in the vice president's diplomatic and policy tasks and the visibility of both the office and its personal occupant. He visited fifty-four countries and met with forty-five heads of state during his eight years in office, attended 217 meetings of the National Security Council while chairing 26, and presided over nineteen cabinet meetings during Eisenhower's various illnesses (Hatfield 1997, 441–446).

In the years since Nixon the vice presidential office has undergone substantial institutional development that has helped transform it into an integral component of the executive branch. Paul Light discusses the major changes that account for this development, including efforts Kennedy originated in 1961 to relocate the vice-presidential office from Capitol Hill into the White House complex. Kennedy assigned the vice president a suite of offices in the Executive Office Building and thus began the gradual process of transforming the vice presidency from a congressional into an executive office. Although the vice president still has some space in the Dirksen Senate Office Building today, the major part of his staff has been located in the White House complex since that move (Light 1984, 63).

In 1969, Nixon took a step as president that led to a substantial enhancement in the institutional strength of the vice presidency. He gave the office a line item in the annual budget of the EOP, a line item of sufficient size to account for the majority of future funding for the vice presidency. Previously, the congressional operating budget had provided for vice presidential expenses. A significant long-term effect of this funding change was to grant vice presidents the opportunity to hire and fire their own professional staff. Previously, vice presidents had limited staff resources and had to rely upon individuals who were often "on loan" from other offices, particularly the president's. This borrowed staff could also be withdrawn at virtually any time, however. Nixon's first vice president, Spiro Agnew, failed to anticipate the potential of this change, but Gerald Ford certainly did. Ford increased the size of the vice presidential staff during his eight-month term from seventeen persons to seventy and then involved this larger staff in a variety of policy roles. Ford's staff expansion became permanent after he assumed the presidency in 1974.

The expanded staff gave the vice president important strategic position in the White House policy process in that he had his own source of independent expertise to use when advising the president. His advisers on national security and domestic issues could supplement those from the presidential staff (Nelson 1988, 37). Light believes an independent staff can be especially influential in policy development when it is functionally integrated with the president's staff. An important step toward this functional integration occurred in 1977 when Jimmy Carter relocated the vice presidential office from the Executive Office Building into the White House West Wing, where it would be in close proximity to the presidential staff. The staff integration that developed from this move was readily apparent in the enhanced role of Walter Mondale, whose top aides regularly attended White House staff meetings with their presidential counterparts while other key aides held important positions with the National Security Council and Domestic Policy staffs (Light 1984, 68–78). The expanded staff also enabled the vice president to prepare for both emergency transitions to the presidency, as happened with Ford, and to train for a future administration, as with George Bush (Light 1984, 63–67).

Finally, the transformation of the vice presidency from a congressional office of limited importance to an executive position of political significance is reflected in a simple clerical change made by the General Services Administration (GSA) in 1972, when the GSA began listing the vice presidential office as part of the executive branch in the *United States Government Organization Manual* (Light 1984, 70).

The enhanced vice presidential role has not been free of troubles, however. Despite these institutional changes, the vice presidency still operates under the direction of the president, who can reduce its role at any time. Moreover, the expanded staff does not translate into greater political power or influence for the vice president. This limitation was made apparent by the unsuccessful attempts by Nelson Rockefeller to control the development of domestic policy during the Ford presidency. Rockefeller convinced Ford to name him vice chairman of the Domestic Council. Since the president was chairman but played a limited role in the council's work, this appointment placed Rockefeller in a position to dominate the activities of the council. Despite holding a strategic administrative office, Rockefeller failed to exert much power over domestic policy development. Instead, he fought a number of divisive political battles with several of Ford's leading aides, including his chief of staff, Dick Cheney, for influence and lost most of them (Light 1984, 9). Ford did not retain Rockefeller as his running mate in 1976.

In addition to Rockefeller's political setbacks, one must also take into account the questionable performances of Spiro Agnew and Dan Quayle in evaluating the nature of the modern vice presidency. A significant number of voters considered them national embarrassments unqualified for office. Nonetheless, Agnew and Quayle took on several important political duties for their presidents, including rallying of the party faithful and key electoral blocs such as foreign policy and religious conservatives (Cronin and Genovese 1998, 337–338).

Most modern vice presidents have been successful in acting as presidential advisers and surrogates and in gaining the confidence of the voting public, however. Walter Mondale was well liked by members of Congress and possessed a strong national political base of his own, an important part of which was his long-standing friendship with Hubert Humphrey. The working relationship between Carter and Mondale was strengthened by the fact that both men trusted and respected one another. Sometimes they disagreed, but Mondale kept those disagreements private and refused to carry them beyond his discussions with Carter (Cronin and Genovese 1998, 331). After leaving office, Mondale told his successors of a variety of methods they could employ to increase their effectiveness in office, such as providing confidential advice to the president and avoiding managerial assignments comparable to Rockefeller's efforts at the Domestic Council (Hatfield 1997, 549).

The potential for significant influence by modern vice presidents was also evident in the actions of George Bush, Sr., and Albert Gore. Both two-term vice presidents had strong personal relationships, with Reagan and Clinton, respectively, that gave them ample opportunities to realize the political potential now inherent in the surrogate role. They offered the president confidential advice on policy matters, played important roles in the formation of administration policy, represented the president in a number of personal diplomatic endeavors, and helped further expand the vice presidential office into an executive branch power center (Cronin and Genovese 1998, 333–337).

The Vice Presidential Role

This extensive institutional development has provided the vice presidency with a significant political role that makes it the most important strategic position from which to seek the nomination of the presidential party when the incumbent retires. The contemporary vice president performs several roles that provide wide-ranging opportunities for generating support for his nomination campaign. Light divides these roles into three categories, the ceremonial, the policy-related, and the political (Light 1984, 28–34). The ceremonial role involves foreign travel, through which the vice president appears as a presidential surrogate and diplomatic representative, and membership on various forums, councils, and task forces. This latter group includes both permanent bodies such as the National Security Council and temporary organizations that function only during particular administrations (Cronin and Genovese 1998, 318–337). The vice president cannot create or implement policy from these activities, but he can use the opportunities offered by them to express his symbolic concerns for the political interests of particular constituencies.

He can be more influential in the development of policy through his advisory role to the president, however. The size, independence, and location of his staff provide significant opportunities for aiding the president in the formation of foreign and domestic policy initiatives. He can use his meetings with the president as forums for presenting alternatives during the agenda setting aspect of policy development. He might also institute some of his own goals through the managerial responsibilities he often acquires with presidential commissions, as did Quayle with the Council on Competitiveness (Light 1984, 44–51).

The political role involves the vice president in a variety of public relations activities as an administrative spokesman, legislative liaison, and campaigner. He strives to rally the party faithful behind the president's policies through his capacity as the most widely sought campaigner of his party and by his appearances at media-related events and televised interviews (Nelson 1988, 74). In addition, he can highlight the importance of specific legislative proposals while serving on the administration's congressional lobbying team. When acting as a campaigner, the vice president is often the most important representative of the national administration at state and local party conventions and events. His efforts are particularly significant during midterm elections and in appeals to voters in specific geographic regions and ideological camps. Sometimes, he can even make a better case among these voters for the election of his party's candidates than the president can (Goldstein 1982, 97–111).

Fulfilling the political role often offers the vice president greatest opportunity for developing support for a future candidacy. "Nothing helps a Vice President look quite as presidential as campaigning, speaking, and public liaison," Light says. "Since Vice Presidents cannot make decisions that the public can see, the political role becomes the best vehicle for gaining name recognition and visibility" (Light 1984, 117).

2

ELECTIONS WITH SURROGATE INCUMBENTS

In a previous work, *Presidential Elections in the Television Age: 1960–1992*, I advanced the argument that the strength of presidential incumbency and the interpretation of that strength by television news media offer a better explanation of the outcomes of recent presidential elections than partisanship. In that work, I depicted the two major political parties as the presidential and the opposition, rather than as the Republican and Democratic. The nominee of each party in a television age election acts more from his strategic position relative to incumbency than from the underlying patterns of partisanship that operate in the American electoral system. News reporters tend to respond to their perceptions of that incumbency, and voters often base their ballot choices on those perceptions. With this in mind, I have argued that modern elections are of three types: those with strong incumbents, weak incumbents, or surrogate incumbents. The first two types occur when an incumbent wins reelection (strong) or fails (weak). The third occurs when the incumbent does not or cannot seek another term and is replaced on the ticket of the presidential party by a candidate from the executive branch of the national government. This candidate, who has been the vice president in every such election, acts as a surrogate of the retiring incumbent and finds that his electoral prospects are highly influenced by the political and personal strength of that incumbent. I devoted one of that book's chapters to explaining how incumbency and televised campaign news reporting intersect in recurring and predictable ways in elections with surrogate incumbents. I drew my conclusions about the nature of these elections from the campaigns of 1960, 1968, and 1988, when the presidential party nominated the vice presidents of the time, Richard Nixon, Hubert Humphrey, and George Bush. I summarize those conclusions in this chapter and advance a framework for observing similar elections in later years, including that of 2000.

Three general patterns distinguish elections with surrogate incumbents; the consistent nomination of the vice president as the standard bearer of the presidential party is the most significant. The development of the vice presidency from an impotent quasi-legislative office into an important and visible executive position, discussed previously, has given vice presidents an important strategic position in which to contest the nomination of the presidential party when an incumbent retires. Every television age vice president who has sought the nomination of his party has successfully used the opportunities provided by his office to convince a majority of his own partisans that he was the leading surrogate and rightful heir of the retiring president.

The second pattern involves the ambiguous nature of the challenge posed by the opposition party. This party enters a surrogate incumbent election hopeful of victory in that it no longer has to face the incumbent who defeated them four years earlier and views the vice president as a far less formidable rival. Nonetheless, their optimism is tempered by the recognition that they lack a strong leader of their own, a unifying leader who possesses the political and personal strength to unite them before a nomination campaign. This problem is not accidental because it derives from the political fact that American opposition parties do not have the institutional capacity to determine their national leaders before an election year. Unlike in European parliamentary democracies, American parties do not have an official leader, often chosen years before an election, who speaks for them and will be their standard bearer in the upcoming election. American party chairs and congressional leaders can speak for their parties only in the limited political contexts for which they are chosen, as committee chairs or as congressional caucus leaders. The spokesperson for the national party, the presidential candidate, is not selected until the national convention, which occurs during the summer of the election year. Whereas the presidential party has such a spokesperson in the person of the incumbent, the opposition party is rarely able to identify its likely nominee with any degree of certainty as late as one year before the election. The party must devote months of time and millions of dollars to potentially divisive primary election campaigns in order to select its nominee. A plethora of candidates, many of whom lack even the basic rudiments of a constituency, quickly leap into the inevitable fights that now accompany the nomination campaign of the modern opposition party. The opposition party might sacrifice its electoral prospects through its own infighting. Despite this threat, the opposition party in surrogate incumbent elections tends to unite behind a nominee who holds out the promise of victory. An important political factor encouraging this behavior is that the opposition party has not held the presidency for at least two terms and is quite willing to set aside its internal differences in order to regain power.

Finally, the fact that neither the vice presidents nor their opposition party challengers enjoy any inherent advantages constitutes the third pattern in surrogate incumbent elections. Regardless of party, the two nominees encounter dilemmas that are unique to their particular strategic positions. The vice presidents have trouble expanding their political support much beyond that of their own partisans; the challengers have such vague and poorly defined public images that many voters who support them during early stages of the campaign may alter their views as the election nears. The vice presidents have to convince millions of skeptical voters that they are more than presidential surrogates, and the challengers need to demonstrate they are qualified for national leadership. Although the voters proclaim they want change, they increasingly appear reluctant to vote for an opposition party candidate who promises it. The final outcomes of surrogate incumbent elections are decided primarily by the ways in which the various candidates overcome, or fail to overcome, their particular dilemmas.

THE ROLE OF TELEVISION NEWS

One of the more significant features of presidential elections is the pervasive role played by television news media in reporting events and defining the contexts and meanings of campaigns. They are influential in all phases of presidential elections, but particularly so during nominations. This is because partisan voters often face more difficulties in choosing from among the variety of similar candidates who seek their party's nomination than in choosing between two major candidates, only one of whom is a member of their own party, in the general election. Moreover, voters often know little about most candidates at the outset of campaigns and rely extensively on media sources for information before making their choices. The influence of television news media can be particularly strong during the early weeks of the primary election season, when voters need information as a large number of aspirants for office rapidly diminishes to a small number of major contenders. The information they receive from television news media can exert a powerful influence on their response to the large number of candidates. It can also help determine which candidates become major contenders and which ones fail.

Television news media do not necessarily decide which of the candidates they prefer to become major contenders. Instead, they observe the performances of the candidates and then stereotype them into a variety of predetermined roles that prove useful for structuring future reporting. Voters can easily learn about which candidate occupies which particular role but often face great difficulties in learning much more about them. Television news media find these candidate roles quite useful when they emphasize the horse race, directing attention to the question of which candidates are "ahead" and which are not.

Television news media use three candidate roles when illustrating nomination campaigns from the horse race perspective: "front-runner," the "leading adversary," and the "others." The front- runner is the one candidate who has enjoyed the greatest success in any or all of the leading measures of campaign effectiveness that television news media employ in determining the status of the horse race. These measures are voter support as recorded in public opinion polls, financial contributions, and endorsements from important party leaders. Once determined, the front-runner then serves as the central political actor in the televised melodrama that becomes the media version of the campaign. He attains more televised news coverage than any of his rivals. On some days, he is the only candidate of his party to receive any mention in a network telecast. In addition, the other candidates and most political events acquire much of their meaning through their relations with the front-runner rather than in their own right.

The leading adversary is the one candidate who has enjoyed the greatest success after the front-runner in the measures of campaign effectiveness. Television news media do not depict the leading adversary as the second strongest candidate with a significant following of his own, however. They prefer to illustrate him in selective ways that often contrast with the manner in which they depict the front-runner. The leading adversary often appears as the antithesis of the front-runner and as the personification of the political attributes the front-runner needs but lacks. He seems mostly to be the main obstacle who stands between the front-runner and the nomination. Television news media seek to telecast and sometimes even create imagery in which the nomination campaign appears to be a personal struggle for power between two role-playing candidates with the front-runner expected to win but facing the need to prove that he actually deserves a victory. In describing the campaigns from this perspective, television news media often attempt to maximize the differences and minimize the similarities of these two main candidates.

The role of others is reserved for the remaining candidates, those who have fared poorly in acquiring poll standing, money, and endorsements. These candidates tend to receive only infrequent televised news coverage, and most of them quickly fade from the consciousness of voters, if they ever entered it. They tend to be the first candidates who withdraw from a campaign.

Although the various roles are stereotypical, it is possible for candidates to move from one role to another as a campaign develops. The identities of the various role players may change, but the media formula for illustrating the campaign remains the same. For example, in 1972 Edmund Muskie began the election year as the Democratic front-runner while George McGovern occupied the role of leading adversary; in contrast, Hubert Humphrey was merely one of the others. Muskie then lost several critical primaries and withdrew, and McGovern, who defeated Muskie, quickly became the new front-runner. Humphrey then became the new leading adversary and soon appeared as the main obstacle between McGovern and the nomination. In 1996 Robert Dole always filled the front-runner role for the Republican nomination but faced three different leading adversaries at various times during the campaign. Phil Gramm occupied the role throughout most of 1995 because of his success in raising money, but he lost that distinction to Steve Forbes in January 1996. Forbes looked strong for several weeks as he spent lavishly from his personal fortune in the Iowa and New Hampshire campaigns but lost the leading adversary status after a fourth-place finish in Iowa. Pat Buchanan succeeded Forbes as the leading adversary after finishing second to Dole in Iowa, then defeating the eventual Republican nominee in New Hampshire one week later.

There is one final feature of televised news reporting that often affects the course of nomination campaigns and the outcomes of general elections. Television news media do not like to illustrate campaigns between two role-playing candidates in both parties; they want only one such campaign. They may focus their attention on the two major candidates of both parties during the early weeks of the primary election season, but they select the one campaign that better conforms to their preference for a battle between two role-playing contenders after the early votes in Iowa and New Hampshire. After making this selection, television news media concentrate their political reporting on the two major candidates of this one party while treating the campaign in the other party as if it has already ended. In every election since 1960, television news media have depicted the latter stages of the primary election season as involving the efforts of only three significant candidates: the front-runner and leading adversary of one party and the front-runner and presumed nominee of the other. This depiction is hardly inconsequential. In nearly every election since 1960, the party that had the misfortune to become the televised choice for political news coverage eventually lost the general election. Voters soon became disenchanted with the leading candidates of this party after watching them fight with one another for many months and then responded by electing the nominee of the other party.

PRESIDENTIAL PARTY NOMINATIONS

The defining characteristic of surrogate incumbent elections is the nomination of the vice president as the standard bearer of the presidential party. This nomination is a direct result of the recent changes in the institutional and rhetorical nature of the presidency and vice presidency discussed previously. In this section, I focus attention on several recurring features of these nominations that are drawn exclusively from the elections of 1960, 1968, and 1988. All were replicated in 2000, however.

An important recurring feature is the credible political status of each vice president before he becomes a presidential running mate. Richard Nixon was a member of the House of Representatives for four years and of the Senate for two before his selection as vice president. He attained valuable national exposure through the highly publicized hearings about Soviet espionage of the House Committee on Un-American Activities and particularly through the events that led to the perjury conviction of Alger Hiss. By 1952 Nixon had already convinced a significant number of Republicans that he was one of the more capable and promising of the party's younger office-holders. Hubert Humphrey had been a senator from Minnesota for sixteen years, a candidate for the 1960 Democratic presidential nomination, and a nationally prominent leader of liberals at the time of his selection as Lyndon Johnson's running mate. He was also one of the major leaders in the Senate battle for enactment of the 1964 civil rights bill. George Bush had held several important governmental positions before 1980, including congressman from Texas, chairman of the Republican National Committee, envoy to China, and director of the Central Intelligence Agency. He had also been Ronald Reagan's major opponent for the Republican presidential nomination prior to his selection as vice president.

The vice president's surrogate role begins when the presidential candidate selects him as the running mate, shortly before or during the first days of the national convention. The selection attracts extensive media attention to the campaign at a time when few other political events are newsworthy. Since nominations are now decided in the primaries, national conventions have become media events the parties use to showcase their tickets. The high point of these "infommercials" is the acceptance speech by the presidential nominee. The speech is followed by a strong and highly emotional show of partisan unity when the two candidates and their spouses appear together on the podium to the cheers of thousands of ecstatic delegates. The imagery of such an event conveys the explicit message that the vice presidential nominee is an integral part of the party leadership and the most important surrogate for the presidential candidate.

The two candidates rarely appear together during most of the campaign events that follow. Instead, their travel and speaking schedules are usually designed to complement one another. The words and actions of the presidential candidates are daily features of network news, but the vice presidential nominees receive only infrequent attention at times other than those involving debates. This dearth of national news is offset by an abundance of local news, however. Public appearances by vice presidential candidates in specific locales are often important events for the local media, who tend to cover them extensively. This coverage provides these candidates with unique opportunities to become known to voters that are not usually available to the rivals they will likely encounter in future nomination campaigns.

This pattern of televised news exposure to the American public, nationally infrequent but locally extensive, does not end with the election. Instead, it continues for the remainder of the term of office as the new vice president performs the role first originated by Theodore Roosevelt of representing the president at rallies of the partisan faithful in order to generate electoral and programmatic support. The vice president speaks to thousands of party activists and millions of other voters, sometimes exclusively through television news, in nearly every state during his term of office. In addition, the vice president engages in the variety of actions that define the modern executive office, as a diplomatic representative, policy adviser, lobbyist, and political spokesman. This proves to be an invaluable resource for generating support for a future campaign. "Occupants of the office receive far greater media coverage than most other public officials," Goldstein writes, comparing the vice presidency to other positions. "Many senators and cabinet members and most governors and members of the House of Representatives toil in obscurity, never in danger of losing their national anonymity" (Goldstein 1982, 256).

Other than members of his own staff, the people most likely to work with the vice president are elected officials and the leaders and activists of state and local parties. The vice president is usually the most important member of the national party who can assist state and local parties in their fund-raising, recruitment, and organizational efforts. Moreover, most party leaders and activists see the vice president as a definite candidate for the first election after the incumbent retires. This visibility helps the vice president emerge as the first candidate in his own party to be successor of the incumbent. The relationship between surrogate and party is symbiotic: the surrogate visits states in order to advance his future candidacy by helping the party with its immediate needs; the party sees him as their future nominee and acts accordingly. Party leaders and activists make their own personal plans to support the vice president when he calls. This is important because these activists are the very people who are most likely to contribute time and money to a presidential candidate and to vote in caucuses and primary elections. They are the ones who control the outcomes of nomination campaigns.

The nomination campaigns of Nixon, Humphrey, and Bush followed similar scenarios: each developed significant followings from among the elected officials, leaders, and activists of his own party while serving as vice president and later translated that support into a victory. Nixon began his 1960 campaign with so much advance support from the activist core of the Republican Party that he convinced all of his potential rivals to abandon the cause even before the primaries began. Foremost among these dropouts were Nelson Rockefeller and Barry Goldwater. Virtually every Republican congressman, governor, and state chairman endorsed Nixon before the national convention gave him a unanimous nomination.

Nixon had an important advantage over his potential Republican rivals in 1960 in the sense that the election occurred in a year when the incumbent was exceptionally popular and more than capable of winning another term had he been constitutionally eligible. Hubert Humphrey was not so fortunate. Humphrey ran for office in a year that was quite the opposite of 1960, when the incumbent was embattled and his reelection was in doubt. Lyndon Johnson was the leader of one faction of a highly divided Democratic Party in 1968 and encountered some very significant opposition from Eugene McCarthy during the New Hampshire primary in his unannounced attempt at renomination. His electoral difficulties in that state and the sudden entry of Robert Kennedy into the campaign within days of McCarthy's surprise showing indicated the depth of the troubles Johnson would have faced if he had chosen to continue his efforts to secure another term. Johnson's departure from the campaign in late March astonished many people, including Humphrey, who announced his own candidacy in early April. Despite this late start, Humphrey won the nomination by relying on the support of his party's elected officials and state leaders, who provided a substantial number of delegate votes at the national convention. The untimely death of Robert Kennedy has led to extensive speculation that the New York senator was destined to become the nominee and would certainly have been had he not been assassinated. The logical conclusion of such an assumption is that Humphrey was an accidental nominee, a defeated candidate whom fate had given a second chance. Although interesting, this argument overlooks strong evidence of the depth of Humphrey's support among key groups of voters and party activists. Humphrey had led both Kennedy and McCarthy among Democratic voters and party leaders in a number of polls compiled shortly before Kennedy's death. Humphrey did not win the nomination by default; he won it by gaining the support of Johnson's most loyal followers, a group of Democratic activists who were far more numerous within their own party than Johnson's detractors. The outcome was a direct result of the four years Humphrey had devoted, as the president's leading political surrogate, to rallying these same people behind Johnson's controversial policies.

The scenario of the Bush nomination was similar to those of both Nixon and Humphrey. Bush was fortunate in that he did not encounter a party as divided as Humphrey's, but unlike Nixon, he was actively opposed by a number of significant rivals. As was true of the two earlier surrogates, Bush gained his strongest backing from the elected officials and state leaders of his party. He relied upon the support of these key groups to overcome a serious political setback that developed in February 1988 when Robert Dole defeated him in the Iowa caucuses. Relying upon the support of the New Hampshire governor, John Sununu, Bush rebounded from his Iowa loss and defeated Dole in the nation's first primary. He beat Dole again several weeks later in South Carolina after receiving the support of that state's Republican governor, Carroll Campbell. This victory was particularly important in the sense that it gave Bush both the momentum and the regional news exposure he needed to compete effectively in the seventeen primaries of "Super Tuesday," only four days later. Since fourteen of those primaries were located in the Southeast, South Carolina helped set the tone for the voting behavior of the region. One week after Super Tuesday and with the assistance of yet another strategically placed Republican governor, in this instance, James Thompson, Bush effectively concluded his nomination campaign by garnering nearly two thirds of the vote in Illinois. The magnitude of Bush's victory convinced Dole, who by now was Bush's only remaining rival, to abandon the race.

In each of these three campaigns a vice president used the institutional and rhetorical opportunities of his office to appeal to the activist core of his own party with the message that he was the political surrogate and rightful heir of the retiring incumbent. The activist core responded favorably to each of these appeals and constituted the crucial support that Nixon, Humphrey, and Bush needed to win their respective nominations.

OPPOSITION PARTY NOMINATIONS

One of the more intriguing aspects of elections that have surrogate incumbents is the campaign for the nomination of the opposition party. This is particularly important in the sense that the nominees of this party won two (Kennedy in 1960, Nixon in 1968) of the three television age elections before 2000 that constitute this category. In addition, the third (Dukakis in 1988) enjoyed a substantial lead in public opinion polls several months before the general election. These results should have encouraged the Republicans of 2000 that their nominee would have an excellent chance of winning the election. Although the opposition party always faces the dilemma that a nomination campaign can be both divisive and threatening to its electoral prospects, each party in the three elections before 2000 avoided these difficulties in ways that appear more recurring than random. The patterns of those elections, described in the following, repeated themselves in 2000 with the nomination of George W. Bush.

The events of a given campaign derive from two factors: the political context of the time and the political needs of the individual candidates in their quest for office. A divisive nomination campaign can occur only if both factors encourage it, but neither factor appears to be very encouraging in surrogate incumbent elections. The campaigns of 1960, 1968, and 1988 were lengthy and competitive, but they always concluded with the party's uniting behind a new or renewed leader who held out the promise of victory. Virtually all of the aspirants who sought nominations in these elections began their efforts as candidates without constituencies. Their support from party activists was limited and often narrow. This occurred because they were relatively new actors on the national stage, as were both John F. Kennedy and Michael Dukakis, or because they were attempting a political comeback after having suffered a previous defeat, as was Richard Nixon. These eventual winners also competed against candidates who seemed very much like them, little known aspirants who frequently lacked constituencies. Instead of acting as spokesmen for ideological factions, each successful nominee addressed himself to the individually pressing demands of fund-raising and organization building so he could compete successfully in the early primaries and caucuses.

The contexts for divisive campaigns were missing in these elections since the opposition parties had not held executive power for eight years and were eager to set aside their own internal differences in order regain it. American parties tend to be broad coalitions of interests, often contradictory in nature, that are held together by the goal of winning office and taking control of government. They can succeed only if they are willing to submerge or downplay a variety of issues about which they may disagree. Although strategies of this nature may lead to electoral successes, they often threaten party unity afterward when the party faces the realities of governing. The party may develop internal divisions over policy preferences grounded in the submerged contradictions that initially helped bring it to power. A strong president can continue to submerge those divisions and even maintain significant unity around the force of his own personality, as did Lyndon Johnson during his first years in office and Dwight Eisenhower and Ronald Reagan throughout the greater part of their two terms. Sometimes the divisions are powerful enough that even a president, for example, Johnson, may become central to them, however. The divisions lead to factional fighting and often contribute to electoral defeat. The fights may also extend to a subsequent election and compromise the party's chances in it as well, but they rarely last much longer. By the time the opposition party has been out of power for eight years, its activists often appear quite willing to overlook their divisions once again and unite behind the candidacy of a new and unifying leader who holds out the promise of victory. The Democrats united behind Kennedy in 1960, the Republicans behind Nixon in 1968, the Democrats behind Carter in 1976, the Democrats behind Dukakis in 1988 and again behind Clinton in 1992 (although the 1976 and 1992 elections did not involve surrogate incumbents). Each of these nominations occurred after the opposition had been out of power for at least eight years.

In a sense, the election of 1960 began in 1952, when the Democrats lost their twenty-year hold on the presidency after the incumbent Harry Truman retired and their new standard bearer, Governor Adlai Stevenson of Illinois, was overwhelmed by the personal and political appeal of General Dwight Eisenhower. They also lost their control of both houses of Congress. The return of the Democrats to power was slow but promising; the first successful step occurred two years later. Here, Democrats quickly brought the newly acquired Republican control of Congress to an abrupt end by winning narrow majorities in both the House of Representatives and the Senate. They enjoyed mixed results in 1956, once again losing the presidency to Eisenhower but recording modest gains in Congress. Two years later, in the middle part of a severe recession, they made substantial gains in Congress, winning nearly forty seats in the House and thirteen in the Senate. These remarkable gains, particularly when coupled with the realization that Eisenhower could not seek another term, encouraged the Democrats to believe the presidency might be theirs in 1960. Unfortunately, they did not appear to have a leader capable of winning the office.

John F. Kennedy was one of five major aspirants for the nomination that year, but he faced strong opposition from Stevenson and three influential members of the Senate, Majority Leader Lyndon Johnson, the liberal spokesman Hubert Humphrey, and Stuart Symington of Missouri, who had been secretary of the Air Force under Truman. Although he led his rivals in public opinion polls at the beginning of the year, Kennedy was a far from certain nominee. He had a valuable asset in that power in the Senate, which his rivals held, was not necessarily applicable in nomination campaigns. Although this may have strengthened his prospects, Kennedy also faced many doubts from voters, particularly related to his religion, age, and personal experience, that he desperately needed to overcome. In responding to them, Kennedy entered several primaries and won them all, including contested battles with Humphrey in Wisconsin and West Virginia. Kennedy's victories convinced Humphrey to withdraw, although the Minnesota senator did not endorse Kennedy while doing so. Kennedy then turned his attention to an even stronger rival, Johnson, who had secured the support of a majority of the delegates from the South and Border regions. In what was one of the most exciting conventions in decades, Kennedy secured a slim majority of the delegate votes on the first ballot and Johnson, Stevenson, and Symington divided the rest. Kennedy, a relatively new and untested actor on the national political stage, quickly united his party after selecting Johnson as his running mate and promising the ecstatic delegates that he would lead them to a "new frontier" if elected.

The Republicans soon faced some unpromising conditions of their own but eventually reversed them and then entered the election of 1968 with optimism comparable to that of the 1960 Democrats. After losing the 1960 election to Kennedy, Republicans engaged in several years of bitter infighting between their conservative and moderate factions that finally contributed to a massive electoral defeat in 1964. They watched in horror as Lyndon Johnson overwhelmed their nominee, Barry Goldwater, by capturing over 60 percent of the popular vote and the electoral votes of forty-four states. Moreover, the Democrats expanded their control of Congress that year from modest to two-thirds majorities in both chambers. The Republicans were not down for long, however. The Democrats quickly began their own public infighting over the Vietnam War and other turmoil of the late 1960s. This infighting helped Republicans garner significant increases in their numbers of elected officials in 1966 and encouraged them that a return to the presidency in 1968 was a strong possibility. As had occurred with the Democrats eight years earlier, Republicans did not have a certain nominee who could guarantee the unity that was so necessary for victory.

There were four major aspirants for the Republican nomination in 1968, who represented virtually every segment of the party's ideological spectrum. Richard Nixon appeared to be the strongest, but his twin losses of the presidency in 1960 and the governor's race in California in 1966 had led to the development of a public image as a loser. Nixon had to contest the primaries that year in order to dispel this image. He did so successfully, first driving Governor George Romney of Michigan from the field of contenders, then defeating his two other rivals at the convention itself. Nixon positioned himself between the appeals of the conservative aspirant Ronald Reagan and the promises of the more moderate Nelson Rockefeller and secured the nomination on a closely contested first ballot. Reagan and Rockefeller were not necessarily allied against Nixon during the convention, but they were cooperating with one another in an attempt to stop his nomination. There was even some speculation about the prospect of their composing the party ticket, one running for president and the other for vice president. The order in which they would appear on the ticket was never clear. Despite this strong opposition, Nixon finally united his partisans by securing the backing of his vanquished rivals; by invoking the imagery of Eisenhower, who was gravely ill at that time; and by promising that he had a "secret plan" to end the war.

The partisan political context of 1988 was similar to those of the earlier elections in the sense that the opposition party believed it had an excellent opportunity to win the presidency after years of political difficulties. Ronald Reagan had given fellow partisans some lengthy coattails in 1980, enabling them to win twelve new Senate seats and control of that chamber and enough House seats to form an ideological majority with the help of some conservative Democrats. The opposition Democrats began their comeback almost immediately by winning twenty-six House seats in 1982, thereby abruptly ending Reagan's ideological majority. They added two Senate seats and expanded their House numbers in 1984 despite losing the presidency to Reagan for a second time. The Democrats' big victory occurred in 1986, when they captured eight Senate seats lost in 1980 and regained majority control. They flexed their new political muscles in 1987 by rejecting the nomination of the conservative jurist Robert Bork to the Supreme Court. These successes, and the political damage to Reagan's credibility of the Iran-Contra scandal, encouraged the Democrats to believe they could win the presidency in 1988. As in other years, all they seemed to need was a strong candidate.

The initial stages of the nomination campaign were not encouraging to Democratic hopes. A number of prominent party members, including Governor Mario Cuomo of New York and Senator Sam Nunn of Georgia, declined to enter the race, and the early front-runner, the former senator Gary Hart of Colorado, withdrew after revelations of extramarital sexual relations led to an abrupt decline in his popularity. The remaining candidates often seemed unimpressive and even acquired the derisive nickname "seven dwarfs." Nonetheless, this group eventually produced a strong front-runner who defeated his rivals and united the party. Governor Michael Dukakis of Massachusetts finished a respectable third in the Iowa caucuses and followed this showing with a victory in the New Hampshire primary. After winning five of the sixteen Super Tuesday contests and over three hundred convention delegates, Dukakis started driving his rivals individually from the race. Congressman Richard Gephardt of Missouri withdrew in late March after losing Michigan; Senator Paul Simon of Illinois quit shortly after his last-place finish in Wisconsin during the first week of April; Senator Al Gore of Tennessee ended his efforts in late April after a defeat in New York. The Reverend Jesse Jackson continued campaigning until the convention but had won far too few delegates to have any realistic chance of stopping Dukakis. After selecting Senator Lloyd Bentsen of Texas, a southerner with a relatively conservative voting record for a Democrat as his running mate, Dukakis united his fellow partisans by emphasizing in his acceptance speech that the election was about competence, not ideology. He also promised to employ on a national scale the same successful economic strategies that he had used to create the "Massachusetts Miracle."

The recurring biases in television news coverage, described earlier, affected the course of these campaigns in ways that frequently enhanced the electoral prospects of the opposition party. Television news media were so preoccupied with the "horse race" that they often depicted these campaigns as little more than strategic battles of solitary individuals who lacked meaningful connections to any ideological or partisan contexts. This can be particularly significant when these contexts are minimized by the events of the campaigns themselves. Television news media depicted the front-runners, Kennedy, Nixon, and Dukakis, as political actors engaged in personal quests for political power and, by virtue of their successes, qualified for the presidency. This enhanced the opposition party's electoral prospects in that its nominees eventually appeared to possess the personal skills needed for uniting their parties and the political virility to lead the nation. Each of these three opposition party nominees seemed to be the new leader the nation said it wanted. In every television age election when the opposition party had been out of power for at least eight years, its nominee managed to prevent the divisive campaign that might compromise a general election. Each of these three nominees united his party by the end of its national convention and then seized the lead in the polls over the nominee of the presidential party. This has taken place far too often and with such regularity that one cannot consider it to be random. It is an important and recurring component of the opposition parties' nomination campaigns in elections with surrogate incumbents.

GENERAL ELECTIONS

Each party faces a significant recurring dilemma in the general election that derives from its unique strategic position. The presidential party has the dilemma that its nominee is an executive branch surrogate of the retiring incumbent who has inherited only some of that incumbent's popularity. The vice president has inherited the most partisan of the incumbent's supporters and has translated that support into a party nomination, but he has not won the support of many weaker partisans and independent voters who backed the incumbent in the previous election. All three vice presidents in surrogate incumbent elections before 2000 could not generate the same level of voter support the party had enjoyed four years earlier.

The limits of surrogate incumbency become apparent in the weeks and sometimes months that transpire between the conclusion of the primary election season and the beginning of the general election campaign. This is the time when the nominees of the two parties are apparent but have yet to receive their official designations from their national conventions. In addition, this is a crucial period because the battle for the presidency has narrowed to the vice president and his one challenger from the opposition party. Voters now have a more clear picture of their choices and many actually make them during this time.

The challenger has a tremendous opportunity to expand his political support and usually possesses the requisite skills for doing so. He no longer appears as simply one of many aspirants for the nomination but instead enjoys an enhanced status as the new and dynamic leader of a unified opposition party. Television news media assist the challenger in the sense that they frequently illustrate him in upbeat scenes making enthusiastic appeals for unity and victory to crowds of his fellow partisans. The powerful and emotional sense of optimism often inherent in such imagery helps make the challenger appear as a capable and inspiring new leader in an election year in which the incumbent's retirement sets the context for just such an expectation. The challenger uses this imagery to expand support among the same weak partisans and independent voters who supported the incumbent in the previous election.

The vice president's dilemma is compounded by his lack of the opportunities presidents enjoy to preempt televised news coverage of his challenger and replace it with alternative imagery in which he appears statesmanlike. Presidents exploit such opportunities when they respond to foreign crises or domestic disasters, conduct White House bill signing ceremonies, announce policy recommendations previously developed by their own commissions, speak at funerals of famous dignitaries, and fulfill patriotic roles on national holidays. Vice presidents cannot order bombing raids, issue executive orders, nominate judges, or engage in most of the trappings of televised executive power that have helped presidents become the formidable candidates they are when they seek reelection. The lack of these opportunities can be particularly damaging to the vice president's electoral prospects during the preconvention period because he cannot compete effectively with the favorable televised imagery his challenger often generates. Nixon and Humphrey lost ground to their challengers during the preconvention period, and neither could reclaim the lead he had once held. Although he eventually regained the lead and won the election, Bush trailed Dukakis during the months preceding the Republican convention.

The campaign is far from over during the summer months, however, for the opposition party has a significant dilemma of its own. The extensive summertime support for its nominee often proves illusory and diminishes as the campaign develops. The illusion of support derives from the context of the nomination campaign and the patterns of televised news coverage that accompany it. The challenger starts to gain support among the general electorate when he changes his appeal from that of a partisan aspirant to that of a unifying new national leader. His appeals are broad but vague and are all too often based on the strength of his own personality and the prospect of victory that he offers partisans. This works for a while, but the national conventions, usually held in July and August, alter the context of the campaign in ways that can reduce the summer advantages of the challenger. A convention provides an excellent opportunity for the vice president to escape from the president's shadow and appear as a true candidate in his own right. The extensive news coverage of both conventions, coupled with the selection of the two running mates, creates a context in which the campaign appears as a battle between two very identifiable party tickets that promise either a continuation of the status quo or some vaguely defined change. The vice president can now present himself as a qualified alternative to the challenger and as a candidate who employs his proven leadership skills to advance a number of successful policies of the current administration. The challenger appears less qualified as skeptical voters wonder about the vagueness of his appeals and question the strength of his personal abilities to lead. He needs to respond to this problem or he may lose the election. Kennedy and Nixon did so effectively, whereas Dukakis failed. Despite their victories, Kennedy and Nixon saw their summer poll leads disappear, and each won the popular vote by less than one percentage point. Kennedy led Nixon in late July by 6 percent; Nixon was ahead of Humphrey by eighteen points in early September. Dukakis fell from a lead of seventeen points over Bush in mid-July to a deficit of seven points in the final vote count. These declines were not accidental but instead derived from the shallow nature of the challenger's initial support and the increased credibility of the vice president's appeal.

The outcome of an election with a surrogate incumbent rests on the ability of the two candidates to overcome their unique dilemmas. The vice president must demonstrate that he is more than a mere surrogate of the retiring incumbent, that he offers a continuation of the best accomplishments of the outgoing administration while escaping the blame for the controversial shortcomings of that administration. The challenger must demonstrate that he is personally qualified for the presidency, that the nation can trust him with the power of its highest office, and that the change he offers amounts to far more than an extensive collection of vague electoral appeals. In 1960 Kennedy used the televised debates as a forum for convincing skeptical voters that he was qualified for the presidency and relied upon an address to the Greater Houston Ministerial Association to convince them that his Roman Catholic religion would not compromise the separation of church and state. In contrast, although Nixon succeeded in establishing some independence as a surrogate from Eisenhower, he failed to convince the additional voters he needed that his administration would address the pressing economic problems caused by recession. The Democrats made some significant gains in the congressional elections of 1958 by blaming the recession of that year on Republican policies. Nixon could not escape blame and suffered accordingly in 1960 despite Eisenhower's wide popularity.

Humphrey left the bitter Democratic convention of 1968 with both a shattered party and bleak electoral prospects but nearly won the election. He convinced numerous voters that he would not continue the unpopular foreign policies of Lyndon Johnson but would instead restore the Great Society programs that had been the central feature of the Democratic agenda before the war. In a sense, Humphrey began as the surrogate of the 1968 version of Lyndon Johnson but tried to transform himself into the surrogate of the vastly more popular 1964 Johnson. He nearly succeeded and almost won the election.

Nixon, the challenger this time, sought to portray himself as a qualified and experienced leader with ties to the recent past and as a person capable of leading the nation in this time of crisis. He held his greatest lead during the very weeks of the most divisive aspects of the Democratic campaign but began losing ground to Humphrey during the last weeks of the campaign. He lost his lead when voters began questioning the vagueness of his "secret" plan for ending the war and remembering the exceptionally partisan behavior he had exhibited during his vice-presidential years.

Bush became the first television age vice president to overcome the dilemma of his office and win the election. His campaign for the Republican nomination in 1988 had been relatively easy. He had eliminated his last remaining rival, Dole, by the end of March. Five months passed before his party held its nominating convention, more than ample time for him to campaign extensively as the new leader of a united party. Despite this advantage, Bush soon fell behind Dukakis and appeared headed for an almost certain defeat. He rebounded through a series of powerful and unanswered televised attacks on Dukakis related to crime, pollution, defense, and patriotism. He reversed the polls by convincing voters that the best of Reagan's policies would continue and that the dangers that seemed present in the undefined appeals of Dukakis would be averted. In contrast, Dukakis is the casebook study of how the summer lead of the challenger can disappear if he fails to address voter doubts about his vague appeals and untested qualifications.

The vice presidency is indeed a double-edged sword. It offers an unusually powerful strategic position from which to seek a party nomination, but it does not provide the same support in the general election that the incumbent president enjoyed in the previous one. The vice president often inherits the partisan friends and political enemies of the president but usually encounters great difficulties in winning the support of the weak partisan and independent voters whose support decides most elections. He can win the support of these voters only after a significant struggle. They are not beyond his reach, however: Bush won many of them to his cause and Nixon and Humphrey almost captured enough of them to win the presidency in their own right.

3

THE CAMPAIGNS FOR THE PARTY NOMINATIONS: 1999

The campaigns for the 2000 party nominations shared two important characteristics that are likely to occur in elections of the immediate future. First, they were resolved far more rapidly than campaigns of previous years. Both concluded with the eleven primaries of March 7. Second, each resulted in the nomination of a candidate whose strategic position reflected the changed dynamics of more recent television age elections and whose selection may very well typify future nominations of the presidential and opposition parties. With respect to the early conclusions, both campaigns began during the early weeks of 1999, when a variety of aspirants announced their intentions. Television news media immediately began depicting each campaign as a battle between two role-playing candidates, a strong but sometimes threatened front-runner and his one leading adversary and political antithesis. Their work was made easy by the fact that one candidate in each party, Bush and Gore, always led his rivals in fund-raising, poll standings, and endorsements of important elected officials. Moreover, since only two Democrats ran for president, the determination of the leading adversary in one campaign was relatively effortless. Television news media faced some difficulties in reporting about the Republicans, however, since the identity of the leading adversary was not obvious. They initially cast Elizabeth Dole in this capacity, later redirected their attention to Steve Forbes when Dole failed, and eventually settled on John McCain during the latter weeks of 1999. They started depicting McCain as the leading adversary of front-runner Bush although several other Republicans who had higher poll standings and more money than the Arizona senator were actively competing for the nomination.

Despite these patterns of news coverage and candidate stereotyping, the campaigns did not last very long. The Democratic one effectively concluded in early February, when Gore won the important electoral tests of Iowa and New Hampshire. After some initial struggles, the Republican battle rapidly moved toward its conclusion after Bush won the hotly contested South Carolina primary on February 19. Television news media responded to these new developments by altering their patterns of coverage in ways that enhanced the generation of consensus within each party behind the candidacy of the eventual nominees. These altered coverage patterns also facilitated the withdrawal of the leading adversaries shortly after the conclusion of the March 7 primaries.

Although it was not the most significant factor in bringing about the early conclusion of the nomination campaigns, the front loading of primaries was certainly an important one. Starting in 1972 and accelerating their efforts in and after 1988, a great number of states advanced their primaries to earlier times in the election calendar with the hope of attracting more attention from the candidates and news media. California, for example, had been conducting its primary in early June for decades but in 1996 changed that date to the last Tuesday in March and then to the first Tuesday in March for 2000. The modern history of primaries began in 1952 when New Hampshire began holding its vote on the second Tuesday in March, a date that made this vote the first primary of an election year. A combination of far-reaching party rule changes in the 1960s and 1970s that required more open delegate selection procedures and the disproportionate amount of candidate and media attention New Hampshire garnered encouraged many states to abandon their caucus methods of delegate selection and adopt primaries instead. Few states initially tried to compete with New Hampshire for the first in the nation status, however; instead they scheduled their primaries for later dates. These expanded numbers of primaries generally took place on various dates between mid-March and early June and frequently resulted in nomination campaigns in which the candidates actively courted their own partisans for about five months, from January to June. In 1972 Iowa joined New Hampshire as an important early electoral test when it began scheduling precinct caucuses at dates earlier than any other state, even New Hampshire. The growing importance of Iowa and New Hampshire in nomination campaigns encouraged some states to reschedule their primaries to earlier dates to compete. Some even tried to schedule primaries on the same day as New Hampshire's. New Hampshire responded by moving its primary to earlier dates.

In an effort to stop this trend and limit the length of the primary season, the Democratic National Committee (DNC) tried unsuccessfully to prevent states other than Iowa and New Hampshire from conducting votes before the second Tuesday in March, the traditional date of the New Hampshire primary. Since 1984, as part of an agreement with the DNC, New Hampshire has been allowed to conduct the first primaries of the election year one week before any other state, and Iowa has been permitted to hold its caucuses eight days before the New Hampshire primary. Several states resisted, but eventually the DNC decided that for 2000 only Iowa and New Hampshire could hold their votes before the first Tuesday in March, a date one week earlier than the one it had preferred. This agreement did not apply to Republicans, however. When Delaware decided to schedule its primary for February 8, Iowa and New Hampshire responded by changing the date of their vote to January 24 and February 1, respectively, from February 14 and 22. Eventually, five other states decided to ignore the DNC rule and scheduled early primaries: South Carolina (February 19), Michigan and Arizona (February 22), and Virginia and Washington (February 29). Since the DNC refused to sanction these primaries, Democrats in those states responded by scheduling caucuses on or after March 7, the first Tuesday in March. These events created an unusual situation in that six states held primaries during February for Republicans only. Depending on a particular state's election laws, the absence of Democratic primaries might encourage Democrats to vote in Republican primaries. Independent voters, who often could choose to participate in either party's primary, would have no choice in these states: they could vote in the Republican primary or not vote at all. This created a political opportunity for a candidate with unusual appeal to Democrats and Independents to compete more effectively in several early Republican primaries of 2000. John McCain would eventually become that candidate. While six states challenged the DNC rules, eleven others, among them California and New York, scheduled Republican and Democratic primaries for March 7, and six more states scheduled primaries for March 14. Eight additional states scheduled caucuses between March 7 and 14. Front-loading of this magnitude meant that over two thirds of the national convention delegates of each party would be chosen by the middle of March.

Although the front-loading of primaries was certainly an important factor in the early resolution of the campaigns, its effect on the eventual selections of Gore and Bush was probably quite limited. These two candidates would have won their party's nomination regardless of the length of the campaigns. Instead, the front-loading appears to have helped Bush in the general election. I discuss this assertion more fully later in chapter 7. Gore and Bush are very typical of the candidates who are likely to emerge as the nominees of the presidential and opposition parties in surrogate incumbent elections. Both held politically advantageous public offices that enhanced their strategic chances for contesting the nomination. Gore, as the sitting vice president, successfully mobilized the vast political resources of the modern presidency and vice presidency, described previously, in his quest for the nomination. This was an advantage that no interparty rival could match. In comparison, Bush was the governor of a major state, Texas, and had the personal backing of a large majority of his fellow Republican governors. Legal changes in the financing of nomination campaigns since 1972 have provided an important, but perhaps unintended, advantage to governors in their efforts to attain the nomination of the opposition party. Bush successfully manipulated this new advantage in 2000 and won the Republican nomination.

The Federal Election Campaign Act, enacted in 1972, limits financial contributions to presidential candidates from individuals to one thousand dollars and from political committees to five thousand dollars and provides limited federal funding for candidates. Two major consequences of this law are that candidates must now start fundraising efforts much earlier than in the past and must solicit funds from a far larger pool of contributors. Possession of a governor's office appears to be a particularly valuable strategic position from which to master these new fund-raising requirements and may well be the most valuable position from which to contest the nomination of the opposition party.

A governor's office gives a candidate several unique advantages. In a time when campaigns have increasingly become candidate-centered, successful aspirants for governor must now more than ever develop individualized networks of contributors within their own states. Although they may obtain some contributions from sources outside their states, candidates for governor are usually less appealing to national interest groups than aspirants for congressional office. Once elected, governors have many opportunities to expand their networks of home state contributors through their association with the executive branch of state government, which is not available to members of Congress. These individualized and home state–based financial networks can then form the foundation of a fund-raising effort for a presidential campaign. Indeed, Bush raised more of his contributions in Texas than in any other state.

In addition, today's governors have many opportunities to work with governors of other states through such forums as governor's associations, intergovernmental organizations, and interstate compacts. Through these, governors can seek electoral and financial support for a presidential campaign from their fellow partisan governors who have developed their own individualized home state financial and political networks. The active support of fellow governors often translates into more fund-raising success when a governor seeks the presidency. One can see evidence of the importance of the governor's office in the campaigns of the opposition party since the passage of the Federal Election Campaign Act. Seven presidential elections have taken place since 1972, and the opposition party nominated a governor or former governor in five of them: Jimmy Carter in 1976, Ronald Reagan in 1980, Michael Dukakis in 1988, Bill Clinton in 1992, and George W. Bush in 2000. Each raised more money from his home state than from any other state, and each gained the endorsements of more of his party's governors than any other candidate. The only two instances since 1972 when the opposition party nominated someone other than a governor or former governor were in 1984, when the Democrats selected the former vice president Walter Mondale, and in 1996, when the Republicans chose Senator Robert Dole, their 1980 vice-presidential nominee. In contrast, the opposition party nominated members of the Senate in three of the four elections that took place immediately before the passage of the Federal Election Campaign Act: John F. Kennedy in 1960, Barry Goldwater in 1964, and George McGovern in 1972.

The central theme of this analysis is that television age presidential elections are decided through the phenomenon of mediated incumbency, that is, the strength of incumbency and the manner in which television news media interpret that strength and illustrate it to their viewing audience. In 2000, incumbency was mediated through

the actions of a surrogate, the vice president, who attempted to succeed a controversial incumbent. As a surrogate, the vice president
found, as earlier vice presidents of the television age had also found,
that his office was a mixed blessing. It provided certain unique opportunities for inheriting some valued attributes of incumbency, but it
also placed other valued attributes of incumbency far beyond his
reach. Gore successfully used his office as a strategic position for rallying his own partisans to his own cause, but he could never employ the
powers and imagery of the modern presidency in ways that would
have distinguished him from his rivals. Instead, he often appeared, as
earlier vice presidents had appeared, as simply another role-filling
aspirant for office. With this in mind, I discuss the nomination campaigns in a manner similar to that in which television news media
presented them through their daily telecasts. The reader can follow
the campaigns in a way that encompasses the messages and imagery
that the television viewer of politics received from the three major
networks. In describing campaign events and related media coverage,
I focus far more attention on the Republicans. I do this because television news media devoted far more of their time to reporting about the
Republicans. On most days, television news media reported about the
Republicans before they looked at the Democrats. All too frequently,
the Democratic campaign seemed to exist in the shadows of the Republican effort. I follow the campaigns from their beginnings in the
early months of 1999 when the candidates announced their intentions and started their fund-raising activities through the conclusions
on March 9, 2000. This date is important because that is when the two
adversaries, Bradley and McCain, withdrew, and the front-runners,
Gore and Bush, claimed victory. I show how television news media
used early successes in fund-raising and polls to stereotype the candidates in their preferred roles of front-runner, leading adversary, and
others. Finally, I demonstrate how television news media used this
stereotyping while reporting on the major campaign events such as
the Iowa caucuses on January 24; the New Hampshire primary on
February 1; several additional Republican primaries in February, including South Carolina; and the concluding primaries of March 7.

REPUBLICANS

The first political developments among Republicans in 1999 that
caught the attention of television news media were the announcements by various aspirants of their intentions to form exploratory
committees. Exploratory committees are organizations that aspirants use to solicit funds and build support and today serve as the

political equivalents of actual announcements of candidacy. The creation of such committees usually results in media coverage of aspirants' intentions and political activities and helps set the stage for actual announcements of candidacy months later. In January, the Red Cross director Elizabeth Dole and the former vice president Dan Quayle announced the formation of their committees. Dole made her intentions known on the fourth, and Quayle spoke on the twenty- first. One network, ABC, devoted about two minutes of its broadcast time on both days to reporting about these announcements, with John Cochran as the correspondent. In contrast, CBS reported only about Dole, with Phil Jones as correspondent, and NBC devoted only twenty seconds of its time each day to mentioning the creation of the two committees. One month later, however, on February 15, the NBC correspondent Lisa Myers reported on the creation of a committee for Congressman John Kasich of Ohio and used this opportunity to describe the efforts and assess the chances of Kasich, Dole, and Quayle. The other two networks made very short mentions of Kasich's announcement.

Several other aspirants formed committees over the next two months, but with one notable exception, television news media paid virtually no attention to any of them. Three unsuccessful contenders for the 1996 nomination, the commentator Pat Buchanan, the former Tennessee governor Lamar Alexander, and the publisher Steve Forbes, announced their intentions during March. They did so on the second, ninth, and sixteenth of the month, respectively. None of them received more than a few seconds of notice on any of the three networks. The one exception to this pattern of a lack of media attention was George W. Bush. Bush also made his announcement in March, but this time each network devoted about two to three minutes of its broadcast time to reporting about it and analyzing Bush's electoral prospects. Peter Jennings introduced the ABC coverage of March 3 by describing Bush as the surprising front-runner. Jackie Judd followed by saying that Bush was so well positioned as a perceived front-runner that Republican leaders believed he could raise about $20 million to $30 million easily and quickly. Judd added that nearly half of the nation's Republican governors had endorsed Bush and were prepared to put their fundraising apparatus to work for him. This news report contained a visual image of Bush's sitting next to the Michigan governor, John Engler, who would later be a major player in the Bush effort in his state's primary. Judd added that many prominent members of the Republican establishment viewed Bush as the candidate with the best chance of winning the election.

Judd outlined four of Bush's political strengths, which included his ability to excel in person-to-person campaigning, and said that Bush connected with moderates without alienating conservatives, was a baby boomer who emphasized issues like education, and appealed to women and Hispanics. The report contained a scene of Bush's speaking Spanish before an audience. Bob McNamara of CBS included scenes in his report of Bush's speaking before a group of supporters about his interest in seeking the presidency. Tom Brokaw of NBC described how a steady stream of politically important visitors had traveled to Texas to see Bush and added that Bush had been getting high approval ratings in Texas after six years as governor.

All three networks used poll standings to support their depictions of Bush as the front-runner. McNamara actually used the term *front-runner*. Brokaw noted that a poll from the Pew Research Institute showed that 72 percent of respondents were willing to consider voting for Bush, whereas only 64 and 52 percent, respectively, had said the same about Elizabeth Dole and Al Gore. One can see the strength of Bush's early support in relation to other Republicans in the results of two surveys by the Gallup-CNN-*USA Today* Poll from 1998. In a poll of May 11 of that year, taken nearly six months before Bush won reelection to a second term as governor, Bush had the support of 30 percent of Republicans and Dole had the backing of only 14 percent. Quayle and Forbes were next at 9 and 7 percent, respectively. In an October 27 poll Bush was ahead of Dole by 39 percent to 17 with Quayle and Forbes at 12 and 7 percent.

The reader should understand that television news media did not create these poll numbers and did not force Republican leaders and voters to see Bush as their party's greatest prospect for winning the election. Instead, they looked at the potential candidates and determined that Bush was the most likely winner of the nomination, drawing their conclusions from his poll standings and support from party leaders. With this, they proclaimed Bush as the front-runner and then structured their reporting to reflect that designation, establishing him as the central political actor in their campaign reporting and evaluating all events and other actors in relation to him. Formation of the exploratory committee had more televised news coverage than that of all of the other Republican candidates. In addition, Elizabeth Dole appeared in these early indicators as the strongest of Bush's rivals. Hence, television news media looked upon her as the leading adversary and directed more attention to her than to any of the other rivals. The total broadcast time the various aspirants received while making their intentions known varied directly with their standings in the polls. Bush received the greatest amount of coverage, Dole the second most. Although they would report extensively about John McCain when he formally announced his candidacy in September, television news media ignored the announcements of Senators Bob Smith of New Hampshire and Orrin Hatch of Utah, the religious spokesman Gary Bauer, and the radio talk show host Allan Keyes.

During the weeks that followed these announcements, television news media occasionally reported new developments in the campaign, but their interest was both infrequent and limited. They usually focused exclusively on Bush, sometimes in contrast to the Democratic front-runner, Al Gore. Only rarely did they look at any of the other Republican aspirants, and when they did, they usually grouped them together and depicted them only as Bush's rivals. For example, on March 7, less than one week after he had announced his intentions, Bush was the focus of an ABC news report on his personal background; correspondent Mike von Fremd identified Bush as the front-runner in this report. Several weeks later, on May 31, von Fremd again reported about Bush, this time looking at his recent statements on foreign policy and his accomplishments as governor of Texas. Von Fremd also analyzed Bush's prospects of winning the nomination and general election. Two weeks later, in mid-June, Bush made his first overtly political trip of the year, to the early test states of Iowa and New Hampshire, and used it as an opportunity to make a formal announcement of candidacy. The trip attracted extensive media coverage. John Roberts, the CBS weekend anchor, began the political reporting on June 12, "The front-runner for the Republican nomination had taken the wraps off his campaigning today as he roared into Iowa." Roberts then introduced Bob McNamara, who looked at Bush's appearance at a statewide Republican meeting. McNamara informed the viewers that Bush was leading in the polls. David Bloom of NBC and Dean Reynolds of ABC, who reported on Bush that day for their respective networks, also identified the Texas governor as the front-runner. Reynolds added that Bush was riding so high in the polls he had no place to go except down. All three networks included scenes of Bush's stepping out of an airplane accompanied by his wife, Laura, and speaking enthusiastically to various crowds when announcing his candidacy. McNamara added that Bush had already raised about $15 million in contributions; Bloom said that Republicans wanted a candidate who they thought could win and Bush seemed to be that candidate. In addition to leading his rivals in the polls, Bush was ahead of them in fund-raising and endorsements from leading Republicans, Bloom added. After showing excerpts of an interview with Bush, Bloom said most Bush supporters acknowledged they did not really know what he stood for; however, many saw him as the candidate who could win the election.

The extensive news coverage of Bush continued two days later when he visited New Hampshire. Peter Jennings of ABC remarked that Bush was attracting an enormous crowd of reporters and camera people in his first day of campaigning for the New Hampshire primary. Dean Reynolds of ABC added that Bush was leading in the polls, had recently had his picture on the covers of *Newsweek* and *Time*, and had supporters who had a sense of inevitability about his nomination. David Bloom of NBC reported on Bush's activities in New Hampshire, and Lisa Myers of NBC focused on his successes in fund-raising. Network correspondents did not completely ignore the other candidates that day but rarely saw them as contenders in their own right. Gary Bauer had some brief comments about Bush on NBC, and Lamar Alexander attacked the Texas governor for his extensive fund-raising and accused him of trying to buy the nomination on CBS.

The horse race theme dominated television news coverage of Bush's rivals. For example, on May 8 John Cochran of ABC described Dole's attempt to make gun control an issue but focused most of his attention on her difficulty in generating support in Iowa. Bob Schieffer on CBS reported on May 19 Dole's troubles in gaining support nationwide, although he did not focus his attention on a specific state. On June 12, while Bush was in Iowa, Lisa Myers of NBC looked at the campaigns of Dole, Alexander, and McCain and pointed out that they were making little headway against Bush. Her report followed David Bloom's review of Bush's Iowa appearance, however. One week later, on June 19, Phil Jones of CBS characterized the other candidates, that is, Alexander, Bauer, Buchanan, Kasich, and Dole, as failing to emerge from behind the Bush shadow. An exception to this theme occurred on May 31 when Jerry Bowen on CBS interviewed McCain and looked at his experiences as a prisoner of war in Vietnam. Finally, one news report that perhaps indicates the difficulties of candidates other than the media-proclaimed front-runner in attaining independent coverage occurred on ABC on June 19. Jane Clayson looked at the various campaigns in California and devoted some time to reviewing the efforts of Dole and McCain. These two candidates received far less attention than the front-runner, however. The front-runner who dominated the news was Al Gore.

Political observers often refer to the year before a presidential election as the "invisible primary." This term derives from the practices of the candidates spending much of their time during it raising money and building support among party leaders and activists and and rarely making direct appeals to voters. Television news media were often quite invisible themselves during 1999, providing limited coverage, or none at all, of the candidates' actually engaging in these necessary campaign practices. They emerged to report about some unusual events, however, such as Bush's trips to Iowa and New Hampshire. The next events after Bush's trips that attracted their attention were the required filings by the candidates of quarterly financial reports with the Federal Election Commission on June 30.

The main story that day was that Bush had actually been more successful at raising money than expected: he had raised $36.2 million in the seventeen weeks since he had formed his exploratory committee, more than twice as much at this stage of the campaign as any other candidate had in history. In contrast, Gore had raised $18.5 million and Bradley had taken in $11.5 million. The various Republican candidates were far behind, McCain at $6.1 million, Dole at $3.4 million and Quayle at $3.1 million. Each network reported the fundraising totals in some detail, and Brian Williams, NBC anchor that day, said that political pros call early fund-raising the first primary and added that "we have a winner in Bush." Jane Clayson of ABC looked at Bush's successes in California, where he had just completed two days of fund-raising with a payoff of $3.7 million. Clayson said funds of that magnitude allowed Bush both to intimidate his rivals and to pay for expensive television advertising. Bush had two goals in his early efforts, Clayson added: to raise enough money that he would not have to rely on federal matching funds to finance his primary efforts and to protect himself from candidates with deep pockets, such as Steve Forbes. With respect to the former, the acceptance of federal matching funds requires candidates to limit their expenditures in each state and their overall spending to $40.5 million for the nomination campaign. If Bush could raise more than that sum, he would not need any federal funding to support his effort. This would permit him to spend as much as he wanted in individual states, particularly those with early primaries. As for the latter, in 1996 Forbes spent over $30 million of his own funds in an extensive advertising campaign that caused serious problems for the eventual nominee Robert Dole. Dole often could not counter Forbes's spending and therefore found the nomination far more difficult to attain. Without the spending limitations forced by matching funds, Bush would be free to counter Forbes if the New Jersey publisher were to engage in yet another big spending quest for the nomination.

Bill Whitaker, reporting that day for CBS, said that Bush was drawing large crowds in California and was confident about his chances. Bush was marching through California, a stronghold of Bill Clinton, and hoping to establish himself firmly as a national candidate, Whitaker added. Whitaker referred to Bush's use of the characterization—Bush's mantra as Whitaker depicted it— "compassionate conservative" to describe himself. Bush was avoiding stands on controversial issues such as affirmative action and immigration and was attempting to stake out more middle ground positions, Whitaker said. Whitaker concluded by remarking that Republicans seemed to like this approach and were jumping on the Bush bandwagon.

The political news of June 30 was not limited to Bush, however, as Bob Schieffer on CBS looked at how McCain had been using his position as chairman of the Senate Commerce Committee to urge lobbyists to contribute to his campaign. Gwen Ifill on NBC focused on the Democrats.

After this, television news media found little of interest to report about Republicans until the Iowa straw poll in mid-August. Occasionally, they referred to Bush's fund-raising successes, and all three networks noted Bush's announcement of July 15 that he would not accept federal funds. The only references to any of Bush's rivals prior to the straw poll were on July 14, when Kasich withdrew from the campaign, and on July 31, when Alexander had a brief comment in an ABC report about how well Bush was running in Iowa. The Iowa straw poll was the ultimate pseudoevent. The Republican State Committee planned to conduct a presidential preference vote at a fund-raising event at the Iowa State Fair. Any Republican could participate simply by making a twenty-five-dollar contribution to the party. The results would not be a part of the process of selecting the actual delegates who would attend the national convention, which would not begin until the caucuses of late January. Instead, the outcome was a test of the organizational strength of individual campaigns and an indication of how well the candidates were faring. Since the candidates considered it important, television and other news media responded with extensive coverage.

Televised news coverage of events related to the straw poll paralleled the standings of the candidates in polls and fund-raising. Since Bush had been most successful in these activities, he received the lion's share of coverage and was the central political actor of virtually all news reports. His rivals received far less coverage and were usually evaluated only in relation to him. Eric Engberg of CBS devoted much of his report of August 13, poll day, to Bush and to his success in fund-raising. Engberg briefly looked at Dole, Alexander, Hatch, Quayle, Forbes, and Bauer but treated all of them only as Bush's rivals. He identified Forbes as the one candidate who had the necessary funds to challenge Bush. Mike von Fremd of ABC also focused on Bush and made only brief reference to Forbes, Dole, Bauer, and Quayle. Lisa Myers of NBC directed her attention to Bush, reporting that he had spent about $1 million in Iowa. Myers questioned whether any candidate could defeat him.

One network, NBC, had a news report that actually featured someone other than Bush as the central political actor, as Anne Thompson looked at the way Elizabeth Dole's campaign was failing. Dole had begun with great promise, Thompson stated, but now seemed to be fading. Thompson described Dole as a Republican star who had lost her luster. She attributed this to Dole's inability to send a clear message that distinguished her from her rivals and to her attacks on the wrong target, Bill Clinton, rather than her Republican rivals. Dole had raised about $3.5 million, only about one tenth of Bush's total. Dole was also running third in various Iowa surveys, Thompson added.

The results of the straw poll were as expected: Bush finished first with 31 percent of the vote, Forbes second at 21 percent, and Dole at 14 percent third. The remaining candidates, particularly Alexander, Bauer, Buchanan, and Quayle, all of whom had actively competed, ran poorly. Television news media reported extensively about the outcomes. Lisa Myers on NBC again identified Bush as the frontrunner in her report of Sunday, August 15, and had more images of him than of any other candidate. Myers included some comments by Forbes and Dole and a minor scene featuring Quayle. Myers said there were three ways to measure the candidates: polls, money, and the Iowa vote. Bush had won all three overwhelmingly. Mike von Fremd of ABC illustrated scenes of the candidates in the order of their finish, Bush first and then Forbes and Dole. He had a brief scene of Bauer. One day later, in looking at the likely effect of the straw poll on the chances of the weaker candidates, Bob Schieffer, anchor for CBS, said that there was a new spin on "who's hot and who's not." He introduced Eric Engberg, who focused on some of the candidates who had lost, particularly Alexander and Quayle. Engberg said several of these candidates would soon be leaving the race. Alexander, in fact, had done just that on that very day. Buchanan would announce on September 11 his intention of joining the Reform Party,

Quayle would end his candidacy on September 26, and Dole would abandon her effort on October 20. The Republican campaign had initially attracted twelve candidates but by the end of October had been reduced to only half that number. Alexander, Buchanan, Quayle, Dole, Kasich, and Smith were gone. The six candidates who remained were Bush, Forbes, Bauer, Hatch, Keyes, and the one candidate who had chosen to bypass Iowa, John McCain.

With the conclusion of the Iowa poll, the Republican campaign increasingly began to look like the story of George W. Bush's running for president against several minor candidates who merely stood as obstacles he had to overcome in his path to political power. This new context was evident in the political reporting of August 19, when the main story was a controversy surrounding Bush that related to his possible past use of cocaine. Bush had told a Dallas reporter that he could pass the drug test standard used by the Clinton administration, which required that persons had not used illegal drugs for the previous seven years. Later, he told a group of reporters that he could have passed the more demanding test in effect during his father's administration, which required persons not to have used drugs for the preceding fifteen years. According to network correspondents who reported this controversy, such a statement meant that Bush had admitted he had not used cocaine since 1974. What about before that date?, some of them asked. Bush would not answer the question. Before the day was over, all three networks looked at Bush and the cocaine controversy in one manner or another. Eric Engberg on CBS said that Bush had opened the door to media inquiry into his possible past use of drugs. Charles Gibson and John Martin of ABC looked at the controversy, and Martin included comments by a variety of people, including Orrin Hatch. David Bloom of NBC said that Bush wanted a "statute of limitations" relating to drug use. Pete Williams on NBC said that both Gore and Bradley had already spoken about their own past use of marijuana and the remaining Republican candidates had denied having ever used illegal drugs. Their statements created little or no controversy.

The media emphasis on Bush continued on August 31, when NBC and CBS once again reported the governor's fund-raising successes. Jane Pauley, NBC anchor, began the political coverage by saying, "Critics may say George W. Bush lacks depth when it comes to his policy positions, but now there is fresh evidence of the incredible depth of his financial support." After defining Bush as the front-runner, Pauley introduced David Bloom, who said that Bush had already raised $50 million, a figure he called considerably higher than the

$38.5 million Clinton and Robert Dole had raised together by this stage of their campaigns four years earlier. Bloom also reported that Bush had raised this money from 108,000 individual contributors, a record number. Gloria Borger on CBS added that Bush might be better known for his money than for his ideas.

McCain soon emerged as the strongest candidate who blocked Bush's path to the nomination. McCain was pursuing an unorthodox strategy that, if successful, promised to pose a serious challenge to Bush. He was concentrating virtually all of his time and resources in New Hampshire while ignoring Iowa. A strong showing in New Hampshire could translate into extensive media coverage that might then enable him to become far better known in other parts of the nation. McCain hoped to use this free media attention to attain the personal recognition that other candidates sought through expensive advertising campaigns. By September, the strategy appeared to be working. McCain had also enhanced his prospects by avoiding the Iowa poll. Other candidates had invested heavily in Iowa, only to lose. The losses drained the finances of Alexander, Buchanan, Dole, and Quayle and encouraged perceptions of them as losers.

Television news media were very attentive when McCain formally announced his candidacy on September 27, focusing their coverage on two themes, McCain's personality and his electoral prospects. With respect to the former, Bill Whitaker of CBS said that McCain prided himself on "going his own way" and was now asking the American people to go with him into the new millennium. He described McCain as a conservative Republican who backed vouchers and tax cuts but who bucked party leaders on campaign finance reform. Lisa Myers on NBC described McCain as "ever the maverick" and as a person who kicked the political establishment of both parties. She added that McCain was critical of both the Republican Congress and the Clinton presidency and believed government had become the spectacle of selfish ambition auctioned to the highest bidder. In exploring electoral prospects, Whitaker said McCain was trailing Bush in both polls and money but hoped to overcome these problems with strong showings in the early primaries in New Hampshire, South Carolina, and California. Myers said the question was whether McCain could win, given Bush's commanding lead. The front-runner would have to stumble, she continued, and Republicans then cast around for an alternative. Myers concluded by saying McCain hoped independent voters in New Hampshire and South Carolina would give him upsets in those states.

Television news media followed a consistent script through the remainder of 1999. In some instances they depicted Bush as the front-runner and reported only about him; on others they looked at both Bush and McCain, treating McCain as the adversary. Sometimes they contrasted the front-runners of the two opposing parties, Bush and Gore, with one another while ignoring all other candidates. For example, on October 5 and 6 the various networks reported about a disagreement Bush had with congressional leaders of his own party over education on ABC and CBS. On October 9 John Palmer on NBC looked at the importance of Hispanic power in presidential politics and included comments by Bush and Gore. Two weeks later, on October 27, Lisa Myers on NBC talked about the most recent NBC poll, which showed that voters preferred Bush to Gore by 49 to 35 percent and that 68 percent of Republicans supported Bush for the nomination compared to only 15 percent who backed McCain. The only significant news coverage McCain received during October in which he was not depicted in a supporting role in a report about Bush occurred in reports on October 15 and 20, in reports about campaign finance reform. McCain commented on the need for reforms and was critical of congressional resistance to enacting them. These patterns of news coverage continued through November and December. In November, network correspondents reported about Bush on education on NBC, about his inability to name certain world leaders when responding to a reporter's question on ABC, and about his first appearance on a Sunday morning talk show on NBC. All three networks reported about his delivery of major speeches about foreign policy on November 19 and about tax cuts on December 1. On December 2, they made Bush the center of attention when reporting about a New Hampshire debate among the six Republican candidates. Anchors Peter Jennings on ABC and Dan Rather on CBS identified Bush as the front-runner when introducing the correspondents who discussed debate preparations. Bush was the central actor in all reports, and in most instances, he was the only candidate to receive any significant news coverage. Finally, ABC reported about recent developments in the campaigns of Gore and Bush on December 5, and CBS described Bush's opposition to campaign finance reform on December 16.

Although television news media focused most of their attention on Bush, they did look more intensively at McCain during the latter weeks of 1999 as the Arizona senator's campaign accelerated and his poll standings increased. Each network looked at McCain at least once between November 22 and December 6 in his new role as Bush's leading adversary. Eric Engberg of CBS described McCain's personal background and mentioned his rise in the polls on November 22. David Bloom on NBC and Linda Douglass on ABC, while reporting for their respective networks on December 6, looked at McCain's growing importance as a candidate. Six days later, Douglass said that people in New Hampshire were lining up to see McCain and that he had already spent forty-three days campaigning as a war hero in this conservative state. Peter Jennings on ABC had prefaced Douglass's remarks by reporting about two polls taken in New Hampshire by the *Boston Herald*. A poll of October 26 had shown Bush ahead of McCain by 44 percent to 26 percent, whereas a new one had Bush ahead by only one point, 34 percent to 33 percent. Finally, in reports that demonstrated that the campaigns for both the Republican and Democratic nominations had developed into two-candidate battles, all three networks looked at the leading adversaries, McCain and Bill Bradley, on December 19. The event that attracted their attention was a joint statement by the candidates of their opposition to the use of "soft money" in New Hampshire (*soft money* is the term often used to describe the unregulated and unlimited contributions that individuals and committees can make to political parties). Television news media were now ready to begin their daily coverage of the Republican campaign in January 2000.

DEMOCRATS

The early phases of the campaign for the Democratic nomination were considerably different from those of the Republicans. The Democratic campaign attracted far fewer candidates and, as a consequence, far less attention from television news media. One constant in both 1999, when the campaigns were in their preparatory stages, and the first weeks of 2000, when the candidates competed in the primaries, was that television news media always found the Democratic race far less interesting than the race among Republicans. The first televised reports about any of the Democratic candidates, other than brief mentions of Gore that lasted only a few seconds, occurred in May. By this time, two candidates had emerged as contenders for the nomination, Vice President Al Gore and the former New Jersey senator Bill Bradley. Absent from network news, the most interesting ongoing story before May might well have been the announcements of noncandidacy by several leading Democrats. Throughout the early months of 1999 five potential candidates—at least potential in the sense that news sources had occasionally reported they might be candidates—made public announcements that they would not run for president. The group included three senators, John Kerry of Massachusetts, Robert Kerrey of Nebraska, and Paul Wellstone of Minnesota, and two party leaders who had, along with Gore, contested the party nomination in 1988: House Minority Leader Richard Gephardt and the Reverend Jesse Jackson.

Television news media, in this instance ABC, looked at Gore on May 16, when the vice president was in Iowa to talk about education in what would be his first major address of the campaign. Another network, CBS, used Gore's appearance as an opportunity to focus attention on Bradley two days later. Gore spoke about new governmental initiatives relating to school violence and financial aid for people who planned careers in teaching, but these topics attracted little media interest. Instead, viewers were introduced to what would become a recurring theme during much of 1999, the troubles of the Gore campaign. Carole Simpson, ABC anchor, on May 16 introduced this topic when she said Gore's supporters believed the speech was what he needed to get his wobbling campaign back on track. John Cochran then focused on Gore's troubles by saying presidents usually announce policy initiatives, then adding that Bill Clinton was having Gore make announcements at this time because the vice president was having trouble starting his campaign. Cochran described several of Gore's problems and then pointed out that about fifty members of Congress had recently warned the vice president that his campaign was faltering and that he needed to take a strong stand on something. Cochran said Clinton was so worried he had told the *New York Times* that he had urged Gore to be less rigid in campaigning. Cochran used these events as evidence to conclude that the Gore campaign was in disarray and was in so much trouble that it needed to bring in a new manager, in the former congressman Tony Coelho. Some of Gore's problems were self-inflicted, Cochran stated, and then provided an example with a recent Gore misstatement, in which the vice president had said that he was responsible for inventing the Internet. After including some scenes of Bradley's shooting basketballs, Cochran said, "Sometimes people simply want change." He concluded by saying that for Gore the five most dangerous words in the English language were "It's time for a change."

Dan Rather began the political component of the CBS news about Bradley by informing viewers that Bradley was trailing Gore in the polls. Phil Jones followed with a report from New Hampshire about the promises and problems facing Bradley. After including scenes of Bradley's playing basketball, Jones said the question was "what kind of shot did he have against Gore." Jones added that many disgruntled Democrats did not trust Gore and wanted an alternative.

With this, Jones included a scene in which Bradley talked about the importance of trust. Although he tended to mention trust in virtually every speech, Bradley was often vague about major issues and did not plan to take major stands until later, Jones said. This approach often resulted in vague answers to questions and often made it difficult for people to see how Bradley differed from Gore. After mentioning that Bradley was behind Gore in both polls and money, Jones said Bradley knew he had to win the first primary of next year or the New Hampshire sun would set on his campaign.

There was little media interest in the Democrats for about a month after this, but interest revived in mid-June, when Gore formally announced his candidacy. Gore chose to make the announcement from his childhood hometown of Carthage, Tennessee. The first network to report about the event was CBS; on June 13, Phil Jones reported on Gore's pending announcement while emphasizing the theme of Gore's troubles. Jones reviewed Gore's political background and then added that the vice president's experiences were not registering in public opinion polls. Gore was trying to reach certain key constituencies, such as women, who had twice supported Clinton but who did not seem particularly supportive of his efforts, Jones added. Jones made these comments while showing images of First Lady Hillary Clinton's introducing Gore to a woman's group. Jones then reviewed what he described as Gore's central problem. He said the vice president had been loyal to Clinton during the past years, including the difficult times of impeachment, but now faced a delicate political necessity. Gore needed to separate himself from Clinton's character but also needed to carry the mantle of the centrist Democrats who had been the key to Clinton's victories. Gore had the organization and money to fight and wage a battle for the nomination but now had a formidable opponent in Bradley, Jones concluded. Jones noted that only one sitting vice president had been elected president during the past century, George Bush.

Gore announced his candidacy three days later and NBC used this opportunity to make their first news report of the year about the Democrats. Claire Shipman also employed the theme of a troubled Gore campaign. Gore, she said, was one of the most recognized men in America, but after twenty-five years of public service voters did not seem to know him. Gore needed to reintroduce himself, she added. Shipman stated that the most critical part of the vice president's message was the theme that whereas he and Clinton might be partners, he was not Clinton. Shipman added that Gore, whom people often considered boring, was trying to create a new image. She then explored three possible images: moral family man, leader of economic prosperity, and real person instead of wooden figure.

Television news media focused only limited attention on the Democratic candidates in the weeks that followed Gore's announcement. Each network looked at Bradley once between mid-June and early September, however. On June 30, after NBC anchor Brian Williams identified Bradley as the challenger running an uphill battle, Gwen Ifill focused attention on his fund-raising efforts. She reported that Bradley had raised about $11.5 million compared to Gore's $18.5 million. Ifill said Bradley had raised his funds without backing from the White House, which had proved helpful to Gore, and was therefore a real challenger to the vice president. Ifill described Bradley as a political rarity, a wild card. She added that he was the only choice for Democrats who wanted an alternative to Gore and pointed out that Bradley had raised his money, and much of his support for that matter, from financiers and the computer industry. Ifill concluded that Bradley was not close to Gore in support among Democrats as measured by any poll, but his money would enable him to give Gore a contest for the nomination. The other two networks had similar reports about Bradley, on July 5 on ABC and on July 11 on CBS. Both emphasized the theme that Bradley was Gore's only adversary, was trailing in the polls, but would give Gore a strong challenge. Neither suggested that he would win the nomination, however.

While using the theme of Bradley as the well financed challenger, television news media continued emphasizing the theme that Gore was the troubled front-runner. On August 3, Phil Jones on CBS looked at Gore and included some remarks about Bradley. Jones talked about another shakeup in Gore's campaign staff, the resignation of his staff director. Jones depicted the Gore campaign as in disarray and used several examples of recent gaffes to support the contention. He mentioned how Gore had been in New Hampshire on a canoe trip for a photo opportunity. State power officials had released some additional water into the river in order to keep Gore's canoe afloat but had done so during a drought. Jones then looked at how Gore had hired a public relations director who had been a publicity director for the same tobacco company Gore had criticized at the 1996 Democratic convention for selling the cigarettes that had contributed to his sister's death. Jones even included a scene in which campaign signs had partially blocked the view that some television cameras had of Gore when the vice president announced his candidacy. In looking at Bradley, Jones emphasized the same theme as other correspondents: that Bradley was trailing in the polls, in this instance by a margin of about two to one, but was confident he could do well.

Bradley announced his candidacy from his childhood home in Missouri on September 8. The news coverage was extensive on this first day, when all three networks focused attention on Bradley simultaneously. Peter Jennings on ABC summed up the media view of the Bradley effort by remarking, "Six months ago, if you asked does this guy have a chance for the Democratic nomination, the answer would be no. Today it is some chance." Dean Reynolds on ABC remarked that the Bradley effort was still a long shot but had a polished look with a good hometown crowd and a cutting message that American prosperity was being wasted. Bradley referred to health care, children in poverty, and people falling behind while the stock market soared. Reynolds then focused on political tactics, mentioning that Gore had a lead of forty-five percentage points over Bradley in the latest ABC poll, 69 percent to 24 percent. Reynolds looked at Bradley's strengths and weaknesses, saying the strengths were his lack of ties to Clinton. Bradley's greatest problems were his alleged lack of party loyalty and the fact that much of his fame was based on basketball rather than politics.

Phil Jones on CBS gave particular emphasis to Bradley's references to health care, race relations, and a soaring economy that had left many people behind. Jones also talked about the fund-raising accomplishments of the two candidates and mentioned the $11.5 million and $18.5 million Bradley and Gore had raised, respectively. He concluded that Bradley faced an uphill battle in knocking off Gore because the vice president enjoyed all the advantages of incumbency.

Anne Thompson of NBC said that Bradley was defining himself as an outsider and was trying to separate himself from the vice president of an administration plagued by scandal. She also described him as an ideological moderate who was trying to appeal to the Democratic Party's left wing on the issues of racial equality, campaign finance reform, and gun control. Thompson added that Bradley was attempting to sell his identity, had surprising strength, and had a chance to win a contest that many political observers had once thought Gore had already won.

Tim Russert on NBC looked at the strategy Bradley might use to win the nomination. He reminded viewers that it is always tough to defeat a sitting vice president for the nomination but then hinted that Bradley might have a chance. Bradley would need to finish close behind Gore in the Iowa caucuses and then win the first primary of the year in New Hampshire. A victory in New Hampshire could propel Bradley to victories in the two big primaries of March 7, California and New York, where successes could make him the front-runner and potential nominee. Russert described Bradley as an outsider, an alternative, and an underdog who needed to appeal to Independent voters of New Hampshire to overcome Gore's strength with the Democratic establishment. Bradley was working this base vigorously, Russert added.

With the Bradley announcement, the Democrats once again faded from media view. They resurfaced in late September with the occurrence of two events, an appearance, but not a debate, by both candidates before the DNC, and Gore's moving his headquarters from Washington, D.C., to Nashville. Lisa Myers reported about the DNC meeting on September 25, saying that Gore had promised "to work his heart out" and Bradley had promised the party leaders "real choices." Myers depicted the people at this meeting, the Democratic establishment in her words, as Gore's crowd. She talked about how Gore had improved his campaign style, adopting a more casual approach, and had "come out from behind the vice presidential seal." Although Gore gave a better than usual speech, he still seemed to be overly choreographed, Myers added. In contrast, Myers described Bradley as low-key and depicted him as comfortable and authentic. She added that much of Bradley's support was due to "Clinton Fatigue," in that many people associated Gore with Clinton. Bradley was also gaining because Gore's uneven performances and sagging poll numbers were creating doubts among Democrats that he could be elected president. Myers referred to an NBC poll that showed that only 32 percent of voters had a favorable view of Gore compared to 36 percent who viewed him unfavorably. Myers cautioned viewers that Gore had powerful advantages, including the support of Clinton and key constituencies of the Democratic Party. Gore's aura of invincibility was gone, however, thus setting up what appeared to be a long fight for the nomination, Myers concluded.

The theme of Gore's troubles resurfaced four days later, when two networks reported about the opening of the new headquarters. Tom Brokaw on NBC said Gore was changing the scenery and writing a new script for the campaign because of the growing popularity of Bradley. Peter Jennings on ABC said Gore's campaign had been stumbling and his lead in New Hampshire had disappeared. John Cochran on ABC said Gore needed a new campaign because the old one was not working. Gore had been spending money, Cochran said, "hand over fist," whereas Bradley had been getting more attention and rising poll numbers. Gore had the problem that far too many people saw him as a Washington insider, Cochran stated. In addition, the campaign staff was top heavy with prominent party officials giving conflicting advice. Cochran gave three examples, including instances of Gore's trying to get out from under Clinton's image, then trying not to. Gore had also attempted to look both presidential and informal and had challenged Bradley to debates and then tried to avoid them. Andrea Mitchell on NBC said that Gore was trying to jump-start his campaign for the third time in the past three months. He was leaving his high-rent Washington headquarters and moving, in Mitchell's words, "lock, stock, and barrel" to Nashville. Mitchell included scenes of a press conference question she had asked Gore about whether this move was an attempt to stop the hemorrhaging of money and support. Mitchell also looked at the New Hampshire campaign and pointed out that Bradley had been getting rave reviews in the press while Gore had been spending much of his money on polls, consultants, and staff. The money drain was so great that Bradley actually had more money available, despite that fact that Gore had actually raised more. Gore's response to Mitchell was "Watch what happens." He then challenged Bradley to a debate. Bradley remarked to reporters that Gore had been refusing to debate him for the past ten months.

Tim Russert on NBC said that it was extremely unusual for a front-runner to acknowledge at this stage of the campaign that his effort was in trouble. Russert wondered how often a front-runner challenges his opponent to a debate and remarked that it was one thing for the vice president to change his address, but he also had to change the attitude of his operation. The operation had to become leaner, meaner, and more aggressive and engage in more one-on-one dialogue with voters if Gore were to maintain his front-runner role, Russert concluded.

Television news media continued their pattern of reporting occasionally about the status of the Democratic campaign through the remainder of 1999, but that coverage remained limited. During the final three months of the year, network evening telecasts contained only twenty-seven reports at least one minute in length involving the Democratic candidates. Nearly one third of these reports included both Democratic and Republican candidates. Five concerned recent developments in the campaigns of the two front-runners Gore and Bush, and three on December 16 described a pledge by both Bradley and McCain to reject "soft money" contributions for their campaigns in New Hampshire. One report focused on Gore only; on October 11 Phil Jones on CBS talked about the American Federation of Labor and Congress of Industrial Organizations (AFL-CIO) endorsement of the vice president. Six were about Bradley, but unfortunately for the challenger, five of them were in mid-December and described his recent difficulties with an irregular heartbeat. The other, by Phil Jones of CBS on November 14, looked at a Bradley fundraiser. The remaining twelve reports focused on both candidates and were generally clustered into three periods.

The first period was October 9–10, when the networks, particularly NBC, looked at the state of the campaign in Iowa. Both candidates had spoken before a meeting of the Iowa Democratic State Committee. Lisa Myers of NBC said Gore was becoming more aggressive in his campaign style and added that Bradley was gaining ground. The scenes from the meeting showed Gore challenging Bradley to a weekly debate, then attacking him for supporting the tax plan of Ronald Reagan in 1981 and leaving the Senate after Republicans won control in 1994. Myers referred to an unnamed Gore strategist who believed Gore should have started attacking Bradley months earlier. With respect to Bradley, Myers looked at his appearance at an African American church, where he talked about shared values and racial healing. Myers said Bradley had received a rousing welcome at the church even though Gore's support was strong among black voters.

Although Gore failed to get a weekly debate with Bradley, the two candidates did meet at Dartmouth College on October 27 for their first debate in New Hampshire. Television news media expressed considerable interest in this event and used it as an opportunity to review the status of the national campaign. Tom Brokaw on NBC said Gore had some encouraging news: Democrats nationwide preferred him for the nomination, 53 percent to 29 percent, in the most recent NBC poll. Lisa Myers later reported that Gore was leading Bradley, 62 percent to 22 percent, among Democrats likely to vote. The polls were not all favorable for Gore as he trailed Bush, 49 percent to 35 percent, nationwide and was actually trailing Bradley by eight points in New Hampshire. Claire Shipman on NBC looked at recent developments in New Hampshire and pointed out that Bradley, whom she identified as the underdog, had made the state a priority. She added that Gore, the front-runner as she called him, was in overdrive. The scenes accompanying these remarks were of Gore's campaigning. John Cochran on ABC offered similar conclusions about the two candidates but focused most of his attention on the debate. Cochran said Gore, whom he identified as "faced with high expectations," needed a clear performance, whereas Bradley, for whom expectations were lower, could get by with a respectable showing. John Roberts of CBS said Bradley was ahead in New Hampshire polls and added that both candidates had a lot at stake in the debate. Gore needed to soften his image and Bradley had to show he was Gore's equal. The networks spent far less time on the aftermath of the debate than they did on its preview, partly because of an upcoming debate among the Republican candidates. They focused much of their attention on remarks related to health care. Lisa Myers on NBC explained that health care had become a campaign issue and included comments by Gore and Bradley in the latter part of her report.

The last day in 1999 when more than one network looked at the Democratic candidates was December 17, a day that featured another debate in New Hampshire. The tone of the debate and the themes of network reporting differed from those of the previous debate, however. This time, the candidates were far more confrontational and willing to attack one another. Tom Brokaw of NBC said that the candidates had engaged in some very tough tactics. Claire Shipman remarked that Gore and Bradley were "regularly exchanging blows and some of them were low." She included several scenes, three of each, of one candidate's attacking the other. Shipman added that Gore had begun his negative campaigning about one month earlier when he had started bashing Bradley's health care program and had not stopped since. She said this change in the nature of the campaign had put Bradley in an awkward position. He had preferred to conduct a high-minded campaign but was now using Gore's attacks. Shipman concluded that the debate had marked the first real side by side display of the candidates' new styles and that the race in New Hampshire was neck and neck. With this network news coverage of the Democratic campaign, 1999 was finished.

4

THE CAMPAIGNS FOR THE
PARTY NOMINATIONS: 2000

THE EARLY TEST STATES: REPUBLICANS

The nomination campaigns took on an added dimension in January 2000 when television news media expanded their coverage from occasional to daily. The campaigns moved from the "invisible primary," in which the actions of the candidates are rarely reported but nominations are frequently won or lost, to the more active part of the campaign as the candidates direct their attention to specific states with upcoming votes. January was a particularly intense month for the campaigns in both parties since the initial voter tests in Iowa and New Hampshire were scheduled for the latter part of the month or the beginning of the next.

By January, the two campaigns had been under way for about one year and had already undergone a number of significant developments. The list of candidates for the Republican nomination had declined by half, from twelve to six, and the race itself seemed nearly over with a Bush victory imminent. Television news media encountered little difficulty in stereotyping the six remaining candidates into the predetermined roles they prefer when illustrating competitive nomination campaigns. Bush was the obvious front-runner, McCain the leading adversary, and everyone else composed the category of others. There was plenty of evidence to support placement of the various candidates in these roles. Bush was leading his rivals in virtually every measurement one could employ in determining the status of the horse race. With respect to national polls, Bush had just garnered the support of 63 percent of Republicans in the Gallup-CNN-*USA Today* Poll of January 12. McCain was in second place but enjoyed the backing of only 18 percent of his fellow Republicans. Forbes finished third with a mere 5 percent, and Bauer, Hatch, and Keyes divided another 5 percent about evenly among themselves. Bush also held a commanding lead in financing. In the quarterly report it filed with the Federal Election Commission, Bush's campaign committee stated it had raised $68.7 million through December 31, 1999; in contrast, McCain's had taken in only $15.7 million. Forbes actually held second place in the financing battle as his campaign had raised $34.1 million, but over $30 million of that money had come from Forbes himself; he had not been successful in generating many contributions from individuals. The financial performances of the remaining three candidates resembled their polling numbers, bleak. Bauer had raised $9.7 million and Keyes checked in with $4.5 million. Hatch finished last with $2.3 million.

One can divide televised news coverage of the campaigns into two distinct periods based on the attention correspondents directed to each of the parties. The first period includes the events related to the early votes in Iowa and New Hampshire, the second, the battles that led to the eleven primaries of March 7. The first period lasted about four weeks and was characterized by an approximately even division of news interest between the two parties. On any given day, for example, one network might begin its political reporting by looking at the Democrats and then consider the Republicans while a rival network would report about the same events but would initially focus on the Republicans. The second period was slightly longer, five weeks, but radically different in tone. Television news media focused the overwhelming majority of their attention on the Republicans while often ignoring the Democrats. When they did look at the Democrats, all three networks considered the candidates of this party only after they had already reported about the Republicans. Moreover, the Democrats received considerably less news time. Often, individual correspondents reported extensively about each of the two major Republican contenders and the network anchor followed by quickly summarizing the actions of the Democratic candidates.

Despite their differences in partisan interest over two periods, television news media employed the same themes in their coverage of both parties throughout these nine weeks. First, they depicted each party's race as a two-candidate struggle between a role-playing front-runner and his role-playing leading adversary. Second, television news media were all too often preoccupied with personal combat between the candidates, devoting an unusual amount of time reporting about when and how each candidate attacked his rival. The theme was one of the candidates' fighting one another in the electoral arena. Correspondents treated statements the candidates made about issues or important events as little more than segments of the larger struggle. There were numerous descriptions of strategy, of how the candidates were responding to the setbacks they had suffered or the successes they had attained, and of how certain strategies they were initiating or continuing might affect they chances. Third, there was the ubiquitous horse race, the constant stream of information about who was ahead and who was behind in either the most recent poll or the actual primary vote and of how these results might affect the chance of each candidate in future events. Together, these themes were held together by one overriding concept: each front-runner would eventually devise and implement the one strategy that would fatally wound his adversary, clinch his nomination, and demonstrate his political competence to president of the United States.

The first network coverage of the Republican race after the beginning of the year was on January 4, when Linda Douglass of ABC emphasized all of those themes. She focused her news report on the televised attack ads that a conservative group, Americans for Tax Reform, was using against McCain in New Hampshire for his advocacy of campaign finance reform. McCain had made limiting soft money a central part of his appeal. Opponents of reform were attacking McCain for allegedly using his position as chairman of the Senate Commerce Committee to pressure lobbyists into contributing to his efforts, Douglass stated. She had some comments from one of those opponents, Grover Norquist, the group's president, and included scenes from the ads while exploring the motives of the interests behind them. Douglass also emphasized the candidate roles theme when she depicted Bush as the "establishment" candidate, that is, the representative of the leadership of the Republican Party, and McCain as a "maverick." In identifying the reasons for the attack ads, Douglass employed the horse race theme when she said McCain had jolted the Republican establishment by building such a strong campaign in New Hampshire that he was running even in several polls with Bush. Several other network reports over the days that followed also focused on attacks against McCain for his advocacy of campaign finance reform; they also referred to the candidate roles and horse race themes. They appeared on NBC on January 4 and 6, on CBS on January 4 and 5, and on ABC on January 9.

The three themes resurfaced in another series of news reports that began on January 7, although this time taxes replaced reform as the principal issue of media interest. Taxes had become an important topic for news attention because of several recent events, including the launching by the Forbes campaign of attack ads in Iowa and New Hampshire aimed at Bush's record. The ads questioned Bush's sincerity on the issue by claiming he had signed laws in Texas that raised some taxes. They also contained a scene of Bush's father's making his famous 1988 campaign pledge "Read my lips, no new taxes." Dean Reynolds on ABC and David Bloom on NBC focused on taxes on January 7 by describing the Forbes ads and Bush's defense. Reynolds added that Bush expected such attacks because Forbes was trailing in the polls. Although Forbes attained some news coverage for his efforts, network correspondents were far more interested in describing a tax controversy as an integral part of the Bush-McCain battle. They started doing so on January 11, when they reported about a New Hampshire debate among the six Republican candidates. All three networks focused more of their attention on the differences between Bush and McCain on taxes than on any other issue. The media interest in taxes continued on January 15, when the networks once again reported about a six-candidate debate, this one in Iowa. The news reports featured several tax-related comments by Bush and McCain but only occasionally by any other candidate. An overriding characteristic of these reports was the depiction of Bush as the central political actor of the campaign. Norah O'Donnell of NBC and Dean Reynolds of ABC identified Bush as the front-runner, had scenes of him talking about tax cuts, and included imagery of McCain's commenting about Bush's proposals. One day later, on January 16, Jonathan Alter of NBC looked at the tax proposals of the four major candidates, that is, Republicans Bush and McCain and Democrats Gore and Bradley. He did not consider the views of the other four Republicans, including Forbes, who had generated the media interest in taxes with his attack ads.

Television news media occasionally focused attention on events that were not necessarily part of the campaign but were newsworthy nonetheless and then illustrated the candidates' responses. This occurred on January 17 in relation to a controversy in South Carolina about flying the Confederate flag above the state's capitol building. On this anniversary of the birthday of the Reverend Martin Luther King, Jr., the National Association for the Advancement of Colored People (NAACP) held a rally in Columbia, South Carolina, where it denounced the flag and demanded its removal. As the most significant political news reports of the day focused on the flag controversy and the statements of the leading speakers, all three networks included comments by the four major candidates. Bush and McCain both evaded the issue by stating that the voters of South Carolina should make the decision about what should be done, as if someone else had the legal and political power to make such a decision for them. Gore and Bradley attacked the Republicans for their unwillingness to oppose the flag display. Network correspondents did not include any flag-related remarks by the four other Republican candidates. Moreover, the flag issue disappeared from the Republican campaign immediately after this one day.

The networks altered their reporting patterns for about one week in mid-January in order to accommodate the Iowa precinct caucuses. They were unable to depict the events in this initial test state exclusively within the context of a Bush-McCain battle because McCain was not competing in Iowa. They had directed most of their coverage during the first half of January to the two-candidate battle for New Hampshire but now needed to focus on Iowa. Nonetheless, they did not ignore McCain. The Arizona senator attained more televised news coverage during this week than any of Bush's rivals.

Two continuing themes dominated network interest during the days preceding the Iowa vote: front-runner Bush's facing a challenge from several candidates with particularly strong appeals to Christian conservatives, and the upcoming battle Bush would face with McCain in New Hampshire after his expected Iowa triumph. On January 20 David Bloom on NBC indicated how these two themes intersected, reporting that Bush's rivals, that is, Forbes, Bauer, Keyes, and Hatch, had made abortion a key issue in Iowa and had been attacking Bush for his unwillingness to use it as a criterion for future court appointments. Bush had been campaigning as an ideological centrist and wanted to avoid issues that might have contradicted this image and thereby cost him support among more moderate voters, Bloom stated. In responding to the growing intensity of these attacks, Bush eventually denounced the *Roe v. Wade* court decision and then promised to appoint conservative judges who would vote to overturn it. Despite this response, Bloom added, Bush had not ruled out appointing prochoice judges. Bloom then identified Forbes as Bush's main rival in Iowa and described how the magazine publisher had built a strong organization in the state and appeared to be catching on with voters. Nonetheless, Forbes was an afterthought with respect to the national campaign, Bloom concluded. With this, he shifted the focus of his report to New Hampshire and described McCain as an even greater threat to Bush than Forbes. Bloom then looked at the variety of attacks Bush and McCain were making against one another over taxes.

The news themes of the other networks were similar. Bill Whitaker of CBS, in reports on January 20 and 21, referred to Bush as the front-runner in Iowa; looked at the abortion controversy in that state, including remarks by Bush, Forbes, and Bauer; and provided scenes of McCain's campaigning in both New York and New Hampshire. Bush was the central actor in the abortion story. Television viewers could see Bush's stating his position on *Roe v. Wade*, but could only see his rivals when they attacked him. In addition, McCain was shown speaking in New York, where he demanded the Republican leadership stop its efforts to block him from appearing on the ballot in several congressional districts in the state's March 7 primary. This had been a growing controversy in the state for several weeks. The party leadership soon responded just as McCain demanded. Finally, on January 22, Linda Douglass on ABC looked at recent events in New Hampshire and South Carolina while downplaying Iowa. She described Bush as the national front-runner, illustrated McCain's campaign among veterans in South Carolina, depicted the New Hampshire campaign as a two-candidate battle between Bush and McCain, and concluded by reviewing Bush's attacks against McCain over taxes.

The horse race theme surfaced one day later, on January 23, when television news media reported the results of a newly released poll in Iowa by the *Des Moines Register*. This poll by the largest newspaper in the state had Bush ahead of Forbes by a margin of 43 percent to 20 percent with McCain and Keyes tied for third at 8 percent. Bauer and Hatch had 6 percent and 1 percent, respectively. The Bush lead was apparent in the themes of the day's network news. The various correspondents reported about the poll, talked about a *Des Moines Register* endorsement of Bush, then looked at the campaign in ways that were quite flattering to Bush. David Bloom on NBC, Bill Whitaker on CBS, and Tom Foreman on ABC focused on the likelihood of a Bush victory while paying little, if any, attention to the other Republican candidates.

One day later Jim Wooten of ABC looked at the closing efforts of Bush and Forbes on this final day of campaigning, giving only scant attention to McCain, Keyes, and Bauer. After Dan Rather on CBS predicted a Bush victory, Bill Whitaker focused on the most recent actions by the two major candidates, Bush in Iowa and McCain in New Hampshire. Finally, David Bloom on NBC made Bush the central political actor in his report, discussing the likelihood of a victory in Iowa by the Texas governor and its implications for the national campaign. As predicted by both the *Des Moines Register* and a variety of network polls, Bush won the Iowa caucuses. He attained 41 percent of the vote and was followed by Forbes with 30 percent, Keyes with 14 percent, Bauer with 9 percent, McCain with 5 percent, and Hatch with only 1 percent. Hatch soon withdrew from the campaign.

One can obtain useful information about voting behavior in the exit polls taken by the Voter News Service and shared by the leading media organizations. Two of the most important differences among participants in the Republican caucuses and primaries related to personal identification with either the Republican Party or the Religious Right. With respect to the first, a number of states had open primaries or caucuses in which a voter could participate in either the Republican or the Democratic elections without being a registered voter of that party. Other states held closed primaries and caucuses that limited participation to party members. These distinctions were important because Bush usually won the support of most Republicans and McCain acquired the backing of many of the Democrats and Independents who chose to vote in the Republican primaries. Bush ran even stronger than McCain among persons who identified with the Religious Right. The absence of McCain from the Iowa vote prevented these patterns from being as distinct in that state as they were in others, but they were present nonetheless. Republicans preferred Bush to Forbes by a margin of 44 percent to 29 percent, and Religious Right identifiers backed the Texas governor over the New Jersey publisher by 33 percent to 27 percent. In contrast, Independents cast 41 percent of their ballots for Forbes and only 29 percent for Bush.

A second-place finish only eleven percentage points behind the national front-runner might have been good enough to attain an infusion of news coverage in other years, but Forbes was not so fortunate this time. His strong performance was virtually ignored by television news media. After Iowa, they moved immediately to New Hampshire and focused even more directly on the two-candidate battle in that state. The dominant theme of televised news reporting was that Bush had won Iowa and had temporarily proved his political virility but now had to step immediately into the next battle. The televised treatment of Bush's Iowa victory was comparable to the coverage of a college basketball team's triumph in a game during the NCAA tournament: intense coverage of the excitement of a game, with an immediate focus on the next game as soon as the first one concludes. On Monday, reporters were in Iowa seeing Bush confront Forbes and abortion; on Tuesday they were in New Hampshire directing attention to the upcoming battle between Bush and McCain and the growing debate over campaign finance reform. Forbes was reduced to the mere status of being the opponent Bush had defeated in yesterday's game.

The post-Iowa reporting from New Hampshire began on January 25 with the various networks' reflecting on both the Iowa results and the nature of the New Hampshire campaign. The leading themes were the status of the horse race and the personal combat of the two leading candidates against one another. The horse race was pervasive and took on some added importance this time because of a major difference that had surfaced recently between national polls and those taken only in New Hampshire. Bush had a large lead over McCain in national polls, as reflected in the 65 percent support level mentioned earlier, but was trailing McCain in New Hampshire. The Gallup-CNN-*USA Today* Poll of January 22 showed McCain ahead of Bush in the state by a margin of nine nine points, 42 percent to 33 percent. Phil Jones of CBS and David Bloom of NBC focused on the horse race and its possible consequences on January 25 when they said McCain would have to win New Hampshire or would have little hope in other states, including South Carolina. The central idea behind their observations was that McCain had spent a considerable amount of time and money in New Hampshire and needed to win the primary or his candidacy would very likely come to an abrupt end. McCain had spent sixty-three days campaigning in New Hampshire and had conducted 114 town meeting during that time in hopes of generating the votes needed for victory. The horse race concept resurfaced several times over the next few days. Dean Reynolds of ABC reported on January 27 that Bush was leading nationally and trailing in New Hampshire and that a loss in the primary could undermine his claim of being able to win in November. One day later Claire Shipman of NBC told viewers Bush was behind in New Hampshire polls, and NBC released a poll of its own on January 30 showing McCain with a lead of 38 percent to 32 percent. Not all news about polls was bad for Bush, however. Bill Whitaker of CBS said on January 29 that Bush was leading in South Carolina, and Norah O'Donnell of NBC said that Bush had a commanding lead in states other than New Hampshire.

The theme of the two candidates' engaging in personal combat was also pervasive in the news coverage during the days immediately before the primary. Sometimes the topics that garnered media attention were generated by remarks made by the candidates themselves; at others they were generated by outside events. McCain instigated a significant amount of controversy on January 26, when he made some inconsistent remarks about abortion, saying he was opposed to abortion but would not prevent his daughter from having one. He also raised media interest on January 30 when he said that his military background had given him the experience to be commander-in-chief, experience Bush lacked. In contrast, the topic of taxes became important on January 28 and remained so through the primary because Clinton had talked about it the previous evening when he delivered his State of the Union Address. Bush and McCain commented on Clinton's remarks and used this opportunity to attack one another and emphasize their own tax plans.

McCain's decision to concentrate his time and money in one early test state paid off as he scored an overwhelming victory over Bush in New Hampshire by a margin of 49 percent to 31 percent. The remaining candidates fared poorly: Forbes, Keyes, and Bauer received only 13 percent, 6 percent, and 1 percent, respectively. Forbes had failed to expand his second place finish in Iowa into a better showing and now had a campaign whose days were numbered. The days of the Bauer campaign were indeed numbered, with none left. He withdrew after this setback. Keyes would remain in the race for several more months, longer even than McCain and Forbes, but would never advance beyond the status of a minor candidate. The exit polls attributed McCain's victory to strong support from Democrats, Independents, and nonidentifiers with the Religious Right. Republicans voted for Bush by a margin of 41 percent to 38 percent; Democrats and Independents, together, supported McCain by 62 percent to 19 percent. Religious Right identifiers were for Bush, 36 percent to 26 percent whereas nonidentifiers backed McCain 54 percent to 28 percent.

The New Hampshire primary had changed the nature of the Republican campaign. McCain had gambled that he might run well and emerge as Bush's main rival, but few observers had expected him to win by an eighteen-point margin. McCain's victory would raise questions about the strength of the Bush effort and the assumed inevitability of his nomination. The Republican primary in New Hampshire had reduced the number of major candidates for the nomination to only two; contributed to the virtual end of the Democratic race, described in the next section; and advanced the Republican campaign to a number of states where only Republicans held primaries. The first state with such a vote was South Carolina, where the vote would take place in less than three weeks on Saturday, February 19.

THE EARLY TEST STATES: DEMOCRATS

There were two different, and somewhat contradictory, indicators of the status of the Democratic campaign at the beginning of 2000, poll standings and fund-raising. With respect to the former, on December 22 the Gallup-CNN-*USA Today* Poll showed Gore with a modest lead over Bradley of 52 percent to 38 percent. The fund-raising story was different, however, as the candidates were considerably closer. Gore had raised $29 million by the end of 1999, and Bradley had $27.8 million. Bradley appeared to have the momentum it that he had raised $8.5 million during the final quarter of 1999 compared to only $4.1 million by Gore. As with McCain in his challenge to Bush, Bradley seemed to have a chance to defeat the front-runner of his party and win the nomination. Bradley, who was closer to Gore in both polls and money than McCain was to Bush, seemed to be the leading adversary with the greater chance of defeating the front-runner of his party and winning the nomination.

The rise of Bradley as a potentially victorious rival of Gore was the theme of the first televised political news report of the year. On January 2, John Yang on ABC looked at Bradley's recent fund-raising success. Yang attributed it to the doubts a number of Democrats had about Gore. Money would be crucial in the later primaries, when television advertising often served as the dominant means of reaching voters, Yang added. He concluded by saying Bradley had actually pulled even with Gore in some New Hampshire polls and was now a legitimate contender for the nomination. Bradley was employing the strategy of a party outsider, that is, a candidate who does not have substantial backing from the key interests of the party. As was McCain, Bradley was concentrating much of his time and money on the early test states of Iowa and New Hampshire in the hope of appealing to the small number of voters who cast ballots in these two states and thereby upsetting the front-runner. Such a strategy, if successful, would translate into intense media coverage and help expand his support throughout the nation. In a sense, both Bradley and McCain were competing against one another. Each was trying to attract Independent voters, particularly in New Hampshire, and attain the intense media coverage that follows a strong performance.

Only one could win, however; at the beginning of January, Bradley seemed more likely to do so.

As a result, television news media found the Gore-Bradley race more newsworthy than the Republican campaign during the first days of January. On January 3, Claire Shipman on NBC emphasized the personal combat theme when she looked at how the two Democrats were blasting one another. She said Gore and Bradley were both trying to sound like visionaries but seemed to be preparing for a brawl. Her report included scenes of Bradley's trying to portray himself as an independent and new thinker and of Gore's trying to rally traditional Democratic voters by creating the image of the fighter he said the nation needed. Shipman also used the horse race when she said Gore was ahead in the most recent Iowa poll by 48 percent to 27 percent, whereas Bradley was ahead 42 percent to 39 percent in New Hampshire. Shipman included comments about campaign strategy by Charles Cook of the *National Journal*, who said that Bradley needed to win New Hampshire and could not survive a loss. In concluding, Shipman said Gore was the favorite in Iowa but had to win by a good margin, whereas Bradley simply needed to stay close.

Two days later, when the major political development relating to Democrats was an endorsement of Gore by Senator Edward Kennedy of Massachusetts, John Roberts of CBS also focused on the personal combat, talking about Bradley's "Big Ideas" campaign and Gore's efforts to depict himself as a fighter. He then reported that Bradley had attacked Gore for interjecting the Willie Horton issue into the 1988 presidential campaign. This issue related to a series of television ads George Bush had run against Michael Dukakis that year about Horton, a prisoner in the Massachusetts penal system who had committed a rape while on a weekend furlough. Many people believed Bush had made a racist appeal since Horton was black. Bradley claimed Gore had introduced the Horton controversy into the Democratic campaign while running against Dukakis for the nomination, Roberts added.

Television news media also focused attention on the candidate roles and horse race themes during January and increasingly saw Gore as the winner. Their reporting started reflecting this view as they constantly told their audiences of how strong Gore was running and how poorly Bradley was. All three networks depicted Gore as the front-runner who would win in both Iowa and New Hampshire and thereby force Bradley out of the race. Terry Moran reported an ABC poll on January 8 that showed Gore leading Bradley among black voters by 63 percent to 31 percent. Moran said Gore's lead among blacks mirrored the condition of the national campaign. Gore was ahead nearly everywhere because he had "organizational muscle and establishment credentials," while Bradley was left to advance the image of an outsider candidacy, Moran concluded. Ten days later, Bob Schieffer reported a CBS poll taken in New Hampshire that showed Gore ahead of Bradley by 47 percent to 39 percent. In his analysis of the poll's meaning, Schieffer said that Gore could very well win in both Iowa and New Hampshire and that Bradley would be severely damaged. When reporting about the campaign in Iowa on January 20, John Roberts on CBS said Gore was building momentum in that state toward "a seemingly impenetrable lead," and Bradley was now fighting to save his political life.

The news for Bradley became even worse on January 21, when television news focused on his health and treatments he had received for an irregular heartbeat. They also reminded viewers of Bradley's poor standings in the polls. Tom Brokaw of NBC introduced the political news that day by saying that Gore and Bush had big leads in Iowa and that the news "was not good for challenger Bradley," who had to explain his irregular heartbeat. Anne Thompson on NBC said Bradley was using medication to get his heartbeat back on rhythm and added that it was questionable whether the Bradley campaign could do the same. Claire Shipman on NBC described Gore as upbeat, especially now that he was in the lead, in contrast to six months earlier. The former White House chief of staff David Gergen, interviewed for Shipman's report, attributed Gore's new political strength to a combination of aggressive campaign efforts and Bradley's passivity in responding to accusations. Shipman illustrated these patterns by first showing scenes of Gore's questioning Bradley during a debate about his opposition to a flood relief bill then showing Bradley's weak response. Shipman stated that Bradley needed some momentum from a good performance in Iowa to run well in New Hampshire.

The other networks had similar reports that day: Dan Rather of CBS said that Bradley had health concerns and that Gore was solidifying his lead and pulling away. John Roberts of CBS described Bradley as "having his hands full" with questions about his heart condition and with fighting perceptions that the heart condition was a metaphor for the troubles of his campaign. Roberts added that Bradley had spent more time and money in Iowa than Gore but was now a distant second in the polls. Gore, Roberts added, had his eyes on a bigger prize, the nomination, and had made a remarkable turnabout from the panic mode his campaign had been in for the past five months. Roberts said Gore now had momentum and could be unstoppable after the Iowa and New Hampshire votes. One day later, Roberts said that Bradley seemed to be a candidate who was just trying to survive. If Gore were to win both Iowa and New Hampshire, Roberts added, he could urge Democrats to unite behind him and put the race to bed. The heart condition story only lasted for one more day, however, but Bradley's horse race problems did not end so abruptly. Jackie Judd on ABC reported on January 22 that Bradley seemed to have regained his footing after having faced the heart questions, but, she added, he was still far behind in the polls.

Television news media emphasized the horse race as the Iowa vote approached. On January 23 John Yang and Jackie Judd of ABC, respectively, reported about how Gore was campaigning door-to-door and was poised to win by a wide margin while Bradley was still bothered by his heart condition and poor electoral prospects. Claire Shipman on NBC looked at the recently published *Des Moines Register* poll that showed Gore leading Bradley 56 percent to 28 percent; John Roberts on CBS talked about Bradley's comment that he would be satisfied with 31 percent of the vote; the 31 percent figure was an Iowa caucus record for an insurgent campaign within the Democratic Party. Edward Kennedy had attained 31 percent of the vote in the 1980 caucuses when he opposed Jimmy Carter in what proved to be an unsuccessful campaign for reelection by a weak incumbent.

Bradley actually exceeded this 31 percent figure: the final results in Iowa were Gore, 63 percent; Bradley, 35 percent. Despite exceeding Kennedy's level of support, Bradley could claim little more. He would now take his campaign to New Hampshire, but television news media would continue focusing their attention on the horse race and depicting Gore as the central political actor in the continuing drama. Bradley seemed to have become little more than a pest Gore had to brush off on his way to the nomination. The only apparent question that remained to be answered in the New Hampshire primary was the size of Gore's victory.

As with the Republicans, the exit polls taken in the caucuses and primaries showed some consistent differences between supporters of the major candidates. Two of the most important were partisan identity and opinions about Bill Clinton the person. Democrats were more likely to support Gore, whereas Independents preferred Bradley. Although most voters who participated in the Democratic caucuses and primaries approved of Clinton's performance in office, a substantial number, often a majority or near majority in most states, disapproved of him as a person. Most of those who approved of Clinton as a person supported Gore; those who disapproved were more likely to vote for Bradley. These patterns first surfaced in Iowa, where Gore won the support of 66 percent of the Democrats who attended the caucuses and Bradley attained the votes of 29 percent. In contrast, Bradley won the votes of 42 percent of the Independents and Gore won the votes of 39 percent. About 17 percent of caucus participants described themselves as Independents. With respect to opinions about Clinton, 49 percent approved of him and 44 percent disapproved. The approval group supported Gore by 76 percent to 19 percent, whereas the disapproval group divided their votes evenly between the two candidates, 45 percent for each.

The horse race and the upcoming Gore victory remained the dominant themes during the week between the Iowa and New Hampshire votes. On January 25, Dan Rather on CBS said that round one, the Iowa caucuses, had gone to Gore and Bush, whom he identified as the front-runners. He added that Bradley needed a comeback victory in New Hampshire. John Roberts on CBS reported that Gore had momentum from his Iowa showing and was seeking to develop an indomitable lead with a New Hampshire victory. Three days later, Tom Brokaw on NBC said Bradley was trying to recover from his defeat in Iowa and Anne Thompson on NBC, reporting the next day, talked about Bradley's being behind in the polls. She told viewers the most recent NBC poll showed that Gore was leading Bradley in New Hampshire by 49 percent to 37 percent.

A particularly significant news story occurred during this week, one that indicates the power of incumbency, even in its surrogate form. Clinton delivered his State of the Union Address before a joint session of Congress and a large national television audience. The timing was not accidental: Thursday, January 28, was three days after the Iowa caucuses and four days before the New Hampshire primary. Clinton's appearance influenced the Democratic campaign in two ways: it erased Bradley from the news for about forty-eight hours, and it placed Gore in a far more central position. Gore was seated at the usual position of a vice president, behind the podium and the president and next to the Speaker of the House, in clear view of the national television audience. Clinton referred to Gore on six different occasions and praised some of his ideas. He also referred to Gore as the vice president. The imagery helped convey the implicit message that Gore was a significant member of a successful Democratic administration and a worthy surrogate and successor of Clinton.

The televised depiction of Bradley as a desperate candidate on the verge of a smashing defeat continued over the few remaining days before the final vote. The main story of January 29 was Bradley's circulating some letters Gore had written several years earlier in which Gore, then a senator, had expressed some reservations about the prochoice view of abortion. Jim Wooten of ABC described this action as an effort by Bradley to weaken Gore's support among women voters. The next day, Anne Thompson of NBC focused on Bradley's attacks against Gore on the themes of trust, character, and consistency. She added that several Democratic congressional leaders, including House and Senate Minority Leaders Richard Gephardt and Tom Daschle, were pressuring Bradley to stop his negative attacks. Phil Jones of CBS raised this same theme while mentioning Bradley's health problems and weak poll standings. Jackie Judd, of ABC, one day later said that Bradley's attacks against Gore were leaving a bad taste among voters.

Television news media employed the ubiquitous polls to structure their reporting and to announce their obituaries of Bradley, but the actual vote was somewhat closer than the polls had suggested. The Gallup-CNN-*USA Today* Poll published ten daily tracking polls between January 22 and January 31 that showed support for Gore ranging between 48 percent and 57 percent with a daily average of 52 percent. These polls had support for Bradley ranging between 39 percent and 47 percent with a daily average of 43 percent. Gore won the primary, although the results were much closer, 52 percent to 48 percent. These results suggest that television news media may have been premature in declaring the Bradley effort over in mid-January.

Gore won the primary by appealing to and repelling many of the same types of voters as he had in Iowa. He attained the backing of most Democrats and of those voters who approved of Clinton as a person. He defeated Bradley by 59 percent to 41 percent among Democrats while losing Independents to him by a nearly identical margin, 56 percent to 41 percent. The turnout of Independents was extensive: 40 percent of the primary voters described themselves as Independents. Gore also won the support of most voters who approved of Clinton as a person while losing the backing of those disapproving. Voters who approved of Clinton supported Gore, 66 percent to 34 percent; those who disapproved backed Bradley, 60 percent to 38 percent. About 42 percent of primary voters disapproved of Clinton the person.

Despite the closeness of the vote and the possibility that Bradley might well continue with his effort, television news media had another story to report and Bill Bradley was not part of it. McCain had won the Republican primary and had made the struggle among Republicans the most exciting political news story of the day. Television news media made a remarkable shift in their coverage patterns after the New Hampshire primary: directing far more of their attention to McCain and his efforts against Bush while virtually ignoring Bradley. The best days of the Bradley campaign were over.

The meaning that television and other news media ascribe to the outcome of the New Hampshire primary is sometimes confusing and inconsistent. The Democratic primary of 1968 eventually became identified as a significant step forward for Eugene McCarthy and a major setback for Lyndon Johnson. Johnson received 49 percent of the vote compared to McCarthy's 42 percent. The difference between Gore and Bradley was much closer, 52 percent to 48 percent, but television news media depicted the outcome as a victory for Gore and a disaster for Bradley.

THE FEBRUARY PRIMARIES: REPUBLICANS

The Republican campaign entered its third phase after the New Hampshire primary. The winnowing period was over and the race now clearly defined as a battle between two role-playing candidates, although television news media had actually made this distinction several weeks earlier. With respect to funds raised and standing in nationwide polls, Bush was clearly the front-runner and McCain was his leading and only significant adversary. McCain's victory and Bradley's defeat changed the nature of the televised aspect of the campaign within both parties. McCain now became the one insurgent candidate who would receive extensive televised news coverage while Bradley quickly became little more than a media afterthought.

Television news media were quick to respond to these changed circumstances as they immediately relegated the Democratic candidates to a secondary role within one day of the New Hampshire vote and placed the two Republican combatants at center stage. For example, NBC focused the first two of its three election-related news reports of February 2 on the Republicans, reserving the final one for the Democrats. David Bloom described Bush as having suddenly become vulnerable. Bloom focused on the personal combat and horse race themes. With respect to combat, Bloom included scenes of Bush's attacking McCain as a Washington, D.C., insider and a candidate far too liberal for the Republican Party. These attacks occurred when Bush was speaking at Bob Jones University in South Carolina. In terms of the horse race, Bloom mentioned that Bush had a lead of twenty-four percentage points in South Carolina, which would be the next contested primary, and had approximately four times as much money available as McCain. The central focus of this news report was that Bush was the candidate with the attributes of a front-runner, that is, money and establishment support. Lisa Myers directed her attention to McCain, whom she depicted as the antithesis of both Bush and Bill Clinton in election 2000, and as a conservative maverick whom the voters of New Hampshire had judged to be authentic.

The other networks emphasized many of the same themes that day. Bill Whitaker on CBS said that Bush's front-runner image now had a black eye. Whitaker also talked about Bush's establishment support, available funding, and poll standings and included scenes of the Texas governor's speech at Bob Jones University. Linda Douglass and Dean Reynolds followed a similar script for ABC. Douglass said Bush had about $31 million to contest the upcoming primaries and added that Bush's father, the former president, was popular among leading South Carolina Republicans and this popularity would prove helpful in the upcoming primary. Reynolds focused on Bush's speech at Bob Jones University and on the attacks the Texas governor had made on McCain's liberal views. Bush had emphasized his own conservative credentials. No correspondent saw in Bush's speech the controversy it would later generate, however; it was considered merely an attempt by Bush to draw distinctions between him and McCain.

The three networks reported daily about the Republican race in South Carolina for most of the next two and one-half weeks and focused virtually all of their attention on the three main themes of candidate roles, personal combat, and the horse race. On February 3 Dean Reynolds on ABC described Bush's directing his appeals to conservatives and veterans and Linda Douglass on ABC focused on McCain and his maverick campaign style on February 3. One day later, Reynolds reported that Bush was trying to recover from his New Hampshire defeat. He had returned to Austin, Texas, for strategy sessions with campaign officials and planned to resume his campaign in South Carolina shortly. John Yang of ABC reported from California the next day and directed much of his attention to McCain's appearance at the Republican Party's state convention. McCain attacked Bush for his absence, although the Florida governor, Jeb Bush, had represented his brother there. Bush resumed his active campaigning in South Carolina on Monday, February 7, and started with some vigorous attacks against McCain over taxes and campaign finance reform. Bob Jamieson of ABC said that Bush was depicting himself as a "reformer with results." Linda Douglass reported that McCain was responding to Bush during this latest phase of personal combat with attack ads of his own. One day later she looked at how McCain had accused Bush of being untrustworthy after Bush had used an armed services veteran to accuse McCain of ignoring the needs of veterans.

Bill Whitaker on CBS reviewed the actions of both candidates on February 3 and informed viewers that McCain had raised new funds in the forty-eight hours since his victory in New Hampshire and was campaigning more intensely in South Carolina. Whitaker also looked at Bush's courtship of conservatives and veterans. One day later, Bryan Pitts emphasized the attacks of each candidate on his opponent. John Blackstone reviewed McCain's speech at the California Republican convention on February 5, and one day later Gloria Borger focused on the question of why Bush was encountering so much trouble with a nomination that had appeared certain only a few weeks earlier. Pitts returned the next day to look at the charges and countercharges each candidate was making against the other in South Carolina. He included references to the veteran's remarks about McCain and to McCain's response.

On February 3, Lisa Myers on NBC focused on how McCain was gaining popularity after his New Hampshire win, but she, and NBC, gave particular emphasis to the increasing bitterness of the campaign. Myers used the personal attacks of the candidates as the central theme of her report of February 4. Tom Brokaw began the telecast of February 8 by saying the Republican race had dropped any pretense of politeness and then compared it to a blood feud. David Bloom followed Brokaw that day with a report that included scenes of each candidate's attacking the other. McCain was shown referring to Bush as the enemy and comparing him, in a television advertisement, to Clinton in terms of trustworthiness. Bloom also talked about how the South Carolina senator Strom Thurmond the former education secretary William Bennett had expressed their disapproval of McCain's attacks. Bloom said the race in South Carolina had gone from "a bare-knuckles to a brass-knuckles fight within the past twenty-four hours."

The Delaware primary on February 8 encouraged television news media to downplay the South Carolina campaign for about two days. This primary was a minor political event because most candidates had invested little money and even less time in the state. Bush had been there once, McCain not at all. In contrast, Forbes had invested both time and money in the hope of reviving his failing candidacy. He had won the Delaware primary in 1996 but not this time. Bush won with 51 percent of the vote and the absent McCain finished second with 25 percent. Forbes was third at 20 percent and left the race. His withdrawal was the main news story of February 9. Forbes received more televised news coverage on the day he withdrew than he had received on any day since the Iowa caucuses. The only network to report about Bush and McCain was NBC, as Lisa Myers reported the media spending by the two candidates in South Carolina: Bush was spending about $2.8 million, and McCain was not far behind at $2.4 million. The personal combat theme was also important as Myers included both candidates' attack ads.

All three networks focused on attack ads on February 10 when McCain blasted Bush for using push polling, in which a campaign worker for one candidate contacts a voter, pretends to be a pollster, then asks for responses to hypothetical questions about the other candidate that are designed to induce negative personal assessments. Push polling allows a candidate to spread lies about his opponent without actually saying anything for which he could be held accountable. Three correspondents, Bill Whitaker on CBS, David Bloom on NBC, and Linda Douglass on ABC, explored McCain's charges. Whitaker included remarks from a woman who claimed her son had received a push poll telephone call that tried to undermine McCain.

The usual patterns of media coverage continued as the South Carolina primary approached. Jim Avila on NBC looked at the use of attack ads by both candidates on February 12; David Bloom on NBC concentrated on the horse race theme two days later. Bloom mentioned that a recent *Los Angeles Times* poll of South Carolina voters showed Bush as leading by 42 percent to 40 percent. Bloom said the poll also indicated that approximately two thirds of Republicans planned to vote for Bush and a comparable percentage of Independents preferred McCain. Tim Russert on NBC reported on difficulties facing the Bush campaign. Bush, he said, had described South Carolina as a "firewall," a place where he needed to defeat and perhaps stop McCain. An underlying theme of Russert's report was that if McCain won in South Carolina—and there seemed to be a strong chance that would actually happen—McCain would very likely follow with victories in Michigan and California. These victories could force an early end to the campaign and lead to the nomination of McCain.

One day later, February 15, Bloom concentrated on the combat theme when he reported that Bush was trying to seize the reform mantle of the campaign finance issue from McCain. Despite his efforts, Bloom said, Bush so disagreed with McCain on a number of key provisions of campaign finance that one could legitimately charge he was not a reformer. Bush wanted to place limits on contributions from labor unions, one of his more powerful adversaries, but not on individuals, who had been greatest contributors. He also did not support an end to soft money contributions. Bloom looked at Bush's record on campaign finance and pointed out that the Texas governor had already raised more money than any other candidate in history and had accepted contributions from lobbyists for companies with extensive pollution records.

Tom Brokaw led off the NBC political reporting on February 17 when he said South Carolina could very well determine the Republican Party nominee and added that Bush and McCain were attacking one another as if this were the defining election. If McCain won, Brokaw added, his insurgent campaign could become "a GOP tidal wave," but if Bush won, it might be very difficult for McCain to recover in the big state primaries in the next few weeks. Bloom once again reported on some of the negative features of the campaign, including scenes of Gary Bauer's endorsing McCain and denouncing Bush's extensive fund-raising and attacks on McCain on finance reform. Bloom also included scenes from a debate of the previous evening in which Bush had confronted McCain about some attack flyers relating to campaign funding that McCain's campaign had distributed. McCain denied any involvement but later acknowledged that his campaign had distributed them.

Lisa Myers on NBC reported the same day about Bush's growing financial difficulties: Bush had raised about $70 million but had already spent about $50 million. This was more money than Senator Robert Dole had spent in the entire nomination campaign of 1996, Myers added. Bush had only $20 million left to spend and McCain had about $10 million. Perhaps the most significant aspect of Bush's financial problems was that he had raised most of his money from individual contributors at the rate of $1000 per person, the legal limit. Although many of these supporters might have been willing to contribute more, federal law prevented them from doing so. Bush would have to defeat McCain relatively soon, perhaps even in South Carolina, or he would be forced to find a new group of contributors to fund what could become a lengthy struggle for the nomination.

Personal combat was the most prominent theme in the ABC coverage during the final days proceeding the vote. Linda Douglass concentrated on candidate attacks on February 11 and 13, and Dean Reynolds looked at them on February 15. Douglass included a taped scene of a Bush campaign official's discussing the campaign staff's use of negative advertising against McCain on February 13. Douglass also referred to poll standings. Reynolds looked at Bush's spending and his use of television, mass mailings, recorded telephone calls, and radio spots as components of an attack strategy.

In a change of focus, but not content, on February 13 CBS reported about the campaign in Michigan, the site of the first primary after South Carolina. After updating viewers about recent polls and candidate attacks in South Carolina, Bill Whitaker described how Bush was relying on Michigan's governor, John Engler, in his attempt to stop McCain. This was necessary because a Bush victory in South Carolina would be so narrow it would have little effect on derailing McCain. Whitaker included scenes of Engler's speaking on behalf of Bush, then informed viewers that a recent poll by the *Detroit News* showed that McCain was leading Bush, 43 percent to 34 percent. Michigan allowed Democrats and Independents to vote in the Republican primary.

A new controversy that would become a major component of the personal combat theme was emerging, Bush's speech at Bob Jones University, and television news media were quick to respond. One day after he lost the New Hampshire primary, Bush had spoken at Bob Jones, where he emphasized his conservative credentials and attacked McCain's allegedly liberal views. At the time, the setting appeared little more than the location for the day's political remarks. This was to change, however. McCain soon started attacking Bush for his appearance at the university, focusing less on the content of Bush's speech than on its location and on what he omitted. Bob Jones University had policies that barred interracial dating by students and depicted the Roman Catholic church as an anti-Christian cult. McCain attacked Bush for his failure to use the appearance to speak out against intolerance. Bill Whitaker on CBS looked at the controversy on February 14 and examined the role of the Religious Right in the Republican Party, which had led Bush to speak at Bob Jones. The Right was supporting Bush and was particularly vociferous in its opposition to McCain. It was also making abortion an issue, but this emphasis seemed odd in that McCain had been identified for years as antiabortion. Whitaker interviewed an opponent of abortion who was also supporting McCain and attributed the Right's anti-McCain stance to the Arizona senator's stand on campaign finance reform. McCain's plans, if enacted, might weaken the political influence of the Religious Right.

Whereas most polls indicated a close race, the results were anything but close. Bush won by 53 percent to 42 percent and captured thirty-four national convention delegates compared to only three for McCain. The differences in candidate preferences between identifiers with the Religious Right and the Republican Party were particularly striking. Identifiers with the Religious Right, who accounted for 34 percent of the primary voters, cast 68 percent of their ballots for Bush and only 24 percent for McCain. McCain won the support of nonidentifiers by 52 percent to 46 percent. Partisanship provided the sharpest difference in support for the two candidates, however. Bush carried the votes of 69 percent of Republicans; McCain won the support of 60 percent of Independents and 70 percent of Democrats. The Republicans accounted for 61 percent of the turnout.

Television news media immediately shifted attention to the upcoming Michigan primary while making no significant changes in their coverage themes. Dean Reynolds on ABC reported on February 12 that Bush had "rolled into Michigan with a full head of steam" and then focused his efforts on Bush's chances and the attacks by the Texas governor on McCain. Linda Douglass on ABC reported that McCain was willing to engage Bush in yet another battle. These two correspondents continued reporting about personal combat and electoral prospects until the primary. Reynolds looked at how McCain's attacks over Bush's appearance at Bob Jones University were causing difficulties for Bush (February 21) and discussed the polarizing effect Governor John Engler was having on the upcoming vote (February 22). Douglas reported that McCain was appealing to Democrats and Independents and discussed how their support might improve his chances: It was possible that the turnout of non-Republicans in Michigan would exceed that of South Carolina.

With respect to the other networks, NBC correspondents David Bloom and Anne Thompson considered how the candidates were using recorded telephone messages as another method for attacking one another in Michigan. Bush was using messages by the Reverend Pat Robertson to question McCain's commitment to conservative religious views; McCain used messages that raised the issue of anti-Catholic bigotry in relation to Bush because of the Bob Jones speech. Bloom described Bush as the "indisputable Republican front-runner" after the South Carolina vote and said his campaign was back on track. He added that Bush was now favored to win the California and New York primaries on March 7 because only Republicans could vote in those states. Thompson depicted Michigan as a crucial state for McCain and explained that he had to defeat the well-organized Bush campaign in order to survive. Such a victory would require large numbers of Democratic and Independent votes, she added. Bob Schieffer on CBS looked at the prospect that Democrats would vote in the Republican primary to embarrass Governor Engler.

McCain was clearly the big winner in the primaries of February 22. He defeated Bush in Michigan by 51 percent to 43 percent and in Arizona by 60 percent to 36 percent. McCain won most of the delegates as well, including fifty-two in Michigan and all thirty in Arizona. The different outcomes in South Carolina and Michigan derive from differences in voter turnout. Bush beat McCain among Republicans by 66 percent to 29 percent but McCain won the votes of 82 percent of Democrats and Independents. This is important because Democrats and Independents cast a majority of the Michigan vote. Only 48 percent of Michigan voters were Republicans; 17 percent were Democrats and 35 percent, Independents. As in South Carolina, Religious Right identifiers voted heavily for Bush, giving him 66 percent of their ballots. Unfortunately for Bush, these identifiers accounted for only 27 percent of the electorate. McCain received 60 percent of the ballots of voters who did not identify with the Religious Right.

THE FINAL PRIMARIES: REPUBLICANS

After the Michigan primary, the Republican race entered what would prove to be its final phase: the two weeks between Bush's losses in Michigan and Arizona and his convincing victories in the major primaries of March 7, which ended the McCain challenge. This phase began quite differently than it concluded, however, because McCain initially looked like a winner. Tom Brokaw said as much when he began the NBC telecast of February 23 by depicting McCain as the new front-runner. Unfortunately, McCain had a serious problem that could, and eventually did, destroy his chance for the nomination. He needed to win the support of a majority of Republican voters, a feat he had thus far failed to accomplish in any state other than Arizona. Anne Thompson, who reported shortly after Brokaw, focused on this problem. She began with scenes of McCain's claiming he was the only Republican who could win the general election but then pointed out that most states with upcoming primaries limited participation to Republicans. McCain would have to win the support of far more Republicans than the 29 percent who voted for him in Michigan if he were to have any chance in these primaries, Thompson concluded. David Bloom then reported on Bush's new troubles with McCain. He said Bush was presently winning the battle for the support of Republicans but losing the war. The implication was that McCain might very well expand his support into the mainstream of Republican voters and secure the nomination. Bloom included scenes of Bush's attacking McCain as not being a real Republican and using recorded telephone messages depicting Bush as anti-Catholic solely on the basis of his appearance at Bob Jones University.

The other networks had similar views of the status of the campaign. Both ABC and CBS featured McCain as the center of their political attention on February 23. Mike von Fremd on ABC and Phil Jones on CBS reported that the now optimistic McCain was trying to define himself as a Reagan Republican in order to expand his party support. These networks also looked at Bush but did so only after they had considered McCain: Bush occupied the position that television news media usually reserved for the leading adversary of the front-runner. Bill Whitaker on CBS and John Yang on ABC focused on Bush's campaigning in California and planning to rebound from his defeat. Both correspondents had scenes of Bush's attacking McCain and claiming to be the real Republican.

The ongoing news theme that Bush was in trouble grew in intensity and was reflected one day later in Dan Rather's opening remarks on CBS. Rather said there were signs that support for Bush was eroding. Eric Engberg reported that Bush had returned to Texas again to meet with campaign strategists, just as he had after his defeat in New Hampshire. Engberg stated that Bush had lost the financial advantage over McCain, since most of his $73 million in campaign funds had already been spent, and the psychological edge that people believed he was unstoppable. Bush once had a clear message, Engberg added, but his appearance at Bob Jones University and his association with Pat Robertson were costing him votes in places that did not care for the Religious Right. Bush was also hurting himself by attacking the Democrats and Independents who were voting in the Republican primaries. These attacks suggested that Bush wanted an exclusionist Republican Party with membership limited to the few, Engberg continued.

Television news media continued directing attention to the theme of Bush's troubles for several more days. They were particularly interested in Bush's appearance at Bob Jones University. Phil Jones on CBS looked at the matter on February 25 and included scenes of Bush stumbling over his words as he tried to explain his actions. One day later, John Yang on ABC and David Gregory on NBC reported that Bush had written a letter to Cardinal John O'Conner of the New York Catholic diocese, apologizing for his failure to address religious bigotry in his Bob Jones appearance and emphasizing that he was not anti-Catholic. O'Connor, who died several months later, was perhaps the most influential Catholic official in the nation.

McCain expanded the importance of the religion and politics issue on February 28, one day before the primaries in Virginia and Washington, when he publicly attacked two of the prominent leaders of the Religious Right, the Reverend Pat Robertson and Jerry Falwell. All three networks devoted a considerable amount of time to this story. McCain attacked Bush for his political alliances with Robertson and Falwell while referring to them as "peddlers of intolerance, division, and smears." McCain also tried to label Bush a "Pat Robertson Republican." This was a risky political move because Virginia was the home state of both men and they appeared to be well liked by many of that state's Republican voters. Using language that seemed intended to emphasize the divisiveness of the religious differences within the Republican Party, Tom Brokaw on NBC spoke of a "holy war" and Dan Rather began the CBS telecast by saying McCain had "given the Religious Right holy hell." Linda Douglass on ABC reported McCain's remarks and his references to Bush and Bush's response denying bigotry. Jim Wooten on ABC spoke of how Bush was trying to distance himself from Robertson while not alienating the Religious Right. Phil Jones on CBS reported that Virginia had become a battleground for what he depicted as an all-out religious war within the Republican Party. Jones said the attack was politically risky for McCain, who would gain little from it in Virginia, though he could gain in some of the primaries in northern states during the coming weeks. Bob Schieffer of CBS said Bush needed to reign in Robertson and make amends to Catholics. Bush had gained supporters earlier in the campaign because many of his partisans had seen him as a "big tent" Republican who could expand the party base. Bush had impressed people with his moderate style in Texas, where he had worked well with minorities and Democrats, and was in danger of losing that image, Schieffer concluded. Anne Thompson of NBC defined Virginia as a battleground in the Republican holy war and included excerpts of an anti-Bush telephone call the McCain camp was distributing. Lisa Myers of NBC reported that Bush was trying to distance himself from Robertson and convince his supporters that he was not an anti-Catholic bigot.

McCain's attacks did not show any immediate payoff, as Bush won the Virginia primary in a manner similar to his earlier victory in South Carolina, defeating McCain by 53 percent to 44 percent and carrying the same demographic and ideological categories of voters that he had previously. Republicans supported him over McCain by 69 percent to 28 percent, whereas 87 percent of Democrats and 64 percent of Independents backed McCain. Bush ran even stronger among Religious Right identifiers than before, receiving 80 percent of their vote. He narrowly lost the support of nonidentifiers, garnering 45 percent of their votes compared to 52 percent for McCain.

Network correspondents used exit polls to review the likely outcome of the Virginia primary on February 29, and as they did on the day of every important primary, focused attention on the winner and the new test he would face in the next stage of the struggle for power. Dan Rather on CBS said that the Religious Right had turned out in force for Bush and added that the Texas governor was running well because Republicans had supported him while the turnout of Democrats and Independents was not sufficient for a strong showing by McCain. Bill Whitaker on CBS, reporting from California, said McCain was campaigning on the issue of campaign finance reform but most Republican activists were satisfied with existing laws and did not want their party reformed. Many of them viewed McCain's strong support from Democrats and Independents as an attempt at a hostile takeover of the party. Linda Douglass of ABC and Anne Thompson of NBC, also reporting from California, pointed out that McCain could not win the crucial primary in that state unless he expanded his support among Republicans.

What a difference a week can make. With a victory in Virginia to bolster his chances, Bush regained the media-proclaimed role of front-runner. Correspondents focused their attention on McCain's diminishing fortunes, the continued use of negative attack ads by both candidates, and the status of the horse race and of the likelihood that Bush would win most of the upcoming primaries. Brian Williams, NBC anchor on March 1, said Bush had the "Big Mo," a term for momentum Bush's father had used in 1980 after he defeated Ronald Reagan in the Iowa caucuses. Lisa Myers of NBC reported that Bush was campaigning with a new confidence and McCain was facing a backlash from a number of Republicans over has attacks on leaders of the Religious Right. She said California could be McCain's last chance. Phil Jones of CBS also spoke of Bush's new confidence and demonstrated it by including scenes of a Bush appearance on the "David Letterman" show. Linda Douglass of ABC focused on McCain's difficulties and his uphill struggle to win the California primary and the nomination; she also suggested McCain's campaign was failing. Bob Schieffer of CBS looked at the campaign in Ohio, where Bush was reported to be ahead and McCain was trying to rebound from his recent defeat. He noted that most Ohio political analysts believed that Bush would win but that McCain, who was drawing large crowds, had a chance.

These themes continued to resurface over the next week. On March 2, Schieffer looked at the likely outcome in the remaining primaries, concluding that McCain might run well in five New England states but that Bush would win the rest. Jim Wooten of ABC described how the candidates were trying to appeal to followers of Ronald Reagan as they campaigned in California and suggested that Bush was winning the battle. Lisa Myers on NBC focused on Bush's efforts to gain support from moderate voters. She said such efforts demonstrated the high level of confidence that now existed in the Bush campaign. Bush believed he had the conservative Republicans and could now seek backing from the moderate voters who had been the foundation of McCain's support, Myers added.

There was extensive media interest in attack ads on March 3 because a Texas supporter of Bush had placed a number of them on New York television, hitting McCain over his record on environmental issues. All three networks had scenes of them and used their existence as the focal point for their news reports. Linda Douglas of ABC directed attention to the question of unregulated soft money and the role it was playing in the campaign. Dean Reynolds on ABC looked at other attack ads in New York, where Bush was hitting McCain's record over his lack of support for funding of breast cancer research. Phil Jones and Bob Schieffer on CBS focused on the attack ads of Bush and McCain, respectively. After describing the ads, Anne Thompson of NBC directed her report to the apparent erosion of support for McCain. In a news segment later in their broadcast that supported this contention, NBC televised the remarks of a Florida attorney who identified with the Religious Right, who said that he had once supported McCain but was angered by his attacks on Pat Robertson and now planned to vote for Bush.

The networks continued emphasizing the roles, combat, and horse race themes in the final days before the primaries of March 7. In general, they projected that McCain would run well in the New England states but would likely lose everywhere else, and this would be the end of his campaign. They attributed Bush's likely successes to his aggressive attacks on McCain and to his powerful support among most Republicans. These projections were correct as McCain won only four states, Connecticut, Massachusetts, Rhode Island, and Vermont, while Bush carried everything else. Bush won California, Georgia, Maine, Maryland, Missouri, New York, and Ohio by margins ranging from 8 percent in New York to 41 percent in Georgia. He won the California primary by 60 percent to 35 percent. McCain's triumphs ranged from 2 percent in Connecticut to 37 percent in Massachusetts. The voting patterns of March 7 reflected those of earlier primaries as most Republicans again backed Bush and McCain gained the support of most Independents. Bush won the backing of Republicans in every primary. His strongest showing was in Georgia, where 77 percent voted for him, and his weakest was in Vermont, where he won only 51 percent. He garnered the votes of 63 percent of California Republicans, 57 percent of New Yorkers, and 68 percent of Ohioans'. He lost the votes of Independents in ten primaries, however, garnering between 21 percent in Massachusetts and 41 percent in California. He won 53 percent in Georgia.

McCain's attacks on the Religious Right appear to have backfired. Bush attained the support of Religious Right identifiers in all eleven states and made substantial gains among nonidentifiers. His support among identifiers ranged between 46 percent in Massachusetts (compared to 44 percent for McCain) and 80 percent in Georgia. He won the support of 73 percent of identifiers in California, 62 percent in New York, and 75 percent in Ohio. Bush won the support of nonidentifiers in five states, including California (56 percent) and Ohio (51 percent). He ran even with McCain in New York at 47 percent. Bush's backing among nonidentifiers ranged between 29 percent in Massachusetts and 60 percent in Georgia.

The Republican campaign ended two days later, when McCain withdrew. Before that happened, however, television news media analyzed Bush's general election prospects in their reporting of March 8. Dean Reynolds on ABC said that Bush's major task would be to run a winning campaign in a year with a booming economy. Reynolds said that Bush would emphasize compassion over conservatism, tolerance, improved public schools, and middle-class tax cuts. He added that Bush could expect attacks from the entire Clinton administration. David Bloom on NBC said that it was an open question whether McCain's supporters would vote for Bush. Lisa Myers of NBC said the key to a Bush victory lay in winning the support of the Independent voters who had been attracted to him until he veered to the political Right. Myers added that Bush had not projected the desire and strength voters usually want in a president.

McCain decided not to endorse Bush immediately after he ended his candidacy. This decision set the stage for a news theme emphasizing the differences between Bush and McCain and Bush's potential difficulty in winning the votes of McCain's followers on March 9. Correspondents from all three networks talked about the differences between Bush and McCain over campaign finance reform and included references to McCain's dedication to the cause and Bush's reluctance to embrace it.

As discussed earlier, television news media prefer to focus much of their attention on one, rather than two, nomination campaigns after the conclusion of the votes in Iowa and New Hampshire. In 2000, that one race was in the Republican Party. In previous television age elections the party that received the most intense televised news coverage after the primaries in the early test states always lost the general election. Voters became increasingly dissatisfied with the combatants and tended to see them as less qualified than their rivals from the opposing party. There was one crucial difference between those earlier elections and this one, however: the amount of time involved in the struggle. The most intense part of the nomination campaign lasted only a few weeks and ended eight months before the general election. The Republicans may very well have enhanced their electoral prospects through their front-loading efforts. Without eleven primaries on March 7, it is quite likely the nomination campaign would have lasted several more months, perhaps even until the national convention in August. With so many primaries so early in the year, the Republicans ended their divisive campaign on the same day the Democrats concluded their far less divisive one. Although Bush did lose some standing in national polls between January and March as a result of his battles with McCain, he had more than enough time to recover. He managed to accomplish exactly that within only a few weeks.

THE FINAL PRIMARIES: DEMOCRATS

The patterns of televised news coverage that would dominate the final stages of the Democratic campaign were evident on February 2, the day after New Hampshire. All three networks began their political reporting that day by looking at McCain's victory and Bush's response and only then focused on the Democrats. Their coverage of the Democrats was far more limited than that of the Republicans as they illustrated little more than the daily activities of the candidates. There were scenes on NBC of Bradley's campaigning in Ohio, where he attacked Gore over abortion and over the rude treatment some of Gore's supporters had given Senator Robert Kerrey in New Hampshire. Gore was shown interrupting his campaign plans and returning to Washington, D.C., because he might have needed to cast a tie breaking vote on an abortion matter on ABC. This tie did not occur. One day later, Dan Rather on CBS briefly put the horse race theme forward as he talked about Gore's lead among automatic convention delegates. Democratic rules permitted several hundred party leaders and elected officials to serve as delegates to the national convention. Rather reported that Gore had been endorsed by nearly six hundred of them compared to about one hundred for Bradley.

The Democratic candidates disappeared from national television for about one week and resurfaced on February 9 when John Cochran on ABC presented a horse race–oriented report. Cochran called Gore the front-runner and talked about his nationwide support by establishment Democrats and labor union leaders while pointing out that Bradley needed to rely on student volunteers to do much of his campaigning. Cochran said this was a frustrating time for Bradley in that McCain was now receiving much of the news coverage he had been attaining only a few months earlier. Cochran added that Gore was trying to avoid mistakes during the weeks leading to the California primary while Bradley was looking for an opening.

Reports with similar themes followed over the next few days. On February 10 Dan Rather on CBS said that Bradley was failing to connect with core Democratic voters and Gore was pulling away from him in polls in states with upcoming primaries. The news was not completely disappointing for Bradley, however, for the next day all three networks showed excerpts from one of his new television advertisements in which he received the endorsement of the basketball star Michael Jordan. Correspondents quickly returned to the usual themes, however. On February 11, John Roberts on CBS said Bradley was down in the polls and running out of options. He referred to a recent California poll in which Gore had a 41 percent lead. In describing Bradley's difficulties and perhaps suggesting media priorities, Roberts said that there was room for only one insurgent candidate and that candidate was McCain.

Three days later, Terry Moran on ABC talked about the difficulties Bradley was encountering in California from attacks by Gore on his health care proposals. Bradley had proposed an extensive health care program with an estimated annual cost of $65 billion. Gore had attacked the plan, pointing out that some of the proposed changes would actually reduce coverage for persons with acquired immunodeficiency syndrome (AIDS). Moran depicted this as one example of a series of similar campaign events in which Gore would zero in on a Bradley position and depict it in the worst possible light. Bradley would respond by crying foul and accuse Gore of negative campaigning but would fail to provide any clarity about his proposals. Gore would move on to the next issue and try the same approach again, and Bradley would respond similarly; this, Moran said, had become the dynamic of the Democratic campaign.

The Democratic candidates disappeared from national television during the days preceding the South Carolina primary but returned shortly afterward. The event that attracted media attention was a debate in Harlem. On February 20, John Roberts of CBS looked at the preparations for the debate and said that Gore had entered it as the clear leader in the New York race and had spent much of the day greeting enthusiastic voters. Roberts identified Bradley as the challenger, described him as more subdued, and said he was trailing in every state that would vote on March 7: a far cry, Roberts pointed out, from his standing two months earlier. Bradley, Roberts informed the viewers, had once had a double-digit lead over Gore in New York. He was now outgunned by Gore's organization and party support, Roberts concluded, and all too often failed to respond adequately to Gore's attacks.

Television news media continued their inconsistent coverage of the Democrats once again as they ignored them in the aftermath of the Michigan primary while concentrating on the Republicans. The event that returned the Democrats to national television was Bradley's quixotic effort in the Washington primary. Washington Democrats had scheduled a nonbinding primary on February 29. Bradley decided to contest it although no convention delegates could be gained. He believed a victory would generate the favorable news coverage that could propel him to victory in some of the primaries of March 7. The strategy appeared to work, at least with respect to news coverage. On February 26, Norah O'Donnell on NBC reported on Bradley's plans to spend six days in the state in an attempt to "stay in the game." She talked about his hopes of halting Gore's momentum in the March 7 primaries but also told viewers of the difficult struggle Bradley faced in trying to do so. O'Donnell referred to several recent polls that showed Bradley running behind Gore: trailing in New York by 56 percent to 32 percent, in Ohio by 68 percent to 24 percent, and in California by 54 percent to 13 percent.

Bradley's foray into Washington continued to attract the attention of network correspondents, but the news was rarely favorable. Over the next two days, each of the three networks looked at Bradley's grim chances and suggested that time was running out on his campaign. On February 29, primary day, Dan Rather said Gore was leading Bradley by 55 percent to 29 percent in New York in the most recent CBS poll and then introduced John Roberts for a report about the campaign in Washington. Roberts said Bradley had generated little fanfare in the state. Also that day, Claire Shipman on NBC said Bradley had spent $1 million in Washington. She called it the political equivalent of a half-court shot during the last minute of a losing basketball game. She had scenes of Bradley's speaking to a small group of workers at a labor union gathering and of Gore's speaking at the same place later to a much larger audience. As expected, Bradley suffered yet another defeat as he lost the primary to Gore 60 percent to 40 percent.

Bradley's poor showing in Washington after his large investment of time and money led to increasing speculation by television news media of his imminent withdrawal from the campaign. Jackie Judd on ABC said on February 29 that the Bradley campaign was in trouble and that the situation was desperate. She referred to the pessimism of some of his advisers and noted that they were speaking of the campaign in the past tense. Tim Russert of NBC also raised this prospect on February 29, Rather on CBS mentioned it on March 1, and Judd on ABC talked about it again on March 4.

The reporting before the March 7 primaries continued with the same themes that Gore would be the big winner and that Bradley would likely withdraw. Many correspondents now began looking at Gore's plans for the general election. On March 6 Terry Moran of ABC looked at Gore's environmental record, Richard Schlesinger of CBS provided a personal background review about the vice president, and Claire Shipman of NBC showed Gore's attacking Bush over health care and campaign finance reform. Each correspondent also referred to how well Gore was expected to perform in the primaries of the next day.

As expected, Gore swept to victory in all primaries on March 7. The closest races were in the five New England states of Connecticut, Maine, Massachusetts, Rhode Island, and Vermont, where he received 55 to 60 percent of the vote compared to Bradley, whose support ranged from 38 percent to 44 percent. Gore attained between 65 percent and 84 percent of the vote in each of the other six states—California, Georgia, Maryland, Missouri, New York, and Ohio—where Bradley's support ranged between 16 percent and 35 percent. Particularly noteworthy was California, where Gore attained 81 percent of the vote compared to Bradley's 18 percent.

There was one unique feature of the California primary that had started and will end with the election of 2000. The state was operating under a law that required one ballot for all voters regardless of party affiliations. This so-called blanket primary was created by initiative in 1998 but was found to be unconstitutional by the Supreme

Court in July 2000. Under this law, all voters would choose from the same list of candidates, and the first-place finisher from each party would win the primary. In order to conform to their national party rules, which prohibited such primaries, the Republican and Democratic Parties both used ballots that limited participation to party members in all votes related to selecting delegates for the national conventions. Nonetheless, the candidates competed among themselves for bragging rights over which one would receive the most popular votes. Gore won with 35 percent, and Bush was second with 28 percent. McCain and Bradley trailed with 23 percent and 9 percent, respectively.

Exit polls once again indicated that two important differences divided Democratic primary voters, partisanship and opinions of Clinton the person. Gore won the votes of self-identified Democrats in every state by margins ranging from 60 percent in Maine to 88 percent in Georgia. He split the votes of Independents with Bradley, carrying five states while losing six. Gore had a low of 39 percent of the Independent vote in Connecticut and a high of 64 percent in California. Voters who approved of Clinton as a person backed Gore by margins that ranged from 68 percent in Maine to 92 percent in Georgia, whereas those who disapproved of Clinton supported Gore by margins between 42 percent in Maine and 72 percent in California.

As in the Republican, the Democratic race ended with the March 7 primaries. Bradley, like McCain, withdrew on March 9. Television news media described the final days of the Democratic campaign in much the same manner as they had described the Republican. They focused attention on the triumphant Gore while speculating about his general election prospects, then spent March 9 describing Bradley's departure. In keeping with the reporting patterns they had employed for the past five weeks, all three networks looked at the Democrats only after they had reported about the Republicans. Viewers did not see Bradley withdraw until they had seen McCain leave.

5

THE GENERAL ELECTION CAMPAIGN BETWEEN MARCH AND AUGUST

Every presidential election has some unique features, and there were certainly many of those in 2000; one of the most unusual was the relatively early conclusion of the nomination campaigns. The simultaneous ending of the quests for both the Republican and Democratic nominations on the same day, March 9, resulted in the longest general election campaign in the history of the American presidency. This next portion of the book looks at the postprimary component of the 2000 election in much the same manner as before, by focusing on how television news media interpreted events and the behavior of political actors and then depicted them to their audiences. Once again, the reader can observe the development of the campaign through the medium of televised network news.

I divide the description into four periods. Of varying length, these periods differ in the nature of their most significant events. The first period encompasses the time between the conclusions of the nomination campaigns on March 9 to the beginning of the televised news interest in the national conventions, July 21. This was a relatively long time, nineteen weeks, but it served mainly as a transition between the nomination and general election campaigns. Bush and Gore had vanquished their partisan rivals, but they were not yet prepared to compete against one another. Neither had been officially nominated, thus preventing them from receiving the $67.5 million in federal funding that accompanied a major party nomination. In addition, neither had yet selected a running mate. The interest of television news media in the campaign was inconsistent during this first period; only rarely did all three networks report about the campaign on the same day.

The second period is the shortest, only four weeks, but quite intense nonetheless. It encompasses events between July 21 and August 17 related to the national conventions. The Republicans met first, in Philadelphia from July 31 to August 3; the Democrats followed with their conclave two weeks later in Los Angeles from August 14 to 17. Television news media expanded their coverage from the relatively limited reporting of the first period by focusing intently on the leading events and political actors of the parties before and during each convention. They started on July 21 by looking at Bush's upcoming selection of a running mate, then devoted about two weeks to reporting about the Republican convention. They then directed about the same amount of time and interest to the Democrats. This second period was characterized by daily news coverage, a pattern of reporting that had not occurred since the conclusion of the nomination campaigns in March. The daily coverage continued after the conventions and lasted through the mid-December conclusion of the legal drama in Florida.

The postconvention time is divided into two distinct periods that are distinguished by the debates. The third period begins on August 18, immediately after the conclusion of the Democratic convention, and runs through the end of September. It encompasses forty-four days and includes the time between the end of the conventions and the onset of the news interest in the first debate involving the two presidential candidates. This period is characterized by numerous instances of each candidate's attempting to develop several key themes for defining his appeal and then placing his rival on the defensive. The fourth period includes the month of October and the first six days of November. It concludes on election eve, November 6, and lasts for thirty-seven days. It is characterized by two features, the debates and the drives by the parties and candidates for getting out the vote. Television news media began their coverage on October 1, two days before the first debate. There were four debates: the presidential candidates met on October 3, 11, and 17 and the vice presidential candidates on October 5. Television news media devoted much of their political reporting during the first seventeen days of October to matters related to the debates. Afterward, they began looking more intently at the probable outcome of the election. They now employed large electoral maps depicting whether each state was likely to vote for Bush, or for Gore, or perhaps might be too close to allow a reliable forecast. In addition, they looked at how the candidates concentrated their efforts on these remaining undecided states.

THE PRECONVENTION PERIOD

The preconvention was the longest period in the campaign, nineteen weeks in all, but was also the least important in terms of political events, televised news reporting, and voter decision making. At the outset, both Bush and Gore needed to direct their efforts to reuniting their respective parties and partisan voter bases after the divisions they had incurred in their nomination battles. Bush, in particular, had a significant problem in that he needed to convince the moderate Republicans and Independents who had supported McCain that he would bring about some meaningful change in American political life. Without their support, Bush would forfeit any chance of winning. Gore's triumph was far less divisive among his own partisans than Bush's, but Gore still needed to appeal to Bradley's followers because many of them were more likely than he to favor private sector solutions to major public problems.

Television news coverage of these efforts was sporadic and often resulted from the occurrence of a particularly significant event such as McCain's endorsing Bush or of a candidate's announcing his position on a major issue such as Social Security. On only six occasions between March 10 and July 20 did all three networks report about the campaign on the same day. Nonetheless, television news media structured their reporting around two central themes during this time and then consistently relied on those same two themes as the campaign advanced into its later periods. These themes were the status of the horse race and the personal combat of the candidates. One news theme noticeably absent both now and later was any effort by reporters to depict Gore as acting in the role of presidential surrogate. Instead, reporters saw Gore as a coequal aspirant for the presidency along with Bush and undeserving of any special treatment because of the nature of his office. This pattern of reporting was partly encouraged by Gore, who wanted to appear as his own man, but it also resulted from the nature of televised news. It was virtually impossible for Gore consistently to create imagery in which he appeared as an incumbent governing the nation. He could appear only as a candidate; hence, television news media illustrated him as one.

Such an illustration contrasts to the televising of an incumbent during this transitional period. In a comparable period of 1996, television news media paid little attention to Robert Dole but reported almost daily about the actions of Bill Clinton's actions as president. Gore had used his role of presidential surrogate during the primaries to rally the party faithful to his banner, but he could not employ that role again in convincing the Independents and Republicans who had supported McCain to back him instead of Bush. He was feeling the limiting effects of the vice presidential office. Gore was inheriting the wrath of the many voters who despised Clinton, but he was trapped in that he could not use his office to engage in actions that would make him appear presidential and perhaps gain their support, such as signing a bill or issuing an executive order. In contrast, Bush was in an excellent position. He was no longer merely an aspirant for the nomination of the opposition party; he was the new leader of that party and a potential president. Voters were now seeing him for what he was, the only viable political alternative to the status quo. While attempting to reunite his opposition Republicans into a cohesive force, Bush was also trying to project a unifying image to the rest of the nation, emphasizing the theme that he was a "uniter, not a divider," and many voters increasingly saw him in that light.

Television news media focused their attention during the remainder of March on one theme related to the horse race and on one involving personal combat. The horse race involved poll standings; the personal combat was illustrated by the troubles the candidates were encountering in winning the support of McCain's backers. The first report looking at poll standings was on March 11, when John Yang described the outcome of the latest ABC poll. Yang advanced the theme that Bush had lost support because of his struggle with McCain. Bush had led Gore by sixteen points (55 percent to 39 percent) in October, saw his lead decline to six points (50 percent to 44 percent) in February, and now trailed Gore by a margin within the polls' 4 percent margin of error (48 percent to 45 percent). In explaining these changes, Yang said many Independents and political moderates had shifted their support from Bush to Gore because the campaign had caused them to believe that Bush was a conservative; many of them had had no clear view of Bush in 1999. In other news that was bad for Bush, these same respondents also viewed the two candidates as equally able to deal with taxes; calls for tax cuts had been one of Bush's strongest appeals. Not all the news was good for

Gore, however. Yang said Gore should have been ahead rather than even because of the strong economy. The fact that the candidates were tied suggested that many voters had doubts about Gore and were looking at Bush as a potentially stronger leader, Yang added. One feature of reporting about the status of the horse race is that the race is never over: both candidates always face challenges to maintain their positions and must strive to overcome them. Bush had to win back the moderates who had abandoned him, and Gore had to win over voters who did not believe he would be a strong leader. The other networks had similar reports about the strength of the two candidates in the days that followed and provided similar analyses. Jonathan Alter on NBC and Bill Whitaker on CBS directed their attention to new polls as they previewed the next round of primaries, six scheduled for March 14, including ones in Texas and Florida.

The polls continued to be close during the remainder of the pre-convention period, but other than during the days that immediately followed the conclusion of the primaries, Bush tended to hold a slight lead. The Gallup-CNN-*USA Today* Poll of March 10 showed Gore as leading Bush 48 percent to 46 percent, a margin similar to those of other polls. Eight other polls taken by this organization between March 13 and July 16 showed Bush's support's ranging between 45 percent and 52 percent and Gore's between 39 percent and 46 percent. Bush's lead over Gore exceeded the margin of error in only four of these, however.

When the primaries concluded, a substantial number of network correspondents appeared to believe that the key to victory rested in attracting McCain's supporters and that the key to winning them was campaign finance reform. Armed with this belief, television news media devoted much of their coverage in the immediate aftermath of the primaries to the personal combat between Bush and Gore over attracting these voters. Gore faced a particularly pressing dilemma: the U.S. Department of Justice had investigated some of his fund-raising activities from the 1996 campaign. Perhaps the most relevant features of those investigations were the inquiries into an allegedly nonpartisan appearance Gore had made at a Buddhist temple that actually resulted in some illegal fund-raising by the Democratic Party and the Clinton-Gore reelection campaign. Gore had denied any wrongdoing, but Republican members of Congress had called for Attorney General Janet Reno to ask for a special prosecutor. She had refused the request and had thereby angered the Republicans. This controversy was several years old, but television news media started reminding their viewers about it in late March, when Gore began advancing proposals about campaign finance reform. Network correspondents viewed Gore's remarks in terms of personal combat with Bush aimed at gaining the support of McCain's backers.

One such example occurred in the March 13 report of Claire Shipman on NBC. Tom Brokaw introduced the personal combat idea when he said Gore was trying to pick up McCain's themes of reform while trying to appear as a reformer. Brokaw added that Gore's actions appeared to have angered Bush. Shipman followed Brokaw and initially focused her report on Gore's remarks about the need for changing the laws governing soft money contributions and then challenging Bush to join him. She included a scene of Bush's attacking Gore's remarks as hypocritical. Afterward, Shipman reminded viewers about the fund-raising controversy at the Buddhist temple by combining her narrative with file film of Gore's appearance. In addition, she updated the audience on several recent developments in the matter, including summaries of memorandums from the Department of Justice relating to Gore's statements during investigations. In her analysis of Gore's present comments on soft money, Shipman said Gore believed he could win the votes of some of McCain's supporters, because he wanted to get the Buddhist temple controversy behind him early in the campaign and because he believed Bush was vulnerable on this issue.

Bush did indeed appear vulnerable. Bush had told the *New York Times* he would make no concessions to McCain on the soft money issue and then attacked Gore for his temple visit. On March 16 David Gregory of NBC reported the negative reactions of some of McCain's advisers to Bush's remarks. Lisa Myers of NBC then reported recent investigations by the Department of Justice into perhaps as many as seventy questionable telephone calls Gore had made in 1996 from his vice presidential office for contributions to the Clinton-Gore campaign. Gore had said the calls were soliciting soft money contributions, which he could legally do in his office, but may have been for hard money, that is, actual contributions to his campaign. Solicitations for hard money contributions on or from federal property were illegal.

The theme of personal combat on the finance campaign issue continued to attract media interest for several more days. Gore proposed a campaign finance reform plan on March 27. Dan Rather began the CBS political reporting that day by saying Gore's plan would set up a $7 million endowment to pay for congressional campaigns, require new disclosure rules for political groups that pay for advertising, and eliminate the use of soft money. Rather added that the Bush campaign was now using television ads to attack Gore on the reform issue. He then turned to correspondent Eric Engberg, who again looked at the controversy about Gore and the Buddhist temple. Engberg also included scenes of Bush's attacking Gore on the campaign finance issue in his report. One day later, CBS directed their attention to Bush's fund-raising actions and controversies. Bill Whitaker reported that Bush had already raised $74 million and had spent $63 million of it. He commented that money seemed to be the message for Bush while showing how a number of energy-related interests had contributed Bush's past campaigns for governor and had then received special treatment in their efforts to seek legislation reducing tort liability awards. Whitaker also looked at Bush's scheduled appearance at an upcoming Republican fund-raiser that might take in about $15 million.

The controversy about Gore's fund-raising, and related media interest, did not subside in the wake of the vice president's soft money proposal. It disappeared from the news for several weeks but eventually resurfaced for two days (June 22 and 23) when Attorney General Janet Reno announced she would not recommend the appointment of a special prosecutor to investigate Gore's testimony to Federal Bureau of Investigation (FBI) agents. Her announcement served as the catalyst for several news reports. Jackie Judd of ABC reviewed the recent events on June 22 and made some references to the Buddhist temple visit. Cokie Roberts of ABC followed Judd and speculated how the matter might affect Gore's electoral prospects. Dan Rather on CBS and Claire Shipman on NBC reported the announcement and provided some analysis of its possible political impact. All three networks included some sharp and negative comments about Gore by Senator Arlen Specter of Pennsylvania, who had been one of the leading members of Congress calling for the appointment of a prosecutor. One day later, Gore responded to Specter's charges and media inquiries by releasing the transcripts of his testimony in which he had denied any lawbreaking. All three networks once again revisited the controversy and included remarks by Specter on why he believed a prosecutor was necessary.

The themes of news coverage would change somewhat during April and May, when television news media began paying more attention to questions of public policy. They did not completely abandon the horse race theme, however, and continued with occasional updates about money and polls. The most significant horse race–related news during this time was McCain's endorsement of Bush on

May 9. That day marked the first time since the end of the primaries that all three networks reported about the campaign at the same time. They employed the same script in doing so, each with scenes of McCain's making his endorsement, and then speculated on how the endorsement might help Bush.

In looking at policy questions, television news media relied almost exclusively on the personal combat theme. They depicted the announcement of a policy position by a candidate as a tactical effort to compete with his rival for the support of a particular bloc of voters. The policy that generated the greatest amount of media interest was Social Security. On May 9 Bush announced his plans for partial privatization of Social Security. His plan would allow for investing some of the program's funds in the stock market rather than in government securities as presently required. Bush believed such an approach would produce more revenue since stock market investments would be subject to higher interest rates. Dean Reynolds on ABC, John Roberts on CBS, and David Gregory on NBC reviewed the plan's main features and focused attention on how possible changes in Social Security might become an important campaign issue. Each included scenes of Bush's speaking in favor of the plan and of Gore's opposing it, of comments by various voters pro and con, and of recent polls about Social Security. Gore advanced his plan about six weeks later, on June 19, and as they had with Bush, all three networks reported extensively on it. John Cochran of ABC and John Roberts of CBS focused their attention on Gore's plan by describing its content and by illustrating Gore's favorable remarks and Bush's unfavorable ones relating to it. Claire Shipman and Lisa Myers of NBC contrasted the opposing plans; Shipman directed her attention at Gore's and Myers focused on Bush's. Each correspondent included comments by both candidates about the merits of his own plan and the limitations of the one advanced by his opponent.

Other policy questions also attracted the interest of network correspondents. The occurrence of a breaking event, such as Bush's and Gore's announcements of their plans for Social Security, was usually the catalyst that encouraged television news media to focus on a specific policy question. Correspondents would summarize the plans of each candidate on the policy issue in question, then illustrate how the candidates were engaging in personal combat in order, as they described it, to gain the support of particular voter blocs. One can see an example of this pattern of reporting in the attention the networks gave to gun control on May 4 and 5. The breaking event that generated media interest was a video of Kayne Robinson, who was the first vice president of the National Rifle Association (NRA). Robinson was seen telling a group of gun owners that the NRA would have easy access to the White House and a more favorable Supreme Court if Bush were to win the election. This video prompted the three networks to look at the gun control issue more closely and to focus attention on some of the more recent remarks by the two candidates. Peter Jennings introduced the ABC political coverage of May 5 by talking about how the candidates were attacking each other's position on guns. He said the NRA was very supportive of Bush but then added that Gore was trying to undermine the value of that support. Dean Reynolds followed Jennings by describing how Gore was attacking Bush for signing a Texas law that prevented cities from suing gun makers for urban violence. Presently, thirty-one cities were suing manufacturers for law enforcement costs associated with gun-related crimes, and the NRA was trying to convince state legislatures to prevent such suits. Reynolds then directed his attention to the breaking event that had encouraged media interest, Robinson's video. After reporting about the video, Reynolds included a scene in which Bush denied he was a political tool of the NRA. Reynolds followed with a scene of Clinton's attacking the NRA and concluded his news report by remarking that the NRA was planning to spend about $30 million in the election. The other two networks had reports similar to that of ABC, but neither included Clinton's remarks. Jim Stewart of CBS and David Gregory of NBC described Robinson's video and remarks and then looked at the controversy about Bush's NRA support. Each also focused some attention on Bush's defensive remarks and Gore's attacks.

This pattern of reporting candidate stands on policy questions within the context of the personal combat theme continued until late July and the onset of the convention period. One can see the functioning of this pattern through several examples. One occurred in mid-May, when network correspondents directed their attention to education after the financier Ted Frostmann offered to donate $500,000 to Bush's and Gore's favorite charities if they would publicly debate the issue. Lisa Myers on NBC reviewed the Frostmann offer on May 14, looking at Gore's willingness and Bush's reluctance to accept the challenge. Four days later Bill Whitaker on CBS directed his attention to the candidates' education proposals. He outlined the main points each was advancing and included brief and contrasting remarks by both candidates. In what seemed to be a departure from the usual pattern of reporting about policy questions, Whitaker then looked at the nature of the policy itself rather than limiting coverage to candidate remarks. He explored several of the more critical education problems facing a school in Los Angeles. Unfortunately, this was the last time that any network would devote a news report to education until after the conclusions of the national conventions.

Another example occurred on May 27 after Gore used his commencement address at the U.S. Military Academy to talk about control of nuclear weapons. Television news media used this address as an opportunity to focus attention on the controversy surrounding Bush's advocacy of a nuclear shield. For some time, Bush had been advocating a limited implementation of what had been known during the Reagan administration as the Strategic Defense Initiative, or "Star Wars." Lee Cowan on CBS and Terry Moran on ABC reviewed the main features of Bush's proposal and illustrated some of his recent remarks. Afterward, they looked at Gore's attacks on that proposal.

In June, after the release of some favorable government statistics about the condition of the economy, Gore sought to link economic growth with the Clinton administration. He also charged that recent successes would be threatened by a Bush victory. On June 13 both John Roberts on CBS and Claire Shipman on NBC described the way Gore was using economic growth as an opportunity to attack Bush and included scenes of Gore's making such attacks in their news reports. A planned execution in Texas encouraged television news media to focus some attention on the death penalty for several days in late June. Dean Reynolds on ABC, Claire Shipman on NBC, and Jim Axelrod on CBS reported about this controversy on June 19, 21, and 22, respectively. All three looked at Bush's record and views but limited their coverage of Gore to a short remark on NBC in which the vice president said he supported the death penalty. There was no controversy to report since the two candidates agreed. Finally, Gore began questioning Bush's record as Texas governor on government spending and balanced budgets. All three networks looked at the charges and Bush's response in their news coverage of July 20. Each network would describe the nature of the charges, show Gore's making his attacks, then include a scene of Bush's or one of his spokesmen's defending the governor's record.

Television news media returned to the horse race in June and July by looking at various efforts of Gore and Bush to win the support of certain targeted voter blocs. They focused their attention on how the two were using both money and policy stands to make their appeals. On June 7, John Cochran of ABC and Phil Jones of CBS looked at the way the Democratic Party was using soft money to purchase television advertising for Gore; Norah O'Donnell reported on June 10 about the way both Gore and Bush were using such advertising. Network correspondents also directed their attention to the Latino vote on July 5; Dean Reynolds on ABC and Bill Whitaker on CBS focused much of their attention on California, where the two candidates had both spoken recently before the National Council of La Raza. The correspondents had scenes of Bush's and Gore's speaking and then speculated on their electoral prospects among Latino voters. Two days later, NBC reported extensively about the efforts of Bush and Gore to win the votes of women. Claire Shipman looked at Gore's activities and included some recent polling about how important the women's vote would be for Democrats. David Gregory described why Bush was running stronger among women than most Republican candidates had in recent elections. Finally, all three networks directed attention to the African American vote after the candidates had spoken before the national convention of the National Association for the Advancement of Colored People (NAACP), Bush on July 10 and Gore on July 12. The underlying theme of the analyses was that Gore would probably win most of these votes and that Bush was trying to explain what he meant by his slogan "compassionate conservative."

One final event during the preconvention period would have an effect in the general election, the nomination of the consumer advocate Ralph Nader as the candidate of the Green Party. This party comprised activists from various environmental and leftist causes who were opposed to what they considered overresponsiveness by the two major parties to the political demands of corporate interests. They met in Denver in late June and chose Nader as their nominee. Tom Foreman of ABC and Phil Jones of CBS reported on the Green convention and Nader's nomination on June 24. Although these correspondents focused some attention on Nader and his proposals and even included scenes in their reports of Nader's attacking both parties, their main emphasis was on how Nader might hurt Gore. Nader might attract votes from liberals who would otherwise back Gore, they said, and thus could help Bush win some states where support was evenly divided between the two candidates. Both correspondents looked at how poorly Gore had been running in recent weeks and how Nader was appealing to some of the liberal and labor constituencies Gore needed in order to win. They included remarks by the Teamsters Union president James Hoffa critical of both Bush and Gore. This was to become the central theme that would appear in virtually all network news reports in the future about Nader. Rather than contrast Nader with Gore and Bush, network correspondents always emphasized Nader's potential to attract votes that would otherwise go to Gore and therefore help elect Bush.

With this, the campaign was ready to enter a new period, the major party conventions.

THE NATIONAL CONVENTION PERIOD

Television news media abruptly changed the themes of their reporting on Friday, July 21, moving from the emphasis on polls and issue stands to matters related to the national conventions. They began by directing their attention to the pending selection of Bush's running mate and followed by looking at the leading events and actors of the Republican convention. Afterward, they devoted about the same amount of time and focused on essentially the same topics while describing the Democratic conclave.

The first convention-related news theme concerned the identity of Bush's running mate. Bush and Gore had spent the four months since the end of the primaries campaigning without running mates. Moreover, neither had indicated whom he might select for the position. With the Republican convention only slightly more than one week away, the time was rapidly approaching for Bush to announce his choice. Network correspondents began openly speculating about his choice on July 21, when they devoted the day to reporting about the possible selection of John McCain. All three networks followed the same basic script: they began with Bush's saying he was still undecided and followed with McCain's remarks that he was not interested. Afterward, they speculated about how McCain might enhance Bush's electoral prospects through his appeal to Independent and Democratic voters.

The speculation on McCain lasted for only one day but did not disappear entirely. Two additional names surfaced on July 22, the former senator John Danforth of Missouri and the man who would eventually get the nod, the former defense secretary Dick Cheney. Television news media devoted most of their reporting that day to the possible selection of Danforth or Cheney but included some references to McCain and continued looking upon him as a possible choice. They narrowed their lists to only Danforth and Cheney one day later but treated Cheney as the probable winner. The next step in the ongoing story occurred the next day, July 24, when the selection of Cheney became a certainty.

Network correspondents employed three themes while reporting about the selection, Cheney's background, ways his choice might bolster Republican chances, and his history of heart trouble. Clearly, they viewed Cheney's background as impressive, although controversial. They saw his presence on the ticket as a gain for Bush but viewed his history of heart problems—he had suffered four heart attacks since 1978—as a matter of some concern. Bob Schieffer on CBS described Cheney as "an intellectual conservative with bipartisan support and a strong record on defense who would be a safe, conventional, and not very exciting candidate." Bill Whitaker of CBS depicted Cheney as a "rock solid conservative who appealed to party moderates." Tom Brokaw of NBC characterized the Bush-Cheney ticket as a "coming together of the young blood and the old guard of the Grand Old Party," and David Gregory of NBC said that Cheney would give a wealth of experience, particularly with respect to foreign policy, to the Republican ticket. Anne Thompson on NBC described Cheney as "sober, serious, and a grown-up," but also pointed out that Cheney's conservative record could cause some problems. She mentioned his opposition to such issues as the Equal Rights Amendment, increased funding for Head Start, abortion, and boycotts of South Africa and his support for school prayer. Thompson said Democrats would see a clear choice. Whitaker made similar remarks, saying Democrats would attack Cheney over guns, the environment, health care, and his business record in their efforts to point him as being "too far to the political Right." Dean Reynolds on ABC included remarks by McCain and Governor Frank Keating of Oklahoma about Cheney's potential strength as a candidate in his report but also focused on Cheney's heart problems. Thompson also described Cheney's health.

Bush announced his choice of Cheney six days before the convention. He followed this announcement with several public appearances that took him from Casper, Wyoming, where he attended a rally with his new running mate at Cheney's old high school, to Philadelphia. The Democrats immediately began to attack Cheney's record and soon attracted the attention of network correspondents. On July 26 Terry Moran on ABC directed attention to Jesse Jackson, who attacked Cheney as a "wolf in sheep's clothing," and to Gore, who depicted the Republican ticket as comprising candidates "with appeal to oil interests, polluters, and price gouging drug companies." Bill Whitaker on CBS continued the media focus on the Democratic attacks one day later by showing how Jackson had compared Cheney to the conservative senator Jesse Helms of North Carolina. Whitaker then described how other Democrats were denouncing Cheney's opposition to outlawing the sale of cop-killer bullets, the Clear Air and Endangered Species Acts, and efforts aimed at freeing

Nelson Mandela when he had been imprisoned by the apartheid government of South Africa.

The media interest in Democratic attacks on Cheney's record was short-lived and ended suddenly on July 28, when network correspondents again directed attention to Bush. The Texas governor was campaigning his way to Philadelphia. Bush left Austin on July 28 with an itinerary that would take him through what Dean Reynolds on ABC depicted as five swing states, Arkansas, Missouri, Kentucky, Ohio, and Pennsylvania. Reynolds said a variety of polls indicated Bush was leading Gore in all five. Bush's first appearances were in northwestern Arkansas and southeastern Missouri, where he talked about character. Cheney talked about restoring dignity to the presidency.

Bush was in Louisville, Kentucky, the next day, where, according to David Gregory on NBC, he emphasized conservatism and compassion. Gregory depicted this as an effort by Bush to "build momentum in the days leading to the convention." Television news media were particularly focused on the horse race that day as they reported the results of a new collection of polls. Terry Moran said Bush was expanding his lead over Gore and was now leading 53 percent to 42 percent in the ABC-*Washington Post* Poll. Bush also led in CBS-*New York Times* (45 percent to 41 percent), NBC-*Wall Street Journal* (44 percent to 38 percent), and Gallup-CNN-*USA Today* (50 percent to 39 percent) polls. Moran described Bush as optimistic about his chances and included scenes in which Bush was emphasizing his lead while speaking before an enthusiastic audience. All the news was not good for Bush, however, as the polls indicated some uncertainty about Cheney. The Democratic attacks were starting to have some effect. Moran said people approved of Cheney when they heard he had headed a large corporation (Halliburton) but disapproved when told that it had been a large oil company. Cheney would run well if people believed he was a former defense secretary and corporation executive but poorly if they believed he was a very conservative former congressman and the former president of an oil company, Moran added.

The horse race theme was pervasive on Sunday, July 30, the eve of the convention. All three networks consistently tried to depict virtually every action by the candidates as an effort aimed at gaining an electoral advantage. David Gregory of NBC talked about Bush's appearance in Cincinnati and mentioned how well Bush was running in the polls. Anne Thompson of NBC told of Cheney's appearances on five Sunday morning news shows in an attempt to refute the characterization of him as a political extremist by Democrats. After Jonathan Alter described the importance of Bush's acceptance speech to the subsequent campaign, NBC correspondents Tom Brokaw, Andrea Mitchell, Claire Shipman, and David Bloom looked at the present state of the Bush's effort. Mitchell said Cheney was having little effect; Shipman said Gore was leaving the attacks on Cheney to other Democrats so he would not look bad during an upbeat convention. Bloom looked at the potential effects of Nader on Gore's chances and concluded that Gore was trailing Bush and having trouble with Nader primarily because he had not consolidated his partisan base as Bush had his. Gore would gain ground if he could consolidate support from liberals, Bloom remarked. George Stephanopoulos on ABC attributed Democratic attacks on Cheney to Gore's need to remain close to Bush in the polls. He said Gore could not afford to be twenty points behind when the Republican convention ended.

The horse race theme continued to be a major component of network reporting the next day. Bill Whitaker of CBS, in Columbus, Ohio, said Bush was attracting big crowds and was now leading Gore in all five of the states in which he had campaigned on his way to the convention. The horse race stories continued throughout the week as NBC looked at Bush's attempts to win the support of women, ABC reviewed the efforts of Christian conservatives on Bush's behalf, and CBS considered how Bush was proposing changes in the Social Security system in the hope of reaching younger voters.

Bush continued using public appearances to generate news as the convention unfolded, although he occasionally had to share the spotlight with Bill Clinton, who attacked him for his position on Medicare and his credentials to be president. Network correspondents were quick to respond because these attacks, and Bush's responses, fit into their theme of personal combat. These attacks were politically significant in that television news media tended to ignore Bush or Gore while the rival's convention was in session but were not willing to ignore the partisan remarks of the president. Clinton used his incumbency at a critical time in that he prevented Bush from using the convention week exclusively to sell his ideas and personality to a national television audience. Clinton received coverage for raising questions about Bush that Gore could not raise or could not raise during this particular week. In addition to being considered newsworthy, Clinton's remarks forced Bush to respond and helped prevent the Texas governor from delivering the messages he wanted. The Clinton attacks were important for the first two days of the convention; he had made them on July 31 and Bush had responded one day later. Bush attacked Clinton for mocking his credentials and for suggesting that he was relying far too much on his father's record. Bush's father, the former president, also entered the fray, an act that virtually guaranteed even more media interest. The elder Bush warned that if Clinton did not stop his attacks, he would publicly announce his opinion of Clinton as a person.

Clinton's attacks may have spoiled the good times for Bush, but they were not the only negative assessments Bush and his party encountered that week. In a departure from the pattern of favorable coverage, on August 2 Dean Reynolds of ABC reviewed some of the contradictions between Bush's pronouncements about compassionate conservatism and his record on a number of related issues. Bush had emphasized the theme of inclusion while speaking at a rally for racial minorities in Philadelphia that day. Reynolds looked at Bush's remarks and then showed scenes from Bush's speech at Bob Jones University. Reynolds added that Bush had arranged to have a gay convention speaker but was opposed to the very issues gays advocated. He also looked at how Bush's advocacy of health care expansion, tax cuts, and environmental protection but had also advanced policies as Texas governor that opposed changes in each. The networks were also quite critical of the management of the convention and of the fund-raising efforts by the Republican leadership. On the convention's first day Dan Rather on CBS said that Republicans were opening a $60 million show designed to emphasize television imagery and the politics of pleasantry. He added that corporate sponsors were providing the money to pay for this appeal to "minorities, moms, and moderates." One day later Tom Brokaw depicted Republican delegates as "continuing to march lock step to the cadence called by Bush." In addition, Brian Ross on ABC narrated a four-part series, "The Money Trail," which looked at Republican leaders' hosting lavish parties for major corporate backers. Lisa Myers on NBC focused her August 1 report on the variety of corporate donors who had provided supplies and services for operating the convention.

Bush's upcoming acceptance speech dominated media interest on August 4, the final day of the convention. All three networks previewed Bush's likely remarks and examined how the speech and the convention might affect the course of the campaign. Dan Rather on CBS depicted the speech as Bush's opportunity to define his vision of where he would take the country and of why he should lead it. Rather added that Bush would speak in the context of the partisan attack Cheney had made the previous evening while delivering his own acceptance speech. Cheney attacked Clinton and, as Bob Schieffer on CBS remarked, "put a sharp needle to the administration." That evening, Bush delivered an upbeat and effective speech that appeared to accomplish the political tasks that network correspondents had said were necessary.

Bush left his convention with a powerful boost in the polls. The Gallup-CNN-*USA Today* Poll of July 24, the last one conducted by this organization before the convention, had Bush ahead by 49 percent to 45 percent. The poll completed by the same organization on August 5, with all questioning done after Bush's speech, showed the Texas governor as enjoying his greatest lead since the beginning of the primaries. Bush was ahead by seventeen points, 54 percent to 37 percent. The minor party candidates trailed far behind: Nader registered 4 percent and Buchanan only 1 percent.

There was a short interim, only two days, between the conclusion of the Republican convention and the beginning of network coverage of the rival Democratic convention. The networks employed the usual horse race and personal combat themes and contrasted the candidates in their various campaign appearances. Bush left Philadelphia for a short whistle stop railroad campaign that took him from Pittsburgh to Akron. Dean Reynolds on ABC, reporting from Ohio, said that Bush was energized by the convention and was "now focused on winning the election." He included scenes of an upbeat Bush's addressing his supporters. Terry Moran on ABC focused on Gore, who was speaking at a Chicago rally of fire fighters. Gore attacked Bush's convention characterization of the Democratic administration as one of lost opportunities. Moran also reminded viewers that Gore was trailing in recent polls.

Bill Clinton reentered the campaign the next day, when he announced a veto of a Republican tax bill that reduced what its sponsors called the "marriage penalty." This so-called penalty was a component of the federal tax code whereby certain married couples with two incomes approximately equal in size might pay higher taxes with their joint filing status than they would if each could file individually. Republicans wanted to reduce the impact of this provision but included other tax reductions Clinton opposed. They had passed the controversial bill shortly before their convention in the hope Clinton would veto it, giving them an opportunity to attack him and, of course, Gore. Clinton waited until after the convention ended to announce his veto. His statement dominated the political news of August 5; all three networks reported both Clinton's remarks and Bush's response.

Network correspondents also focused on Bush as he continued his whistle stop trip through the Midwest. Bill Whitaker on CBS reported that Bush, campaigning in Michigan, was using the Clinton veto as the centerpiece of his daily remarks. Whitaker also looked at the problems Bush was encountering in attempting to win the presidency from an incumbent administration during a time of prosperity. Bush had secured the support of his Republican base, but this was not enough to win, Whitaker concluded. He added that Bush was campaigning in places where elections were won, "in the middle of the political road in the middle of the country." Bush, Whitaker said, was replacing "the old Republican hard line with the soft sounds of compassionate conservatism" and was aiming his appeals at middle-class moderates who found the old Republican Party mean-spirited but were dispirited about the Clinton administration.

The political news of August 5 was not limited to the remarks of Bush and Clinton. There was also significant media speculation about the identity of Gore's running mate. Two networks, CBS and NBC, focused on three senators who apparently had emerged at the "finalists" for the position, John Kerry of Massachusetts, John Edwards of North Carolina, and the senator who would eventually receive the invitation, Joseph Lieberman of Connecticut.

The speculation did not last long as Gore announced his choice of Lieberman on August 8. Except for health-related questions, the news themes related to this announcement were similar to those that followed Bush's designation of Cheney. Network correspondents looked at the stronger features of Lieberman's personal and political background and explained why his candidacy might improve Gore's electoral prospects. John Roberts on CBS described Lieberman as having "a moderate voting record in the Senate and high moral standards" and then depicted him as a strong critic of Clinton during the Lewinsky scandal. Roberts said that Gore had chosen Lieberman "in an attempt to shake up his campaign and turn around a growing spread in the polls." Claire Shipman on NBC referred to Lieberman as a revered figure in the Senate and added, "Republicans could barely come up with criticism." Lieberman was popular with Republicans because he was a political moderate, a hawk on foreign policy, and a critic of sex and violence on television, Shipman added. Shipman attributed the Lieberman choice to Gore's need for winning support from Independent and Republican voters to counter Bush's appeal to Democrats. The choice would also provide some moral authority to the Democratic ticket, Shipman concluded. Anne Thompson, who reviewed Lieberman's performance in the Senate for NBC that day, added that he differed from Gore on several issues, among them school vouchers, privatization of Social Security, and tax cuts on capital gains, and in 1994 had opposed the Clinton health care plan. Finally, network analysis of Gore's electoral prospects was not limited to his attempts to bolster his image of moral leadership: it included his presently bleak poll standings. Each network reported on its latest poll, which showed Gore as trailing Bush by a double-digit margin, with an average deficit of about 15 percent.

Gore made his announcement of his selection of Lieberman in Nashville before a large and enthusiastic crowd; Terry Moran on ABC said that it appeared to have galvanized the campaign. After illustrating the remarks of both candidates, Moran focused his attention on the political strategy behind the choice. He said Gore was talking about values and morals in an attempt to move his campaign toward the political center and to distance himself from Clinton. John Roberts on CBS once again spoke of how Gore was trying to light a fire under his campaign. All three networks also reiterated their previous remarks about Lieberman's moderate Senate voting record and his continuing emphasis on moral values. They focused their attention on Lieberman for one more day, briefly looking at some anti-Semitic statements that had appeared on a variety of Internet web sites. Despite these statements, network correspondents generally concluded that Lieberman's Jewish religion would not be considered a liability in the campaign.

The Democratic convention was not scheduled to begin for another six days after the Lieberman announcement, but there was another political convention at this time that quickly attracted the interest of television news media. The Reform Party was holding its convention in Long Beach, California, during the interim between the two major party conventions. Ross Perot had started the party after his independent candidacy in 1992 as an organizational vehicle for advancing political aspirations and the goals he had annunciated during his unusual presidential bid. Perot was the initial presidential nominee of this party in 1996, when he attained 7.8 percent of the popular vote. This showing helped qualify the Reform Party for $12.6 million in federal funding for the 2000 election. Since Perot had announced that he would not be a candidate this time, the nomination appeared to have some political value. This assumption was eventually shown to be wildly inaccurate because the party disintegrated in front of a national audience in a manner that would have a profound effect on the outcome of the general election.

Two networks looked at the Reform convention on August 8, and their reports were exceptionally unflattering. Jim Stewart on CBS and Morton Dean on ABC directed attention to a bitter credentials fight between supporters and opponents of Pat Buchanan. Since he had left the Republican Party in October 1999, Buchanan had spent much of his time organizing his followers to take control of the various state conventions where the delegates who would be attending the national convention of the Reform Party were chosen. Buchanan won a majority of those delegates and with it, a strong claim to the nomination. In addition, he had won a national vote-by-mail party primary with 63 percent of the vote. His angry opponents were supporting John Hagelin, the founder of the Natural Law Party. Stewart said some of Buchanan's rivals were charging that he was trying to turn the party into a fund-raising organization for social conservatives and were challenging the seating of many of his delegates. Both correspondents focused on an intense shouting match of Buchanan and Hagelin supporters at a credentials committee meeting. The outcome, when the committee ruled in Buchanan's favor, led to a significant split within the party and an eventual walkout from the convention by Buchanan's enemies, who held a separate meeting and nominated Hagelin. Dean said the tidal wave of discord and disunity was expected to roll on.

The actual walkout of Hagelin supporters and the formal nomination of Buchanan occurred two days later. Television news media were there once again to report on the chaos as Lisa Myers on NBC and Jerry Bowen on CBS described the convention as a circus and a free-for-all, respectively. Myers focused on Buchanan's enemies' charging that he had stolen their party and was taking it too far to the political Right on issues such as abortion and immigration and their threatening a lawsuit in federal court to prevent Buchanan from receiving federal funds. Bowen looked at the depth of the party split, mentioning that forty states had sent competing delegations to the convention. Both Myers and Bowen remarked that Buchanan's support had declined to only 1 percent in national polls. Myers concluded her report by describing Buchanan as "politically irrelevant."

Eventually, Buchanan won the legal right to the federal funds but then attained only 0.43 percent of the popular vote. He was not a factor in the electoral outcome in any state. This was important because the leading minor party candidates, Buchanan and Nader, had been attracting about the same level of support earlier in the year. The collapse of the Reform Party as a viable political entity meant that Bush would lose far fewer votes to a party on his right flank than Gore would lose to one on his left. Nader would eventually attain 2.9 percent of the popular vote, perhaps half of it at Gore's expense.

Bush had dominated the political news during the days immediately preceding the Republican convention through the naming of Cheney as his running mate and his five-state tour en route to Philadelphia. Gore was not so fortunate; most network correspondents found other events and actors far more newsworthy during the final days before the Democratic convention. One such was the controversy related to a convention fund-raiser that had been scheduled at the Playboy mansion of the publisher Hugh Hefner. After several days of media-centered debate among party officials over the propriety of such a gathering, the party forced its organizers to cancel their plans. Even more distracting for Gore were the fund-raising activities in the Hollywood movie community by Bill and Hillary Clinton. The president was raising money for his library while the first lady was soliciting funds for her Senate campaign. Hardly improper, these efforts garnered considerable attention at a time when network correspondents were particularly focused on Democrats. The Clinton efforts reduced the amount of television time available for Gore; moreover, Gore would have to begin the convention under Clinton's shadow. The president was scheduled to speak to the delegates on opening night. Clinton's presence, both in Los Angeles in the days before the convention and at the convention itself, nearly erased Gore from all network news coverage.

Gore did generate some favorable imagery, however, when he visited the Pennsylvania home of the environmentalist Rachel Carson on August 12, but he also encountered some difficulty in sustaining it. One day later Gore traveled to Cleveland, where he emphasized health care, and then to Missouri, where he talked about a variety of issues in a move that Terry Moran on ABC said was designed to create strength out of weakness. Moran attributed the weakness to Gore's lackluster image and inability to inspire and excite voters. After several failed attempts at creating a new image, Gore was now trying to appear as a policy expert, Moran added.

Television news media followed much the same script in reporting on the Democratic convention that they had used for the Republicans. They profiled convention speakers, speculated about Gore's acceptance speech, raised questions about corporate contributions to the party and its packaging of the convention and reported the results of their latest polls. One of these polls, by ABC, related to Gore's "Clinton problem": The poll indicated that voters were very mixed in their assessments of Clinton. A strong majority, 61 percent, liked his policies, but a much smaller group, only 34 percent, approved of him as a person. Moreover, about half of those who approved of Clinton's policies, but not of him, said they planned to vote for Bush. John Cochran on ABC described this phenomenon as "Clinton fatigue." He said voters were happy with the policy agenda and direction of the country but were tired of Clinton and wanted to forget him. Casting their votes for Bush and not for Clinton's surrogate, Gore, was one way to bring about this preferred change, Cochran concluded.

Democrats tended to approve of both Clinton and his policies, and this approval occasionally proved valuable to Gore. It was particularly evident on the second day of the convention, when Clinton and Gore jointly appeared before a very partisan audience in Monroe, Michigan. Several network correspondents, including John Roberts of CBS, described this event as a "passing of the torch of party leadership." Clinton introduced Gore as the new party leader, mentioned that the vice president had been involved in every important achievement of his administration, and then left the rally. Gore, who was charged up, in Roberts's words, took the podium and delivered a strong and forceful speech in which he said he would not let Republicans wreck Clinton's accomplishments. Gore then headed for Los Angeles, where his arrival served as the leading news story for the next day and his acceptance speech the dominant one a day later.

The nationally televised acceptance speech by the presidential nominee has become the most important event at a contemporary political convention. It provides a unique opportunity for the nominee to introduce or reintroduce himself to what is often the largest television audience of the campaign for a political speech. For Gore, given his image and Clinton problems, this speech was particularly important. Network correspondents focused their attention on the problems Gore faced and his need to address them. Tom Brokaw began the NBC news telecast by referring to this evening as "the very night that Gore wants to reintroduce himself to America as his own man." Claire Shipman said Gore needed to do two things with his speech, outline his policy agenda and tell voters who he is. Lisa Myers then interviewed Gore's wife, Tipper, who planned to introduce him to the convention. Myers said Mrs. Gore needed to convince voters that "the stiff guy in the suit that they often saw was something more." Myers said Mrs. Gore tries to humanize her husband and embodies qualities he is said to lack.

Tipper Gore's introduction, Al Gore's speech, and their long kiss immediately after the introduction appears to have worked. Gore's support as measured in the polls increased significantly after the convention. The Gallup-CNN-*USA Today* Poll of August 19 showed Gore's leading Bush by one point, 47 percent to 46 percent. This was clearly within the poll's margin of error of 4 percent, so one would have to conclude that support for the two candidates was approximately even. This pattern was not temporary: eight days later another poll by this same organization had similar results, although this time Bush had the one-point lead, 46 percent to 45 percent. Despite the difficulties he had encountered with Clinton, Gore had closed the gap between him and Bush and was now ready to contest the general election on more even terms.

6

THE GENERAL ELECTION CAMPAIGN BETWEEN AUGUST AND NOVEMBER

THE PREDEBATE PERIOD

The conclusion of the Democratic convention on August 17 signaled the beginning of the most intense part of the general election campaign. Each party had nominated its ticket and was now eligible for $67.5 million in federal funding. With this, the candidates were ready to embark on the final twelve weeks of the quadrennial struggle for national power.

The variety of network polls taken during the first half of the postconvention period indicated that voters were dividing their support about equally between Gore and Bush and neither candidate seemed to have an enduring advantage over his rival. The Gallup-CNN-*USA Today* Poll instituted a series of daily tracking polls on September 4, Labor Day. The organization would interview daily and include results from three consecutive days in its polls. The twenty-five tracking polls conducted September 6–30 always indicated that the outcome might be close. During this time, Gore registered a daily average of 47 percent and Bush garnered 44 percent, but there was considerable variation in the results. Gore led Bush in most of the polls taken before September 22 but ran even with his rival in polls taken after that date. One could not conclude that Gore was necessarily ahead in very many of these polls, however, because his average lead was usually less than the 4 percent margin of error. At best, neither candidate seemed to be losing at this stage of the campaign.

The September polls showing a competitive and even race were vastly different from earlier ones, noted previously, which indicated a strong Bush lead. Gore had gained ground on Bush precisely because he had effectively used the media coverage of the Democratic convention as an opportunity to distinguish himself from Clinton. This was most pronounced in his acceptance speech, when he claimed he was his own man. He was no longer seen as a mere surrogate of a president but was instead projecting political and personal imagery in which he looked like a potential president himself. This was the first instance during the campaign when Gore had received the sustained attention of television news media and had appeared as the central political actor in an ongoing drama. He had managed to accomplish this feat despite Clinton's domination of media during the days immediately before the convention. The existence of a competitive Republican campaign between Bush and McCain and a Democratic campaign whose the outcome was obvious even before the New Hampshire primary had contributed to a significant public relations problem for Gore during the early months of the election year. These events had helped make Gore appear to be acting in a supporting role as a candidate at a time when he also appeared to be acting in a supporting role as a national executive. The battle between Bush and McCain had dominated much of the electoral news during the first three months of 2000 while Clinton, in his role as president, dominated much of the remaining political news. Gore did not seem to be a particularly significant actor in either context. With television news media now focusing daily attention on the two major candidates while reducing their coverage of Clinton, Gore looked more like the star and thereby gained personal and political respect. His stronger poll standings reflected his changed status in this altered pattern of news reporting.

Gore was the center of media political attention for several days after the Democratic convention as he undertook a four-day riverboat journey with his running mate along the Mississippi River. The trip carried the Democrats through Wisconsin, Iowa, and Missouri and provided several opportunities for speaking to large and enthusiastic crowds. Gore emphasized populist themes in his efforts to appeal to working families, Chip Reid of NBC reported. Gore also attacked a number of powerful interests, including big oil, drug companies, and health maintenance organizations (HMOs). Network correspondents could not resist the appeal of the latest polls, which illustrated the success of Gore's recent actions. Reid said Gore was riding a surge in the polls, and Terry Moran on ABC referred to the same phenomenon as a postconvention bounce. John Roberts on CBS described Gore as buoyed by new poll numbers showing him in a dead heat with Bush. Roberts also said the Gore campaign had taken on a new energy not seen before. Moran remarked that Gore was drawing large crowds in small towns and was generating the kind of excitement the campaign had not seen in months. In addition to emphasizing populist themes, Gore attacked Bush on a number of tax and economic issues, including his plans for financing Social Security. Bush, meanwhile, spoke in Tennessee about how Gore was trying to exploit class divisions and then traveled to New Mexico, where he talked about improving education.

All three networks released new polls on August 21 that continued to show strong gains for Gore and then used them to define their horse race–related reporting. Charles Gibson of ABC attributed Gore's gains to three factors, including the belief of many voters that Gore had separated himself from Clinton. A response to a question of whether Gore was too close to Clinton had produced a yes answer in only 39 percent compared to 58 percent who had responded no. Gibson said this was the first time the ABC poll had shown the yes response as in the minority. Gore's new appeals to working families also helped as a majority of respondents said he understood their problems. Gore led Bush by twelve points in responses to this question. Finally, more people now trusted Gore on the economy, Gibson concluded.

Television news media did not ignore Bush during this time, although they seemed less interested in his campaign. When looking at him, they illustrated his responses to Gore and focused attention on his campaign strategy. On August 21 Dean Reynolds on ABC reported that Bush was planning a twenty-one-state advertising campaign targeting women and independent voters on the issue of education. Reynolds said eighteen of these states—he did not identify which—had voted for Clinton in the previous election. A leading component of the Bush electoral strategy, Reynolds stated, was to win the twenty states Robert Dole had captured in 1996 and then supplement that Republican base with several of the eighteen states subject to this latest advertising effort.

There were several consistent patterns in the reporting preferences of television news media during this phase of the campaign.

They would concentrate virtually all of their coverage on the actions of the two presidential candidates of the major parties and downplay or even ignore all others. The others category were the vice presidential nominees of the major parties and the presidential nominees of the two leading minor parties, Nader (Green) and Buchanan (Reform). The networks tended to limit their coverage of the running mates to those instances when they appeared in public settings with the presidential candidates. They looked at the minor party nominees only in the context of how those nominees might harm the electoral hopes of someone else. With the virtual collapse of the Buchanan effort, television news media limited their occasional glances at the minor parties to the one theme of how much Nader might hurt Gore. As they had before the conventions, television news media emphasized two themes in reporting about the two main presidential candidates, the status of the horse race and the ongoing personal combat between Bush and Gore.

A one-day news theme occurred on August 23, when Gore received some good news with an announcement that Attorney General Janet Reno would not seek a special prosecutor for the fund-raising controversies of the 1996 election. With this, television news media directed their attention for the next three days to the issue of taxes while reiterating the usual themes. The event that encouraged this interest was an announcement by the Clinton administration of plans for the president to veto a Republican bill providing for a cut in the estate tax that had recently passed Congress. Claire Shipman on NBC reported about Gore's comments of August 24, when the vice president said he would not support large tax cuts that would wreck the economy. Gore's remarks were clearly aimed at Bush, who had been advocating just such a tax cut. David Gregory on NBC focused on Bush's proposed tax cut of $1.3 trillion and featured the contrasting comments of both major candidates. He then looked at the status of the horse race by examining some of the problems that seemed to explain why Bush had lost his lead. Gregory said Bush was "faltering in his bid to regain the spotlight in a campaign where the polls now showed him trailing." He used a number of gaffes Bush had made in recent days, including a remark in Des Moines about how terrorists and rogue nations should not be able to hold this nation "hostile" to illustrate his point.

The media interest shifted to foreign policy on August 25 after Bush delivered a speech in Miami directed at Latin American relations. Bill Whitaker on CBS said Bush was facing nagging doubts about his grasp of foreign affairs and had set out to dispel them by focusing on Latin America, the region he says affects the United States most and claims to know best. Whitaker included scenes of Bush's speaking and summarized his remarks by describing them as offering Latin American nations free trade, a helping hand for democracy, a clenched fist to Castro, and thumbs down on Clinton's policies. In his analysis, Whitaker said Bush's plans were not much different from Gore's and were actually aimed at winning support among the large Latino populations of Florida, Texas, and California. He concluded by saying the speech might improve Bush's foreign policy credentials but would not help him gain the support of many Latino voters, most of whom were already planning to vote for Gore.

Gore dominated the news on August 28, when he spoke to a group of senior Americans in a Tallahassee, Florida, pharmacy about the high prices of prescription drugs and attacked the drug companies for convincing Congress to extend the protected life of patents. Gore attributed high drug prices to these longer patents and said he would veto any bills extending them. He also denounced Bush for failing to advance a plan for prescription drug benefits for senior citizens. Terry Moran on ABC said Gore had made this attack in Florida, a state where he believed he had a chance of winning. Bush, meanwhile, spoke about education that day but received far less coverage than Gore. After looking at Gore's actions, Phil Jones on CBS focused on Bush's comments and added that the Texas governor was trailing in the polls.

The candidates were not always successful in creating the one event that would enable them to dominated network news for a day, as Bush had with his speech about Latin America and Gore had with the pharmacy visit. Often, the individual networks would find different matters of interest on the same day. Nonetheless, they would report them with the same horse race and personal combat perspectives. During the next two days ABC looked at candidates fighting over education, CBS focused on battles over taxes and health care, and NBC directed attention to health care and controversies about the scheduling of debates. All three networks expressed a strong interest in a new Bush attack ad on August 31, which attacked Gore on campaign finance reform, with scenes from the Buddhist temple gathering, and his constant efforts to create a new public image. All three networks had remarks from representatives of each campaign, who either denounced or defended the ad. John Cochran on ABC emphasized the horse race motivation of the ad when he said it was aimed at winning support for Bush from independent swing voters.

The shift in media attention from one event to another continued in September. The networks were particularly fascinated on September 1 with a recent poll by *Newsweek* that showed Gore as holding a ten-point lead, unlike other polls, which indicated a much closer race. Bush won the battle for the leading news event on September 4, although it was probably one he later regretted. He was heard whispering to Dick Cheney that a reporter who had just asked a question was "Adam Clymer, a major league asshole from the *New York Times*." Bush's remark, which all three networks reported, was the most common theme but not the only one that day. Each network also looked at the Labor Day actions of both candidates. Claire Shipman on NBC focused her attention on the status of the campaign by reporting how various states were likely to vote. She concluded that the race was too close to call and that the outcome in eleven states was uncertain. Television news media would eventually describe these eleven as swing states and proclaim to their viewing audiences that they would decide the election. Bush and Gore would devote much of their time, particularly in October, to winning them. The states were New Jersey, Pennsylvania, Ohio, Michigan, Wisconsin, Illinois, Missouri, Arkansas, Louisiana, Georgia, and Florida. On election day Gore would clearly win in five of them, New Jersey, Pennsylvania, Michigan, Wisconsin, and Illinois, for eighty-nine electoral votes; Bush would win Ohio, Missouri, Arkansas, Louisiana, and Georgia for sixty electoral votes. Florida, of course, would be disputed but would eventually provide Bush with twenty-five electoral votes. The nearly even division of the swing states mirrored national results that were also very even.

Bush finally found his opportunity to dominate the news on a domestic policy issue when he announced his plans on September 5 for prescription drug coverage for seniors. Bill Whitaker on CBS included scenes of Bush's speaking about his plan and attacking the Clinton administration. Whitaker also reviewed the differences between the Bush and Gore plans by pointing out that Bush's plan would rely more on the private sector than Gore's, would offer senior citizens a greater range of choices, but would lead to higher prices. John Roberts on CBS followed Whitaker by reporting on the more negative features of the campaign, including remarks by Gore attacking Bush's plan.

It was Gore's turn the next day, when he announced his economic plan in a two-hundred-page booklet. The networks followed the same script: each looked at Gore's remarks about the contents of his own plan and the shortcomings of Bush's, and then at Bush's attacks against Gore.

Polls rapidly returned to the forefront of network interest, however, with the release of several new surveys on September 7. That most had been conducted since Labor Day, was an important factor in gauging their significance. The convention bounce, when a candidate registers sharp gains in the polls during the time of his party's national convention, has been a common phenomenon in modern election campaigns. By now, enough time had passed since the conclusion of the Democratic convention that no real bounce could still exist. The results of these latest polls should have been a more accurate reflection of national opinion than those of earlier ones; consequently, television news media focused extensive attention on them. Two facts stood out about these polls: they did not always agree, and the networks interpreted them in a negative light for Bush. One poll, taken by Zogby International and reported by NBC, showed Gore's leading Bush by 46 percent to 40 percent, a difference greater than the margin of error. Another poll, by ABC, placed the two candidates in an even race, each at 47 percent. David Gregory on NBC explained Bush's poor showing by controversies related to the timing of debates and his attack ads; Lisa Myers on NBC analyzed how Gore had gained significant ground among women voters. Bill Whitaker on CBS attributed Bush's declines to his prescription drug issue, his off-color remarks about a reporter, and the perception among many voters that his campaign was arrogant. Bush's failure to convince people of the merits of his proposed tax cut, along with negative advertising and the inability of Cheney to catch fire, were the reasons Dean Reynolds on CBS saw for Bush's recent declines. Despite the negative nature of their reports, network correspondents quickly saw Bush begin his "recovery." Within days, Bush was appearing less formal and was campaigning in a style that CBS and NBC correspondents described as "one-on-one with voters."

Television news media found two issues in mid-September on which one of the candidates appeared to be having some particular difficulties. They responded by directing attention to that candidate. On September 11, the Federal Trade Commission (FTC) issued a report critical of the movie industry for marketing violent movies and video games to young children. Gore spoke in support of the FTC ruling, but television news media focused on his hypocrisy on the issue. Terry Moran on ABC and Claire Shipman on NBC described it as an issue that would be particularly appealing to women voters and attributed Gore's remarks to that political end. Both also looked at the strong financial connection between the Democratic Party and the movie industry. Shipman said Gore was attacking Hollywood during the day and attending fund-raisers there at night.

Bush faced media scrutiny over a controversy about his campaign's use of a subliminal television message. The message was about health care and included remarks about how the Bush health care plan would rely more on private sector efforts than those of government. The ad was critical of governmental bureaucrats and included a few frames of film in which the camera focused on the last four letters of the word *bureaucrats*, so that the word *rats* appeared, perhaps as an attack on the character of government officials. There was extensive criticism of Bush by a number of people that day, including representatives of the Gore campaign. Bush officials denied any deliberate effort to create the subliminal message. All three networks reported the controversy and concluded that it had prevented Bush from talking about what he had wanted to on that day, Medicare.

The news theme quickly returned to poll standings in response to the appearance of a new round of network- and other media-generated surveys. In general, these polls had Gore ahead by a margin that was beyond the margin of error. In a *Newsweek* poll Gore registered a fourteen-point lead, 52 percent to 38 percent. In addition, the daily results of the Gallup-CNN-*USA Today* Poll consistently showed Gore ahead during this time. His daily showings September 10–20 ranged between 48 percent and 51 percent with a daily average of 49 percent. In contrast, Bush's support ranged between 41 percent and 44 percent with a daily average of 42 percent. Gore had moved from a deficit in the polls before the Democratic convention to a statistical tie immediately after it and eventually into an actual lead one month later. To some observers the race appeared over and Gore now looking like a certain winner. The themes of network news reflected this growing perception.

Bill Whitaker of CBS began his report of September 17 by remarking, "It has been a tough couple of weeks for Bush." Whitaker then directed attention to several of Bush's recent problems, including more verbal gaffes such as the awkward language Bush used in attempting to describe his tax cut plan and the vulgar remarks about a *New York Times* reporter. Bush had suffered a number of blows, Whitaker concluded, and added that many were self-inflicted. He called attention to the controversy over the subliminal messages, to the debate over whether there should even be debates when Bush seemed to be avoiding them, and to the constant questions about Cheney's congressional voting record and oil industry ties.

One day later Dean Reynolds and Terry Moran of ABC reported on the different receptions the two candidates were receiving from women voters. Reynolds told viewers Bush had led Gore among women shortly after the Republican convention by a margin of 49 percent to 40 percent but now trailed, 56 percent to 38 percent. He looked at how Gore was effectively using the tax issue and how Bush was trying to reemphasize his tax message. Moran reviewed Gore's successes among women by focusing on the vice president's calls for patients' rights for women and mandatory minimum hospital stays and on his efforts to appear more frequently in the role of family man. The media interest in women was not accidental because Bush was scheduled to appear on Oprah Winfrey's show, which regularly attracts one of the largest audiences of women viewers of any television program in the nation, one day later. Dan Rather began the CBS political reporting of September 18 by depicting Bush's appearance on the show as an effort to close the gender gap. He added that if women voters would not go to the candidate, then the candidate must go to them. All networks included scenes of the banter between Bush and Winfrey and explanations of Bush's failure to attract much support from women.

After several days of interest in the difficulties of the Bush campaign, television news media changed their focus to Gore's problems. Betsy Stark on ABC and John Roberts on CBS focused their reports of September 20 on several of Gore's misstatements. Stark talked about how Gore had been employing a populist appeal by attacking big business but then added how he had also supported measures of interest to business such as the North American Free Trade Agreement (NAFTA). Stark said Gore would need the support of business in order to govern but believed that antibusiness appeals to working families could help him win the election. Roberts focused on Gore's pursuing a "front-runner strategy": "Keep on script and run out the clock." Gore was trying to maintain strict control of his message and focus on a daily theme. Roberts said the goal of this strategy was to prevent attention from being directed to any matters other than the messages that Gore wanted to send. He then illustrated why the strategy had been failing; Gore had made several factual misstatements about such matters as drug costs and union labels that had eventually generated attacks from the Bush campaign and greater media scrutiny.

Despite these troubles, Gore's alleged message control strategy appeared to work well for the next few days. Gore garnered the major political headlines on September 21 by calling on Clinton to order a temporary tapping of the nation's strategic oil reserves to reduce rapidly increasing prices of petroleum-based fuels. All three networks looked at Gore's remarks and described what they understood to be his motives. Claire Shipman on NBC, through comments by the former White House chief of staff David Gergen, suggested that Gore was trying to protect himself from charges that the Clinton administration was responsible for the higher oil prices. Bush said as much when he attacked Gore on the issue. Shipman then focused her attention on several of the factual misstatements Gore had made in recent days. The oil reserve story dominated political news for several days, and Clinton eventually acted on Gore's call. Each network included remarks by the two candidates in their coverage of Clinton's actions and the possible effects of those actions.

The oil reserve story ended shortly afterward, about one week before the candidates stopped their daily speeches and concentrated their efforts on the first debate. The main themes of media interest during the last week of September were the usual, the horse race and personal combat. With respect to the race, Campbell Brown of NBC looked at the campaign in Florida on September 23 and reported that Bush had been leading in the state during July but the race there was now a "dead heat." Gore's popularity had surged in Florida since the Democratic convention, Brown continued. She attributed this to Gore's aggressive efforts among young working families on the issues of education and health care and to Lieberman's popularity among Jewish voters. Bush was trying to counter this change by appealing to Cuban voters, Brown added. She said that Bush's increased efforts in Florida might hurt his chances in other battleground states. This was not an isolated news report, for many in television news were now taking a greater interest in the Florida campaign.

The horse race garnered more interest as new polls indicated that Gore's lead of mid-September was gone. On September 24 Jacqueline Adams of CBS, while directing much of her attention to the campaign in Florida, also looked at recent national polls that showed the race as tightening. This change was reflected in the daily results from the Gallup-CNN-*USA Today* Poll. Bush's daily average for the final ten days of September was 45.8 percent compared to Gore's 45.1. Adams attributed this change to Bush's appearance on the Oprah Winfrey program. She pointed out that a CNN poll taken before Bush's appearance had shown Gore ahead of Bush among women voters by 58 percent to 34 percent, but that lead had now declined to only 48 percent to 44 percent. In her analysis of the status of the Florida campaign, Adams said Bush had spent $2.2 million and six days in the state since the Republican convention. As did reporters at the other networks, Adams concluded that such an investment of money and time could hurt Bush in other battleground states. Of course, Bush needed to campaign extensively in Florida because of Gore's efforts. Terry Moran on ABC looked at the state in his report of September 25 and reported that Gore had spent nine days there since he had clinched the Democratic nomination in March.

The final horse race–related story that attracted media attention before the first debate was the status of the campaign in Michigan. Peter Jennings on ABC introduced this story on September 26 by saying that Michigan was "an enormously important battleground state and the country's economic boom was more than evident here." This makes a challenge by Bush difficult, he added. Jim Wooten on ABC followed Jennings by directing his attention to the likely outcome in the modest-sized suburban town of Plymouth. He described the town of ten thousand as "a good place to live, given its low crime rate and good schools." Wooten said Plymouth tends to vote Republican but might support Gore this year because of the good economy. He continued that many people who were once planning to vote for Bush had changed their minds because they liked Gore's stands on education and health care. Gore was ahead in statewide polls, Wooten concluded.

Bob Schieffer of CBS also looked at Michigan but focused his attention on the statewide vote and how it might fit into a larger national pattern. He depicted Michigan as one of six battleground states where the election would probably be decided. Pennsylvania, Illinois, Ohio, Missouri, and, of course, Florida were the others. Bush had been leading in Michigan during the summer but had now lost that lead to Gore, Schieffer added. Schieffer pointed out that Gore was particularly strong in union households, which were about one third of all households in the state.

The personal combat theme resurfaced on September 25, when television news media directed their attention to what appeared to be unrelated campaign activities. Gore and Bush were emphasizing different issues in their appearances, but network correspondents depicted the candidates' remarks as combat and attempted to illustrate how those remarks were actually important components of a much larger pattern of strategic efforts. Gore had spent the day campaign in Florida emphasizing Medicare while Bush was in the Pacific Northwest states of Oregon and Washington talking about education. Terry Moran on ABC and John Roberts on CBS were with Gore; Bill Whitaker on CBS and Dean Reynolds on ABC looked at Bush. In contrast, NBC focused its political attention that day on Lieberman's campaign in Connecticut for reelection to the Senate.

Moran and Roberts both mentioned that Gore was aiming his remarks about Medicare at Florida's 2.5 million seniors, who could cast as much as one third of that state's votes, and then showed scenes of contrasting remarks by the two candidates. Gore was shown attacking Bush over the Texas governor's recent verbal gaffe, that Medicare was a government-run HMO. Gore said he would never support any move to change Medicare in ways that would make it an HMO. Gore also attempted to link Bush's proposals with ideas advanced several years earlier by the former House speaker Newt Gingrich. Moran included previous comments about Medicare by Bush in his report. In addition, Roberts looked at some other aspects of the Florida campaign, particularly Gore's efforts to win the support of younger voters. The networks had similar themes in their reports about Bush's efforts. Bush had emphasized greater funding, accountability, vouchers, and standardized testing in his educational speeches that day. Whitaker and Reynolds both included scenes of Bush's talking about an education recession, and each outlined the major differences between the two candidates on educational funding and related issues.

The contrasts between the two candidates continued for several more days, but the candidates were not always able to select the issues used in the contrasts. The high cost of prescription drugs was the issue of September 27, but it became important primarily because an elderly woman had made a spontaneous remark during a question and answer period. Winifred Skinner, while raising a question to Gore in Des Moines, said she had been collecting cans and bottles along Iowa highways for years in order to afford the prescription drugs she needs. After the various network correspondents had reported Skinner's remarks, they contrasted recent statements by Bush and Gore about drug prices.

Network correspondents concluded their reporting before the first debate by illustrating the personal combat of the candidates on two additional issues. The issue on September 28 was the economy, with the coverage directed to the various proposals on taxing and spending. One day later the issue was energy supplies, with some attention focused on Bush's preference for opening the Arctic National Wildlife Refuge for oil drilling and on Gore's opposition to this proposal. With this, the campaign and television news media were ready for the first presidential debate.

THE DEBATES AND THE FINAL WEEKS

The first of the four nationally televised debates was scheduled for October 3, a Tuesday; the second, between the vice presidential candidates, would follow two days later. In response, the candidates devoted much of their time and television news media their attention to preparations during the initial week of October to the debates themselves, and to the outcomes and political effects. All three networks devoted much of their news coverage during the first three days of October to debate preparations. The candidates spent that time practicing their remarks and conducting debate simulations with staff members. Both generated several "made for media" events that illustrated these preparations. Correspondents described the events and explored the strategies of the candidates.

Gore prepared in Longboat Key, Florida, with a group of voters, "citizen advisers" as he called them, whom he had recruited to advise him on popular responses. The networks included scenes of Gore's walking along a beach with this group of approximately twelve persons. Terry Moran on ABC said they had told Gore to "loosen up" and added that Gore seemed to be relaxed as the debates approached. Claire Shipman on NBC said Gore would try to make his debate remarks a repeat of his successful convention speech, upbeat and specific. John Roberts on CBS suggested Gore would focus on issues such as debt reduction, economic growth, and targeted tax cuts while trying to cast doubt on Bush's proposals. Bush prepared in Austin, Texas, and had an occasional scene of practice sessions with staff members. Bill Whitaker on CBS said Bush wanted to remove all doubts about his ability and would emphasize the conservative aspects of his philosophy, particularly those that related to private sector efforts, and would talk about military spending and education. Bush had been preparing for this debate since May, Dean Reynolds of ABC reported; he added that the Texas governor was now as ready as he would ever be. David Gregory on NBC said Bush wanted to appear natural and to show voters that he was "up to the job" of being president.

Although debates are certainly significant events in any presidential election campaign, the political consequences of the media analysis that follows may be comparable to those of the debates themselves. This appears to be true with respect to the aftermath of the first debate. Television news media devoted much of their political reporting of October 4 to debate analysis and again relied on their usual themes of personal combat and the horse race. They did not declare a definitive winner; Tom Brokaw on NBC indicated this when he remarked that neither candidate seemed to have moved many undecided voters. All three networks concentrated their political reporting on reviewing the debate performances and daily actions of the candidates. In each instance, an individual correspondent analyzed a particular candidate's actions. David Gregory and Claire Shipman of NBC directed their attention to the candidates' postdebate remarks. Bush spent the day campaigning in Pennsylvania and Ohio in search of what Gregory described as "undecided independent voters." Since most of these voters were women, Gregory added, Bush would focus on such issues as education, health care, and values. Gore, in contrast, directed his appeals to seniors and talked about prescription drug benefits under Medicare while campaigning in Ohio. Shipman looked at Gore's growing support among seniors, indicated by several NBC polls. Terry Moran and Dean Reynolds of ABC focused their attention on the personal combat theme. Moran said Gore believed he had out-pointed Bush on taxes and education and was emphasizing his differences with Bush on those issues. Reynolds illustrated Bush's attempts to depict Gore as a big-spending liberal, a move he described as "a typical Republican approach." Bob Schieffer, John Roberts, and Bill Whitaker of CBS spent much of their time reviewing the debate performances of the two candidates; Schieffer summarized debate highlights and included remarks by Bush and Gore about their opinions of their own personal performances. Roberts and Whitaker looked at the plans of the Gore and Bush campaigns, respectively, for future debates. Although they differed in the topics they reviewed, all three networks viewed the debates and the candidates' remarks that followed as components of election-related strategies, evaluating all candidate remarks as efforts designed to win the support of specifically targeted voter blocs.

There was one news report that day that would prove to have some staying power and even highlight what would become a campaign issue. Gore had made several factual errors in his debate remarks about the cost of his proposals and where he had been on specific days. Lisa Myers of NBC, in a segment entitled "The Truth Squad," looked at inaccuracies in Gore's statements about the costs of tax reduction; crowding in the schools of Sarasota, Florida; and a trip Gore had said he had taken to Texas in order to inspect fire damage. She repeated a debate remark Bush had made about Gore's "fuzzy math." This issue of Gore's truthfulness would resurface several more times over the next few weeks. Not reported on that day, one additional feature of the debate, Gore's behavior, would also affect the course of the campaign. Gore had been particularly aggressive, perhaps even overly scripted, while attacking Bush's position on a number of issues and in his reluctance to relinquish his own speaking time. He had also appeared condescending and perhaps even arrogant while employing some very audible signs, facial expressions, and eye movements after several of Bush's remarks. In time, these factual misstatements and nonverbal actions would contribute to a growing public perception that Gore had lost the initial debate.

The presidential candidates had to assume supporting roles for the next three days as the debate of the vice presidential candidates dominated political coverage on October 5, 6, and 7. Network correspondents reviewed the personal backgrounds of Dick Cheney and Joseph Lieberman on October 5 and summarized their debate remarks and campaign activities during the next two days. The coverage tended to emphasize that each candidate had reiterated the major issues the presidential candidates were using for targeting voter blocs and to analyze the effectiveness of their campaign efforts. Anne Thompson on NBC concluded that Lieberman had helped humanize Gore, whereas Cheney often appeared to come across as too formal and sounding as if he were providing a news briefing at the Defense Department.

There were three campaign days between the end of the media interest in the vice presidential candidates and the second presidential debate on October 11. This was a time for reporting about the most recent horse race and personal combat developments. Guns and polls dominated ABC coverage during these days. Peter Jennings looked at the battle between the NRA and Gore in the feature "A Closer Look: The Gun Fight" on October 9. Jennings looked at how the NRA was actively attempting to persuade gun owners to oppose Gore by emphasizing that the federal government would attempt to confiscate guns if Gore were to win the election. One day later, ABC reported that their latest poll showed Bush ahead by less than the poll's margin of error, 48 percent to 45 percent. Jennings said Bush had improved his position since the end of the first debate. The intensity of the battle in Florida was of particular interest to both CBS and NBC during these days. Bill Whitaker on CBS reported on October 7 that the race was close in Florida and then directed attention to the way the candidates were engaging one another on Social Security, Medicare, and education vouchers. One day later John Roberts of CBS, also in Florida, directed attention to the difficulties each candidate was encountering over his remarks on specific issues. He looked again at the controversial misstatements by Gore in the first debate and at some of Bush's verbal gaffes about Medicare and taxes. Claire Shipman of NBC also reported about the misstatements and gaffes but directed much of her attention on October 10 to the tight status of the Florida campaign. She looked at recent polls emphasizing the even division of support for both candidates and described the extensive use of resources such as time and money that each campaign was now devoting to Florida. Tom Brokaw added to the horse race theme as he reported that Bush was now leading Gore by one point, 43 percent to 42 percent, in the most recent NBC poll. Finally, David Gregory of NBC focused on personal combat, looking at the growing use of negative advertising by both campaigns.

The second debate differed from the first in two ways. First, the candidates were seated at a table rather than standing at podiums as in the more traditional debate format. Second, they received very limited news coverage for their performances because most election-related news was overshadowed by a significant breaking event from the Middle East, a terrorist bombing of the U.S.S. *Cole* in Yemen. Nonetheless, there was some news coverage of the debate and it was not favorable to Gore. The bombing of the *Cole* occurred on October 12, the day after the debate, thus limiting most debate coverage to the network previews of October 11. Television news media by now had concluded that Gore had lost the first debate and their commentary reflected this view. Peter Jennings on ABC said that Bush had "improved his position and was ahead in nearly every national poll since the first debate." He then introduced Terry Moran, who talked about Gore's need to relax and to appear less aggressive in this debate than he had in the first one. Moran included scenes from a satire about the debate on the NBC comedy *Saturday Night Live*, which had mocked Gore for his aggressive performance. John Roberts on CBS emphasized that Gore needed to "lighten up and make fewer exaggerations"; Bob Schieffer on CBS added that in a close election "voters often support the candidate with whom they feel more comfortable." Currently, that candidate seemed to be Bush.

Gore appears to have added yet another debate loss to his record. He was hardly as aggressive as before; in fact, he was so subdued he sometimes appeared zombielike and was perhaps far too agreeable with Bush on a number of key issues. The most widely discussed issue this time was foreign affairs, which accounted for forty-one minutes of the ninety-minute encounter. Unfortunately for Gore, the two candidates had such similar views he failed to convince voters he possessed any special expertise or experience that would distinguish him from his rival. The two had agreed on sixteen occasions in their responses to real or potential foreign problems. The fact that the bombing of the *Cole* occurred one day later eventually turned the debate into a lost opportunity for Gore. A strong performance, particularly with respect to the most widely discussed issue, foreign affairs, might well have convinced a number of undecided or uncertain voters that Gore had the skills needed to lead a national response. As the two candidates appeared even, Gore lost all chance of appearing as a strong leader during a crisis. Since he was not the incumbent, he could not preempt the political news during a crisis as a president could. Instead, Gore had needed to use his position of surrogate to convince voters that his executive branch experience had provided him with unique opportunities not available to his rival that qualified him to lead the nation during an emergency. Gore's failure was even more unsettling in that it was against a man whose running mate had been defense secretary during the Persian Gulf War and whose probable secretary of state, Colin Powell, had been the wartime chairman of the joint chiefs of staff. On the day of the *Cole* bombing, Tom Brokaw reported that a postdebate poll by NBC indicated that 46 percent of viewers thought Bush had won compared to only 41 percent who saw Gore as the victor.

Network news began looking at the campaign once again on October 15 as the final debate approached. This one, to be held on October 17, with the more traditional format of the candidates' speaking from podiums, would allow Gore one final opportunity to use his surrogate position effectively to prove his worth as a presidential successor. Several network news reports that preceded this debate focused on each candidate's practicing objectives and particular needs. The general theme was that Gore needed to avoid appearing overprepared or overly aggressive and appear more truthful, whereas Bush was reported to be confident and to believe that the crisis in Yemen could highlight his calls for military preparedness.

There was one unusual news theme on debate day as ABC looked at recent developments in the Nader campaign. There had been little coverage of Nader in recent weeks as many observers expected his support to dwindle to virtually nothing, perhaps in the range of the support that Buchanan was now registering. Nader refused to quit, and his support in the polls remained constant, about 3 percent to 4 percent in most national surveys. Linda Douglass on ABC had scenes of Nader's speaking to a rally at Madison Square Garden to a crowd of about fifteen thousand with Tim Robbins and Susan Sarandon present as the leading performers. Douglass summarized Nader's major themes: that "Americans had become powerless in a nation dominated by corporate power and that both major party candidates were corrupt." Nader was shown denouncing his two rivals. Although this report was unusual in that it focused more attention on Nader's issues and political goals, including winning major party status for the Green Party, than had earlier reports, it also echoed the usual theme of all televised reports about Nader. Nader was seen as a threat to Gore who might deny him victory in a number of competitive states. Introducing Douglass, Peter Jennings said Nader could make the difference in the outcome in several states. Douglass referred to the possibility but also had scenes of Nader's arguing that the Democrats had no one to blame but themselves for their troubles.

The final debate was inconsequential in that it had the smallest audience of any debate and that the audience was nearly evenly divided in its assessments. Viewers saw Gore as the winner over Bush by a margin of 45 percent to 40 percent (CBS). It was too late for Gore to recover from his poor performances in the earlier debates, however. By now, most voters had already made their electoral choices, thus forcing the candidates and parties to concentrate their final efforts on convincing their followers to show up at the polls and vote. Political activists refer to this as "getting out the vote."

The two candidates differed in the varieties of people on whom they concentrated their get out the vote efforts. First, each focused his attention on a small number of states that polls indicated were either too close for one candidate to be adjudged ahead or one candidate held a slight and perhaps insecure lead. The candidates sought to win those uncertain states by targeting rhetorical appeals to particular blocs of voters who appeared to hold the balance of power. Sometimes it was necessary for both candidates to motivate certain people actually to cast ballots; in other instances they needed to frighten probable voters that certain real or imagined disasters would befall the nation if they cast their ballots for another candidate. Television news media viewed these efforts, including travel and statements by the candidates, as the final components of the horse race and personal combat themes. This last portion of the campaign, slightly less than three weeks in duration, began with the conclusion of the news coverage of the final debate and extended to the eve of the election, from October 19 to November 6.

Gore used the economy as his theme on October 19, when he spoke at Columbia University. Accompanied by the former Treasury secretary Robert Rubin, Gore said that "prosperity was on the ballot." Terry Moran of ABC said Gore was trying to make the election a choice on economic policies, taxes, size of government, and Social Security. This speech was also a continuation of the class-related appeals Gore had been making since the Democratic convention. There were televised scenes of Gore's attacking Bush on these issues and of Bush's responding. Most of the televised news coverage of the day involved

Gore's statements; Bush was shown only in contrast to Gore. The only televised remarks about Bush were of his responses to Gore.

Two other matters that resulted from unusual events attracted media interest the next day, October 20. One was already a major factor and would contribute to the election outcome: Clinton's absence from the campaign. It is now expected that retiring presidents will attempt to improve the electoral prospects of their vice presidents in surrogate incumbent elections. Ronald Reagan certainly did so in 1988 as he devoted much of his time during the final two weeks of the campaign to making public appearances on behalf of George Bush. The three major networks had nine references during the first week of November to Reagan's actions as a campaigner. The election that year was held on November 8. On November 1 Reagan accused Michael Dukakis of not being a liberal in the tradition of Harry S Truman and Franklin D. Roosevelt on NBC. Reagan campaigned in Ohio on November 2 (reported by ABC), in New Jersey one day later (reported by NBC), and then in Michigan and Texas over the days that followed (reported by NBC). His travels encouraged two networks to broadcast news reports that focused exclusively on these campaign appearances, CBS on November 5 and ABC on November 7. The other network, NBC, included coverage of Reagan's activities in four news reports during the final week of the campaign. All three networks had scenes of Reagan's speaking in San Diego on the final day before the election. There may well have been a political payoff for these travels: every state where Reagan campaigned in the days before the election voted for Bush.

Such extensive efforts by the incumbent president were not present in 2000, however, as Clinton had been notably absent. Clinton had made an occasional speech on Gore's behalf, such as his address on the first evening of the Democratic convention and in Michigan the next day, but he usually did little for Gore and sometimes even detracted from the vice president's efforts. His preconvention fundraising on behalf of Hillary Clinton's Senate campaign and the construction of his presidential library had encouraged some unneeded publicity about the presence of soft money in politics. Moreover, it had helped push Gore out of the news for several days at a time when the national media were focusing their attention on the Democrats. Gore wanted to prevent Clinton from campaigning on his behalf because of the threat Clinton's personal behavior posed to his efforts to attract support from undecided Independent voters. On most days, television news media focused political coverage on the remarks, strategies, and poll standings of the two major candidates while ignoring Clinton except on matters that appeared unrelated to the campaign.

The event that attracted media interest about Clinton's role was a joint appearance by Clinton and Gore at the funeral of the Missouri governor Mel Carnahan. Carnahan had been the Democratic candidate for the Senate but had died in an airplane crash. The presence of Clinton and Gore at the funeral encouraged the networks to discuss Clinton's absence from the campaign and describe the controversy that existed among Democratic Party strategists over his participation. John Roberts of CBS said that Clinton had been reduced to a supporting role, such as working on fund-raising, but could have been far more valuable. Roberts remarked that some Democrats believed it was a waste of talent to leave Clinton out because he could attack Bush and mobilize the Democratic vote. Roberts said Gore believed including Clinton would hurt his effort to appear to be his own man, an idea Gore had emphasized since accepting the nomination.

The other matter related to Bush's appeals to women. Bush's mother, Barbara, and wife, Laura, visited some suburban cities in various states of the Midwest and emphasized the slogan "W stands for Women." Ron Claiborne of ABC depicted this an as attempt to attract local television coverage.

New polls were now available, and network correspondents used them as major components of their political reporting on October 22, a Sunday. There was a general pattern in all polls: Bush held a slight lead that was within the margin of error of 4 percent. The Gallup-CNN-*USA Today* Poll had Bush ahead by 46 percent to 44 percent, Nader at 4 percent, and Buchanan at 1 percent. The three major networks had similar results: NBC had Bush ahead by 4 percent, CBS at 3 percent, and ABC at 2 percent. Besides their similarity, these results had been consistent through much of October. The Gallup-CNN-*USA Today* Poll had shown Gore with an 8 percent lead immediately prior to the first debate, but it had also shown that lead disappear in the first poll after the debate. Bush had led Gore by 3 percent on October 9 (47 percent to 44 percent) and now led by 2 percent. After reporting the results of its own polls, each network then looked at how the two candidates were working on their get out the vote efforts. Gore was in Philadelphia trying to encourage blacks and union members to vote and was once again employing the prosperity theme. Chip Reid on NBC reported that Gore was leading in states with a total of 208 electoral votes and was now spending $4 million weekly telling voters about Bush's economic record as governor of Texas. Campbell Brown on NBC focused on Bush, describing the twenty-eight Republican governors campaigning in a number of undecided states on his behalf. Bush described these governors as examples of people who could lead and solve problems. Brown reported that Bush was leading in states with a total of 209 electoral votes.

One unusual event can dominate network news for a day, and one such event occurred on October 23. Gore indicated his concern about the possibility that Nader might hurt his chances in several states by raising the threat that a vote for Nader could help Bush and result in the appointment of more conservatives to the Supreme Court. Gore made his remarks to reporters while traveling via airplane to the Pacific Northwest. Gore was careful not to attack Nader directly— he left that task to others—but his concern was a signal to network reporters to direct their attention to the Nader candidacy. Terry Moran on ABC depicted Nader as an electoral shadow stalking Gore. Moran said Nader had enough support in six states, Washington, Oregon, Minnesota, Wisconsin, Michigan, and Maine, to cost Gore the election. Lisa Myers on NBC said that Nader was attracting about 5 percent of the national vote and running even stronger in several states Gore needed to win. She said Nader was winning support at Gore's expense because the vice president had failed to connect with those voters. Myers pointed out that perhaps as many as half of Nader's supporters might eventually vote for Gore, however. Phil Jones on CBS included scenes of Nader's attacking both major candidates in his report that day and said Nader's target was the Democratic Party base.

Media interest in Nader was limited to the one theme of how his candidacy might harm Gore's chances. That theme was actually part of the larger and increasingly dominant pattern of horse race–related coverage that was rapidly becoming the only matter of interest to television news media. All three networks were now employing electoral maps illustrating, in different colors, how each state was likely to vote. The campaign was now centering on the small number of undecided states. Network correspondents were beginning nearly all of their daily news reports by referring to the most recent polls and to the projected number of electoral votes each candidate was likely to win. On October 23 Tom Brokaw depicted the race as a "sprint to the finish." One day later Dan Rather on CBS said each candidate was ahead in states with 205 electoral votes and Peter Jennings on ABC proclaimed that more states were becoming undecided. Individual correspondents directed their attention to the candidates' personal combat in the undecided states. Linda Douglass on ABC said Bush was campaigning in Illinois because Gore's lead in the state had diminished and he now thought he had a chance. David Gregory on NBC reported on Bush's efforts on October 25 along the I-4 corridor in Florida, a group of suburban cities between Tampa and Orlando and the home of many of the state's undecided voters. Bill Whitaker on CBS reported comments about Bush's chances in Florida by John McCain, who was with Bush and Jeb Bush, the state's governor and candidate's brother.

One of the undecided states was Tennessee, and the fact that Gore might fail to carry his home state was not lost on network correspondents. Claire Shipman on NBC, reporting from Nashville that day, looked at how close the race had become in Tennessee. She referred to some contradictory polls, some showing Bush ahead, other placing Gore in the lead, and then reviewed the chance of Gore carrying his home state, which was not good. She described Tennessee as a state that had been voting Republican in recent years and referred to the fact that both of the state's U.S. senators and governor were Republicans. Shipman mentioned that George McGovern had been the last presidential candidate to lose his home state. John Roberts on CBS considered many of the same themes in his report about Gore and Tennessee and added that the last winning presidential candidate to lose his home state had been Woodrow Wilson. Jim Wooten on CBS strongly hinted that Gore would lose in Tennessee and even interviewed the vice president's state campaign manager about this prospect.

This pattern of candidate activities and news reporting continued for the final two weeks of the campaign. Gore was in Wisconsin on October 26 talking about global warming; network correspondents depicted this as yet another attempt by Gore to appeal to Nader supporters. Gore moved on to Pennsylvania, Michigan, and Florida over the days that followed and focused his appeals on economic issues aimed at traditional Democratic voters. Bush was in Pennsylvania, Indiana, Missouri, and California, where he emphasized tax cuts and the need for political change. Television news media continued looking at both candidates' daily activities and depicting them as horse race–related efforts to energize particular blocs of voters. They also had numerous, almost daily, reports about the outcomes of new polls and employed their electoral map illustrations of the likely outcome of the state-by-state vote. The polls continued to show the candidates nearly even, some with Gore ahead, others with Bush first, but the leads were always within the margin of error. The electoral vote projections showed each candidate as winning about 200 votes, but there were far too many undecided states to permit any network to project a winner.

In addition to candidate actions and poll results, the networks had several election-related features during the final days of October. The role of television advertising in these late stages of the campaign was of interest to ABC. This network offered a two-part report about the advertising efforts of the candidates and their special interest supporters. In addition, this network also looked at the undecided vote in Wisconsin and Missouri, business support for the two candidates, and potential effects of the various Social Security proposals. Social Security and the economy were of interest to CBS and NBC, and NBC also focused on the contrasting positions of the candidates on taxes, energy, and abortion.

The closeness of the polls encouraged television news media to devote even more time to the horse race. In the imagery of this sports metaphor, the campaign was now in the home stretch of a race that appeared headed for a photo finish of the two major contenders. Each horse, that is, candidate, was struggling to reach the finish line before his embattled rival. The race announcers, who in this instance were the network correspondents, were trying to generate excitement and intensity among the race viewers. Of course, there are many differences between an actual horse race and a political campaign. A horse race is a real event, whereas the "race" aspect of a campaign is an artificial creation of media and other observers. Perhaps one way to recognize the difference between the two is to compare the late stages of the 2000 campaign with an important race that actually occurred about that time, the Breeders' Cup Classic, the richest thoroughbred event in the nation and a major event in the determination of the year's racing titles. It was held at Louisville, Kentucky, on November 4, three days before the election. This race was telecast by NBC and lived up to its advance billing as the "race of the year." The two fastest horses in the world fought one another through the entire length of the home stretch only to end in a photo finish. The American star Tiznow defeated the European champion Giant's Causeway by a few inches. Unlike in this actual race, in which each horse fought his rival in order to reach the finish line first, in a political campaign the candidates rush around frantically in media view trying to rally voters who have already decided how they will cast their ballots. Since most voters had already made their choice, the political race was actually a creation of its observers, who sought to create a sense of excitement in their viewers about an election in which the voters had yet to cast ballots. Media interest was focused primarily on the candidates' final attempts to break open what appeared to be a pending photo finish rather than on the kind of president either would be.

The first week of November was similar to what passed before, although television news media began looking at the prospect of a split vote. A split vote would occur if one candidate won the popular vote and the other captured the electoral vote and the presidency. This new concern was added to the usual themes of the candidates' fighting with one another in the final days of the race. On November 1, Peter Jennings started the ABC political reporting by saying that thirteen states were toss-ups and mentioned the possibility of a split vote. Later in the broadcast, Barry Serafin described some of the circumstances that might lead to such an outcome. With this, ABC focused on the political combat of the day. Terry Moran, reporting from Florida, said Gore was making his nineteenth visit to the state and believed he had a chance of winning it. Gore was directing his appeals to seniors by emphasizing Social Security and using the environmental theme with younger voters along the I-4 corridor by talking about how he would ban off-shore oil drilling. Moran said the vote in Florida was too close to call. On that day Bush was in Minnesota and Washington, where he attacked Gore's spending plans and was photographed talking with a sales clerk at a Seattle fish market. After reporting these events, Dean Reynolds on ABC talked about Bush's electoral prospects in those two states. Meanwhile, Dan Harris on ABC was with Nader in Madison, Wisconsin. After summarizing Nader's main statements, Harris returned to the usual theme of how the consumer advocate might hurt Gore and how some liberals were attacking him for continuing his candidacy. In yet another look at the horse race that day, Linda Douglass on ABC reported about the ongoing battle between the NRA and the United Mine Workers to win the support of gun-owning union members in West Virginia for either Bush or Gore.

One day later Dan Rather began the CBS telecast by depicting the campaign as "hot, tight, and negative." He added that Bush had questioned Gore's character and Gore had questioned Bush's ability. Bill Whitaker then reported that Bush's crowds were getting bigger and more enthusiastic because Republicans believed they were going to win. Bush was then shown attacking Gore over the inability of the Democrats to lead the nation. Bush had campaigned in two states that day, Illinois and Missouri. Whitaker said Gore was ahead in Illinois but the race was even in Missouri. John Roberts on CBS talked about Gore's trying to lure Bush into campaigning in states that had voted twice for Clinton. The goal was to have Bush spend time and money in these states and for the Democrats to win them with strong get out the vote efforts.

Bush soon found himself with a character problem of his own, however. The news of Friday, November 3, was dominated by the revelation that Bush had been arrested for driving under the influence of alcohol (DUI) in Maine in 1976. David Gregory began the NBC coverage by a report about the reaction of the Bush campaign. He had remarks by Bush, by his campaign communications director Karen Hughes, and by Bush's father. Pete Williams followed Gregory and looked at the details of the arrest, including comments by police and the individual who had made the arrest public. Claire Shipman followed, directing her attention to the Gore campaign and its reaction. The other networks followed this same script of using three correspondents who individually focused on the incident itself and the reaction of each campaign.

The drunk driving controversy proved to be a minor one-day event, which had virtually disappeared from network news by November 4. Television news media returned to their usual themes then with the first political information the status of the horse race. One network, NBC, began its telecast with an electoral map showing the probable state-by-state outcome, and CBS had the results of its latest poll. The polls had been consistent for weeks: Bush had recorded a daily average of 47 percent and Gore 44 in the Gallup-CNN-*USA Today* Poll between October 1 and November 6. The final poll by this group had Bush ahead 47 percent to 45 percent, a difference within the margin of error. Bush spent the day attacking Gore on accountability and Social Security while attempting to energize core Republican voters in Pennsylvania, New Jersey, and Florida. Bill Whitaker of CBS said recent polls showed Bush as trailing in Pennsylvania, New Jersey, Michigan, and Florida. Gore spent the day in Tennessee and West Virginia, where he tried to mobilize black voters and address the charges the NRA had been making against him on gun control. One day later, ABC and NBC began their telecasts by reviewing their latest polls and electoral maps and then focused on the candidates. Gore talked about economics that day while speaking to black voters in Pennsylvania and Michigan; Bush emphasized Social Security in Orlando and Tampa, Florida. Each network correspondent who reported informed viewers of the latest polls in particular states. Ron Claiborne on ABC and Campbell Brown on NBC described Florida as close but added that Bush was confident he could win. Chip Reid on NBC said Gore was leading in Pennsylvania and

Florida but Bush was ahead in Missouri and Wisconsin. John Yang on ABC proclaimed that Gore had to win at least two of the three major toss-up states of Florida, Pennsylvania, and Michigan in order to have any chance of winning the election. Joe Johns on NBC looked at Nader's support in several midwestern and Pacific Northwest states, where he appeared to threaten Gore's chances.

Finally, CBS began its telecast of November 6 with new polls and an electoral map containing results similar to those of the other two networks. John Roberts looked at Gore's Michigan efforts to energize black and union voters, and Bill Whitaker focused on Bush's campaigning in Tennessee, where he appeared to be ahead in the latest state polls. With this, it was time for the votes to be cast, for the confusing network projections of the probable outcomes, and for a thirty-six-day legal battle that would cast doubt on the legitimacy of the whole process.

7

THE GENERAL ELECTION: OUTCOME AND MEANING

THE NATIONAL OUTCOME

The general election of 2000 had a most unusual ending. It concluded in a virtual dead heat between the two major candidates after an acrimonious thirty-six-day legal struggle over the outcome in Florida. This chapter describes the national distribution of popular and electoral votes and analyzes the candidate preferences of several important demographic and political groups. It also reviews the leading features of the Florida controversy and summarizes the rulings of the various courts involved. It does not attempt to explore the constitutional complexity and long-term legal significance of the issues raised before the Supreme Court. The reader should consult law reviews and other similar publications for answers to the questions relating to due process and equal protection that arose from this controversy.

With respect to the aggregate nationwide outcome, Gore defeated Bush by 470,383 votes, a margin of less than 0.5 percent. The count showed Gore at 50,902,900 (48.26 percent) and Bush at 50,432,517 (47.81 percent). The minor party candidates were far behind, as Nader garnered 3,084,542 votes (2.92 percent) and Buchanan 448,808 (0.43

percent). The electoral vote, and therefore the election, went to Bush 271 to 267. The official tally in Florida provided Bush with a final and legal lead of 537 votes out of more than 6 million that had been cast and all of the state's twenty-five electors. This election marked the fourth time in American history and the first in 112 years, since 1888, when the popular vote winner failed to win the presidency.

Although the outcome may have been close at the national level, it was anything but close in many locales and among numerous demographic and ideological groups. Each candidate won most of his electoral votes from specific regions of the country that have been consistent supporters of his party for many years. Gore ran best in states in the Northeast, Midwest, and Pacific Coast regions; Bush dominated the vote among the southeastern, Border, Plains, and Mountain states. The Northeast was Gore's strongest region. With one exception—and it proved to be an important one—Gore won every state in the region by a wide margin. His showings in Massachusetts, New York, and Rhode Island stand out because they were his three largest statewide victories. Gore defeated Bush by nearly two to one (61 percent to 32 percent) in Rhode Island while winning Massachusetts by 60 percent to 33 percent and New York by 60 percent to 36 percent. Gore overwhelmed Bush in Vermont (51 percent to 41 percent), Connecticut (56 percent to 39 percent), New Jersey (56 percent to 41 percent), Delaware (55 percent to 42 percent), Maryland (57 percent to 40 percent), and the District of Columbia (86 percent to 9 percent) and won modest victories in Maine (49 percent to 44 percent) and Pennsylvania (51 percent to 47 percent). Unfortunately for Gore, he lost New Hampshire by 7282 votes and one percentage point (47 percent to 48 percent). A victory there would have been particularly valuable for Gore because the state's four electoral votes would have given him the presidency outright and would also have eliminated the need for any recounts in Florida. The northeastern states have been Democratic in recent elections. Clinton carried all of them, including New Hampshire, in both 1992 and 1996.

Gore also dominated two other regions, although his support in them was less extensive than in the Northeast. He carried five Midwest states, four from the Pacific Coast, and New Mexico. California was the prize of the Pacific Coast, and Gore won it with a sweeping victory of 1.3 million votes (54 percent to 42 percent percent). He also ran well in Hawaii (56 percent to 38 percent) and added two states from the Pacific Northwest, winning Washington by a solid margin (50 percent to 45 percent) and Oregon by a cliffhanger (47 percent to 47 percent). He won New Mexico in the Mountain region in another close race (48 percent to 48 percent). These states have been reliably Democratic in recent elections: Hawaii, Washington, and Oregon have voted Democratic four consecutive times (1988 through 2000), and California and New Mexico have backed the Democratic nominee in the past three national tallies (1992 through 2000).

Television news media often depicted the Midwest as a battleground region, and the electoral outcomes certainly supported that view. Gore won five of seven Midwest states while making his strongest showing in Illinois (52 percent to 43 percent). He had a comfortable lead in Michigan (51 percent to 47 percent) and much closer victories in Minnesota (48 percent to 46 percent), Iowa (49 percent to 48 percent) and Wisconsin (48 percent to 48 percent). He suffered his greatest Midwest defeat in Indiana (41 percent to 57 percent) and lost Ohio by four points (46 percent to 50 percent). As in the Pacific Coast, many of the states Gore carried in the Midwest have been voting Democratic for some time. Minnesota has not supported a Republican presidential candidate since 1972; Iowa and Wisconsin have voted Democratic in the last four elections. Illinois and Michigan have backed the Democrats three consecutive times. Indiana is somewhat unusual among Midwest states in that it has been reliable for the Republicans. They have carried it in every election since Lyndon Johnson won it in 1964. Ohio has not been a Republican state, however: it cast twenty-one electoral votes for Clinton in both 1992 and 1996. The loss of this major industrial state was a particularly strong setback for Gore. He failed to add any new states to the Democratic list from those Clinton had carried; instead, he lost eleven states that had voted for Clinton in 1996 and nine states that had supported Clinton in both elections. Ohio was the largest state that voted for Bush after having twice backed Clinton. New Hampshire, as discussed, was also one of the nine states that voted for Clinton in both elections.

Bush won a majority of the electoral vote by forging a coalition between two groups of states. One group consisted of those that had supported Robert Dole in 1996; the second comprised the eleven states that switched from a Democratic preference in 1996 to Republican in 2000. With respect to the first group, Dole and Bush won the electoral votes of most Southeast, Plains, and Mountain states. Bush swept eight Southeast states that had voted for Dole by margins ranging from a low of seven points in Virginia to twenty-two points in Oklahoma. Included in this group are Virginia (52 percent to 45 percent), North Carolina (56 percent to 43 percent), South Carolina (57 percent to 41 percent) Georgia (55 percent to 43 percent), Alabama (57 percent to 42 percent), Mississippi (57 percent to 42 percent), Oklahoma (60 percent to 38 percent), and Bush's home state of Texas (59 percent to 38 percent). These states have also been strong supporters of Republican candidates for some time. Virginia and Oklahoma last voted Democratic in 1964. With only one exception, the remaining six states have voted Republican in every election since 1976, when they supported Jimmy Carter. Georgia is the one exception: it voted for Clinton in 1992 but not in 1996.

The four Plains states that supported Bush, North Dakota (61 percent to 33 percent), South Dakota (60 percent to 28 percent), Nebraska (63 percent to 33 percent), and Kansas (58 percent to 37 percent), are also Republican strongholds. Each has voted Republican in every election since 1964. The same partisanship record also exists in the Mountain states Bush won, Alaska (59 percent to 28 percent), Idaho (69 percent to 28 percent), Utah (67 percent to 26 percent) and Wyoming (69 percent to 29 percent). The remaining Mountain states that favored Bush, Colorado (51 percent to 42 percent) and Montana (59 percent to 34 percent), have also been consistent members of the Republican presidential coalition. With but one exception, 1992, both have voted Republican in every election since 1964. The exception occurred when Ross Perot attracted the support of so many Republicans that he helped Clinton carry both states.

Most of the states that voted for Clinton in 1996 and Bush in 2000 are located in the Border region. The loss of these states, particularly since Gore himself is a Border resident and political actor, was a significant factor in Gore's defeat. A victory in even one of these states would have made the controversy in Florida moot. Bush won West Virginia (52 percent to 46 percent), Kentucky (57 percent to 41 percent), Missouri (51 percent to 47 percent), Arkansas (51 percent to 46 percent), Louisiana (53 percent to 45 percent) and Gore's home state of Tennessee (51 percent to 48 percent). His victory in West Virginia was unusual because the state has been consistently Democratic for nearly seven decades. Between 1932, when Franklin D. Roosevelt won his initial term, through 1996 and Clinton's reelection, West Virginia voted Republican on only three occasions. These were in 1956, 1972, and 1984, when Dwight Eisenhower, Richard Nixon, and Ronald Reagan won reelection by sweeping margins. Until 2000, West Virginia had not voted for a first-term Republican presidential candidate since Herbert Hoover in 1928. The remaining five states in this region that voted for Clinton in 1992 and 1996 have not been Democratic strongholds. Instead, they have been Republican or competitive, but they did respond to the personal appeals of a Border region political actor in Clinton. Gore's inability to retain them for the Democrats is indicative of how he failed to use the advantages of surrogate incumbency. Finally, three other states, Arizona (51 percent to 45 percent), Nevada (50 percent to 46 percent), and, of course, Florida (49 percent to 49 percent), that had voted for Clinton in 1996 also moved into the Republican column in 2000. They also have Republican histories. Florida and Nevada had voted Democratic on only three occasions during the past half-century and Arizona had done so only once. These states appear to have returned to their long-term Republican preferences in 2000.

Although state differences in voting behavior are always important, particularly since they determine the allocation of the electoral vote, they often result from variations in the mixes of people who reside in specific locales. The determination of the electoral choices of those mixes of people can prove quite valuable to understanding the appeals of specific candidates and parties. The choices are usually measured by exit polls and observed by subdividing voters into categories based on population characteristics, class differences, ideology, religion, and policy preferences.

One of the more significant population characteristics dividing voters was place of residence. Gore drew much of his support from urban residents; Bush was particularly attractive to residents of more rural places. Suburban voters divided about evenly between the two. Gore won many of the votes cast by residents of large cities (61 percent to 36 percent) but lost the support of rural voters by a nearly identical margin (38 percent to 59 percent). He garnered 47 percent of the suburban vote, and Bush acquired 49 percent. This divide resurfaced over an issue that has urban-rural undertones, gun control. Voters who support stronger gun control laws, and who tend to reside in large cities or their suburbs, supported Gore (62 percent to 34 percent), whereas persons opposed to stronger gun control, and who are often rural residents, favored Bush (74 percent to 23 percent).

There were significant racial and ethnic differences as most whites supported Bush (54 percent to 42 percent) and members of other races or ethnic groups backed Gore. Despite Bush's attempts to appeal to minority groups, Gore dominated the votes of African Americans (90 percent to 8 percent) and attained clear majorities from Hispanics (62 percent to 35 percent) and Asians (55 percent to 41 percent). Patterns of this nature were particularly important in California, where the 2000 census had demonstrated that only 47 percent of the state's residents are white. The gender gap that first surfaced in 1980 was important once again as most men voted for

Bush (53 percent to 42 percent) and most women preferred Gore (54 percent to 43 percent).

It is often difficult to measure social class patterns in American voting behavior since far too many people define themselves as "middle-class." Surrogate variables that reflect rather than ask for class differences frequently prove to be the best approximations of class-related voting. Income, marital status, and labor union membership are particularly useful measurements. The questionnaires had six income categories ranging from "under $15,000" to "over $100,000." Gore attained his strongest support, 57 percent, from the former and his weakest, 43 percent, from the latter, whereas Bush's support ranged from 37 percent to 54 percent among these same categories. Gore's support diminished over the categories as incomes increased while Bush's support expanded. Gore also dominated the votes of the unmarried (57 percent to 38 percent) and of persons from union households (59 percent to 37 percent), whereas Bush won the backing of married voters (53 percent to 44 percent) and of those from nonunion homes (52 percent to 44 percent).

Voting patterns also differed on ideology and a variety of ideologically related issues. Gore won the support of self-described liberals (80 percent to 13 percent) and moderates (52 percent to 44 percent), and conservatives preferred Bush (81 percent to 17 percent). Gore ran strongest among voters who considered economically related issues as being most important; Bush dominated the preferences of those persons who considered taxes or noneconomic issues as top priorities for the next president. Voters who believed that prescription drug benefits for seniors (60 percent to 38 percent), health care (64 percent to 33 percent), jobs (59 percent to 37 percent) education (52 percent to 44 percent), or Social Security (58 percent to 39 percent) was the issue that mattered most supported Gore. Bush received the support of those who considered taxes (80 percent to 17 percent) or foreign affairs (54 percent to 40 percent) as most important. Bush won the support of voters who thought abortion should always be illegal (74 percent to 23 percent), whereas Gore ran very well among voters who believed abortion should always be legal (70 percent to 25 percent). Religion was a factor as Bush won the backing of those persons who attended religious services more than weekly (63 percent to 36 percent), whereas voters who never attended services preferred Gore by a similar margin (61 percent to 32 percent). Protestants, who constitute a majority of the electorate, were the only religious group who preferred Bush. Identifiers with the Religious Right, who tend to be Protestants, were among the strongest supporters of Bush as they backed him by a margin of 80 percent to 18 percent.

Voters reacted differently to the personal qualities of the candidates. Gore attracted the votes of those people who believed that understanding issues (75 percent to 19 percent), caring about people (63 percent to 31 percent), or being experienced (82 percent to 17 percent) was the quality that mattered most. Bush won the votes of people who considered being honest (80 percent to 15 percent), being likeable (60 percent to 38 percent), or being a strong leader (64 percent to 34 percent) the preferred quality.

Finally, Bill Clinton was an issue. As discussed in earlier chapters, many voters had contradictory views of the incumbent president. They approved of his performance in office but disliked his personal behavior. These views had been of some importance in the Democratic primaries when voters who tended to approve of Clinton's performance but not of him had frequently voted for Bill Bradley rather than Gore. Gore had suffered in his surrogate role. He had not been harmed much, however, since most of the primary voters were Democrats who approved of Clinton, and they were the ones who usually voted for Gore. The problem was far more serious in the general election, however, because the ambivalent voters were more numerous and not necessarily Democratic. With respect to the distribution of opinions, 57 percent of all voters approved of Clinton's job performance compared to 41 percent who disapproved, but only 36 percent approved of Clinton as a person compared to 60 percent who disapproved.

These two opinions can be subdivided into four possible combinations. The largest, with 39 percent of all voters, consisted of persons holding two negative views of Clinton, disapproval of both his performance and his personality. As one might suspect, this heavily Republican group voted overwhelming for Bush (89 percent to 7 percent). A second combination, 35 percent, consisted of voters with two positive views of Clinton, approval of both his performance and his personality. This strongly Democratic group favored Gore (85 percent to 12 percent). The critical group, and the one that appears to have held the balance in the election, comprised voters with favorable views of Clinton's performance and unfavorable views of his personality. They constituted 20 percent of the electorate and voted for Gore by a margin of 63 percent to 33 percent. These results appear to favor Gore, but a closer look reveals a troubling problem for the vice president. Gore lost the votes of one third of the members of this group, which amounts to approximately 7 percent of the electorate. These were some of the so-called swing voters to whom each party structured its appeals. The policy successes of the Clinton administration appear to have resonated well with these voters, who responded by telling pollsters of their favorable views of the political status quo. These voters should have acted upon their favorable retrospective evaluations of Clinton's policies and elected the surrogate of the incumbent as the next chief executive. Unfortunately for Gore, they refused to do so. Instead, they rejected the vice president as a successor because he appeared to be a personal surrogate of a political actor for whom they had lost respect. They liked the policies of the immediate past but were ready for a change of personalities in the executive branch. Gore's failure to provide a convincing argument, for this critical 7 percent of the electorate, that he would perpetuate the desirable aspects of the Clinton presidency while eliminating its scandals appears to have contributed more to his loss of the presidency than any electoral irregularities in Florida.

THE FLORIDA VOTE CONTROVERSY

The Florida controversy involved an interrelated set of events that appear to have developed from the manner in which Florida, and probably every other state in the nation, conducted its elections. Five events that occurred in a variety of different Florida counties became significant enough to generate some legal action by the Gore campaign or its supporters and attract the interest of television news media. Under the American federal system the conducting of elections, including those for members of the Electoral College, is the responsibility of the states. Specifically, the Constitution requires that electors be chosen in a manner determined by the legislatures of the respective states. Congress is allowed to set a uniform date for choosing those electors, however. Congress exercised its prerogative in 1845 by establishing a national election date and in 1887 by enacting the Electoral Count Act. This law requires electors to be chosen according to provisions of state laws enacted before an election occurs. States have subsequently assigned many of their electoral responsibilities to local governments, with counties often being the government of choice. Counties perform the major electoral functions of registering voters, printing ballots, operating polling stations, and counting results. A county clerk usually performs these functions. A state election official, most often a secretary of state, supervises these county clerks and certifies the various electoral features, such as a final vote count, as legal. Moreover, states often choose their county clerks and secretaries of state through partisan elections. This practice virtually guarantees that the supervision of elections is enmeshed in politics. Each party attempts to win these positions and use them in ways that enhance their electoral advantages. Finally, most county governments have very limited financial resources. Federal systems in general, including the American, employ taxing structures that generate far more revenue for higher-level governments, such as national and state, than they generate for lower-level governments, such as counties. Many counties have limited financial resources and often must choose among demands for public services such as transportation, social services, law enforcement, and elections. Elections usually rank toward the bottom of the list of priorities for county government spending. Such was the case of Florida. Much of the state's voting equipment was outdated and poorly maintained.

The vote count in four urban and heavily Democratic counties on Florida's eastern coast was the most important of the five electoral events that constituted the vote controversy. Under Florida law, an automatic recount of votes must occur in any election or jurisdiction if the two leading candidates are separated by less than 0.5 percent in the unofficial tally. Consequently, there had to be a statewide recount in the presidential balloting because Bush led Gore by only 1784 votes. The recount would be by mechanical means, however, and the votes once again tabulated by counting machines. These counting machines would be the same ones that had been used to tabulate the ballots initially. The fundamental problem, at least from the perspective of the Gore campaign, was that the machines had failed to tabulate presidential votes on approximately sixty thousand ballots in Broward, Palm Beach, Miami-Dade, and Volusia Counties and would probably fail to tabulate them again through mechanical recounts. These counties had used punch card ballots, which are an outdated and often unreliable method for casting votes. Punch card ballots contain a detachable box, called a *chad*, beside the candidate's name that can be removed by punching it with a needlelike instrument called a *stylus*. In all, twenty-two of Florida's fifty-nine counties had used this type of ballot; the larger and poorer counties were among the most likely to have done so. Occasionally, chads remained attached to ballots after voters punched them with a stylus. In some instances the chads remained attached because voters had not punched them hard enough to force their removal, but in other instances they remained attached because election officials had failed to clean the voting machines. These failures could lead to accumulations of chads that would make the detachment of newly produced chads more difficult. The Gore campaign believed mechanical counts would again fail to tabulate the attached chads. In response, it demanded manual recounts in these four counties with election clerks' visually inspecting uncounted ballots in order to determine voter intent. The Bush campaign argued that most of these uncounted ballots simply did not contain presidential votes. The Gore request set off a series of legal battles between the two campaigns that lasted for thirty-six days.

The counties honored Gore's request and began manual recounts. The Bush campaign responded by complaining about inconsistency in the standards employed by these counties for determining voter intent. The most lenient standard allowed a ballot to be counted if there was any mark or indentation on the attached chad. The terms *pregnant* and *dimpled* were often used to describe chads of this nature. Three of the four counties employed this standard; Palm Beach County used a modified version in which presidential votes were counted only if there were comparable marks or indentations on the chads relating to other offices. More demanding standards frequently used in other states required that two or in some cases three corners of the chad be removed for a vote to be recorded. The Bush campaign said the Gore campaign was trying to recount votes selectively until it had its desired result. There were, of course, unrecorded votes in eighteen other counties with punch card ballots, but no one demanded that any of these be recounted manually. On November 13 a federal district court ruled against a Bush motion to stop the recounts and a state court responded similarly to a Bush request two days later. The Bush campaign then appealed to the Florida Supreme Court but also received an unfavorable ruling from that tribunal. Meanwhile, Katherine Harris, the Florida secretary of state and a partisan Republican who had served as an official of the Bush campaign, interpreted state law to require that all recounts had to be completed by November 14, seven days after the election. She announced that she would then certify the election as official. Most of the recounts had not been completed by this time, but the recording of those that were finished reduced Bush's statewide lead to only 300 votes. The Florida Supreme Court, whose seven members had been appointed by Democratic governors, overruled Harris on November 17 and ordered her to extend the time available for completing recounts to November 26.

At this time, a second event suddenly became important in the controversy. Florida law allowed absentee ballots to arrive from overseas locations within ten days after an election and be counted. Most of the 4000 or so ballots of this nature had come from military bases and were likely to favor Bush. They were counted on November 17 and increased Bush's lead to 930 votes. Despite these gains, the Bush campaign responded that about 600 of these ballots had been disqualified because they did not contain required postmark dates or signatures of military election officials. It accused the Gore campaign of trying to prevent servicemen from voting. The Florida Supreme Court had found the ten days permitted for military ballots and the seven days allowed for all other ballots to be inconsistent and had used this inconsistency as a reason for extending the certification date.

The November 26 date arrived, and only Broward County had completed its manual recounts. Harris included these in her official certification, which resulted in a Bush lead of 537 votes. This would be the final and official tabulation of the Florida vote. The remainder of the battle over recounts was conducted in courtrooms, where Gore generally suffered a series of defeats. The Gore campaign responded by filing suit in Florida court attempting to have Harris's certification overturned and the recounts completed in the other three counties. The Bush campaign filed suit with the U.S. Supreme Court requesting an end to the recounts because the Florida law specified that certification must occur seven days after an election. The rulings on both lawsuits occurred on the same day, December 4, and were unfavorable to Gore. A Florida judge, Sander Sauls, refused to extend the deadline set by the Florida Supreme Court beyond November 26. The U.S. Supreme Court vacated the order of the Florida Supreme Court and ordered that court to provide clearer standards relating to its extension of the time available for completing the recounts beyond the initial seven days.

The Gore campaign now took its case to the Florida Supreme Court. This court responded by overruling Judge Sauls and extending the time available for concluding the recounts to December 10. Bush asked the U.S. Supreme Court to overturn this decision. The court did so and issued an order on December 9 temporarily halting the recounts pending its review of the controversy. Three days later, the federal court permanently ended the recount, although it accepted the previous decision of the Florida Supreme Court establishing November 26 as the certification date. The federal court ruled that Florida lacked uniform standards for determining voter intent on ballots with attached chads. The practice of each county's establishing its own standards for determining voter intent was arbitrary and violated the Equal Protection Clause of the Fourteenth Amendment. This ruling ended the election but not the controversy. Every justice who voted in the majority of the five to four decision had been appointed to the court by a Republican president. Critics of the court, as well as angry Democrats, charged that the justices had made a partisan decision comparable to the infamous *Dred Scott v. Sanford* decision of pre–Civil War times and proclaimed that such a decision would eventually undermine the court's reputation for political neutrality. In *Dred Scott*, five southern justices formed a majority favoring a proslavery position that slaves could never become American citizens. This ruling was so unpopular that it had the effect of severely damaging the court's reputation for many decades. The decision also appeared to contain a Catch-22 feature: some votes could not be counted because of defective procedures, but efforts to correct the defective procedures were not permissible because they violated the federal Constitution.

Although the battles over manual recounts and overseas ballots were the most significant components of the Florida election controversy, they were not the only ones that raised questions about the legitimacy of the outcome. The other events were not part of any legal battles between the Gore and Bush campaigns but resulted in litigation nonetheless. The most widely publicized of these related to the so-called butterfly ballot in Palm Beach County. In this instance, a Democratic county clerk had designed a ballot that appeared to violate certain features of Florida law about ballot structure. The law requires that ballots list the names of candidates on the left side with the corresponding punch numbers placed immediately to their right. The butterfly ballot had the punch holes in the middle with the names of the candidates listed on both sides. Many voters were confused about which numbers were associated with which candidates. Perhaps as many as nineteen thousand voters eventually cast their ballots for someone other than the candidate of their choice. Gore may have been the greater victim here. He appears to have lost about thirteen thousand votes through this error compared to Bush, who may have lost approximately six thousand.

Another problem occurred in Seminole County, where a Republican clerk had allowed representatives of his party to fill in some missing voter identification numbers on about five thousand absentee ballot applications that had been submitted by registered Republican voters. The general practice is Florida is to reject incomplete applications. In response, some local Democrats sued to have those votes disqualified. The Gore campaign refused to become involved in this case because it had been arguing that all votes in the four urban counties should have been counted and wanted to prevent the appearance of hypocrisy. The Democratic suit might have had significant electoral implications: the loss of those votes would have cost Bush the election. A Florida trial court eventually rejected the Democrats' case and let the results stand.

Finally, one event had overtones of racial discrimination. Various political groups had made extensive efforts to increase the voter registration of African Americans and seemed to have succeeded as the turnout of these voters reached record highs. Unfortunately, the capacity of various county clerks' offices to process these new registrations was far too limited. Hundreds of minority voters had been listed on the centralized registration roles in their respective counties, but information about these new registrations had not been transmitted to polling stations where voters reported for their ballots. The clerks' offices were greatly understaffed. The available remedy for such a problem was for polling station workers to contact the county clerk's office, either by telephone or by laptop computer, then verify the registrations. Many of the polling stations in the lower-income areas of urban counties were not supplied with laptops, in contrast to stations in the higher-income areas, which always seemed to have them. Moreover, attempts by voters to telephone clerks' offices to verify registrations were often futile because of the large number of calls being made and the limited number of election personnel available to answer them. Many newly registered minority voters simply gave up in frustration and did not vote, perhaps costing Gore even more votes. Civil rights organizations responded by suing Florida in federal court, charging violations of the Voting Rights Act. How many thousands of votes Gore may have lost because of the butterfly ballot and the inability of many late-registering African Americans to cast their ballots will forever remain uncertain. They also will continue to cast doubt on the legitimacy of the Florida outcome and the election of 2000.

THE SIGNIFICANCE OF THE PARTY NOMINATIONS

Despite the uniqueness of the Florida controversies, most of the leading events of Election 2000 conformed to the usual patterns of mediated campaigns in the television age. Again television news media were not mere observers dispassionately reporting the outcomes of political events to their viewing audiences but were significant participants in a process that helped determine the course of the campaign itself. Probably unintentionally, they might well have enhanced the electoral prospects of George W. Bush through their definitions of political news and their assignments of stereotypical roles to the candidates. In addition, the three features that characterized earlier elections with surrogate incumbents also characterized the election of 2000. The defining feature of elections of this nature is the nomination of the vice president as the standard bearer of the presidential party. The second is the nomination by an eager opposition party of a unifying challenger who holds out the promise of electoral victory. The third is the lack of inherent advantages enjoyed by either side in a political context in which both candidates must overcome dilemmas unique to their particular position of incumbent, or challenger. The vice president must convince voters that he is more than a mere surrogate of a retiring incumbent, but he must do so without undermining the value of incumbency. The challenger must convince voters who become increasingly skeptical as the campaign develops that he is personally and politically qualified for the presidency.

The defining feature was met with the nomination of Gore. The vice president led all of his real or potential rivals in every measurement of political strength between the 1996 election and the end of the campaign in March 2000. He outpaced them in fund-raising, endorsements from party leaders and elected officials, and support from party voters, as determined by national polls. He had already developed an extensive following even before the campaign began in January 1999 by utilizing the institutional and rhetorical opportunities provided by the modern presidential office. A significant component of the Democratic Party's activist core had already identified Gore as the leading political surrogate and designated successor of Bill Clinton long before the struggle for succession had even begun and quickly rallied to his banner when it did. Gore devoted a considerable part of the first six years of his tenure in office representing the president in a variety of political settings with his party's activist core. He also operated a personal staff that was integrated into the policy-making apparatus of the Clinton administration and relied on the foreign, budgetary, and economic expertise of the EOP to project imagery to his partisans that he should be Clinton's successor. After realizing the difficulty of duplicating these advantages, five potential rivals eventually decided against opposing Gore. Only one, Bill Bradley, stepped forward to issue a challenge. As a candidate, Bradley was far less effective than he was when depicted by television news media.

A fundamental difference existed between the televised version of the campaign and the one that actually occurred among the party activists. The televised campaign had two major themes, one of them the charge that front-runner Gore was running a disorganized and confused effort that might fail after an attack from Bradley. The second theme was that Bradley might successfully appeal to Independent voters in the early test states of Iowa and New Hampshire and translate their support into a larger national following. In retrospect, this version of the campaign does not appear ever to have existed. Although Gore's staff and personal actions may indeed have been disorganized, a occurrence far more common in campaigns than television news media indicated to their audiences, Gore was acquiring the support of those persons who count most in nomination struggles, the activist core of his own party. Television news media could not direct their coverage to the processes whereby Gore had actually won the support of this activist core. He had accomplished this by performing the partisan duties of the contemporary vice president over the previous six years. Since they could not show Gore's acquiring this support, and since it was far too early in the election cycle to show Gore in any capacity other than as the surrogate of the incumbent, television news media directed their attention to trivial matters. They focused on Gore's expensive consultants, talked about the high rents on his Washington office, and remarked on the gaffes of his campaign staff. Although perhaps interesting, these stories were of little importance to the development of the campaign but may have contributed to a perception that Gore lacked leadership skills.

Bradley directed his campaign to the one overriding goal of winning in Iowa or New Hampshire. He concentrated virtually all of his time and money in these two states. This is a long-shot strategy as the candidate gambles that a strong showing in one state will generate expanded, and free, media coverage in other states. A significant political cost characterizes this strategy: Bradley lacked effective organizational efforts in most of the remaining states. Candidates frequently encounter great difficulty in developing personalized organizations in most states and must instead rely on some existing political entities, such as party committees or partisan-oriented interest groups, to advance their efforts. Gore had the support of numerous elected officials and such Democratic oriented groups as labor unions and civil rights and women's groups. Bradley had limited support among these people, who saw a possible Gore administration as a continuation of the Clinton presidency. Bradley lost both of the early test states, and for all intents and purposes, his effort ended.

Television news media assigned the two stereotypical roles they employ when describing nomination campaigns to both Gore and Bradley and then structured future reporting around them. They depicted the campaign as an ongoing struggle between the front-runner Gore, who constantly tried to deflect challenges, and his leading adversary, Bradley. This pseudocampaign outlived its usefulness with Bradley's loss of Iowa and New Hampshire, however. These outcomes encouraged network correspondents to focus more of their attention on the intense two-candidate battle within the Republican Party and downplay their coverage of the Democrats. Although television news media had probably not attempted to favor one candidate over others, their actions may have harmed Gore because they occurred at a time when the vice president was still unable to escape from his image as a Clinton surrogate. Gore needed extensive television exposure at this time in order to develop imagery through which he would appear as a political actor in his own right. Whereas the surrogate image had proved useful to Gore during his attempts at winning the support of his fellow partisans, it was less advantageous when he tried to expand that support to other voters. Gore occupied two public roles: he was a high-ranking official of the national administration and he was a candidate for the presidency. Bill Clinton constantly overshadowed Gore when the vice president was acting in the first role, and George W. Bush frequently did so with the second. Consider the 2000 State of the Union Address as an example. Although Clinton referred to Gore on six occasions during the speech, Gore performed in the role of supporting actor during the evening's festivities as he sat at his desk behind the president and had no opportunity to speak. Gore also appeared in the supporting actor role during most of the nominating campaign. Bush led all candidates, including even Gore, in televised news coverage of political actions throughout 1999 and during the post–New Hampshire phase of the primary season. The Texas governor all too often appeared as the central actor in the televised version of the battle for succession. The vice presidency was a mixed blessing for Gore during the nomination campaign. It proved useful as a forum for mobilizing his partisans but was limiting when it trapped him in a supporting role in a televised drama that appeared to exist between the actions of the incumbent Bill Clinton and the leading man who would be president, George W. Bush.

The Republicans entered the campaign encountering the same problem the opposition party always faces in elections with surrogate incumbents, contradictory circumstances that held out the promise of victory while threatening defeat. They were encouraged by the forced retirement of Clinton and the realization that their likely rival this time, Gore, lacked Clinton's personal and political appeal. Moreover, the scandals of the Clinton administration, including those that eventually led to impeachment, encouraged Republicans in the belief that voters might be ready to demand a change of parties to accompany the required constitutional change in political actors in the White House. The one drawback to this promising scenario was the uncertainty accompanying the naming of the party's new leadership. As with opposition parties in every American election, the Republicans of 2000 had no easily identifiable political actor comparable to an incumbent around whom it could quickly unite in its attempt to regain executive power. The controversial government shutdown in 1995 over the content of federal spending and the failed impeachment attempt four years later had damaged the image of congressional Republicans among many of the nation's voters. Far too many people saw the legislative component of the Republican Party as ideologically extreme and politically irresponsible. The party's most respected component was its governors, but far too many of them were unknown outside their own state. The lack of a strong and unifying leader meant the Republicans would probably have to engage in a lengthy and divisive nomination struggle that might attract numerous aspirants and competing factions. Such a campaign could very well compromise the party's electoral prospects. The existence of twelve candidacies in early 1999 suggested this might become the Republican fate in 2000.

Despite these candidacies and an intense fight between Bush and John McCain during the primaries of February and March, this threat did not materialize. Instead, Bush united his party fairly easily and successfully led them to their desired victory. As with the three previous elections with surrogate incumbents, the opposition party this time was also quite eager to regain power. Consequently, most of its activist core found little difficulty in supporting Bush after he convinced them he could win the election. Relying upon contributors who had supported his two successful campaigns for governor, on connections from his father's previous presidential quests, and on the backing of most of his fellow governors, Bush quickly seized the lead in every important measurement of candidate strength and became the early front-runner for the nomination. Television news media indirectly assisted Bush in his efforts to generate a consensus among his partisans through the manner in which they depicted his actions and those of his opponents. They stereotyped Bush in the front-runner role and constantly illustrated his as possessing all the attributes that occupants of this media-defined role must have. Bush received the greatest quantity and quality of media coverage of any candidate during the nomination campaign. Network correspondents focused significant attention on him in March 1999, when he formed his exploratory committee, and in June the same year, when he made his initial political visits to Iowa and New Hampshire. No other candidate received such attention, even those who had visited those two early test states on several occasions. With respect to the quality of coverage, network correspondents were unusually deferential to Bush in August 1999 while reporting his actions relating to the Iowa straw poll. They telecast numerous scenes of the Texas governor speaking to his supporters at upbeat rallies, they talked extensively about Bush's successes at attaining the status of front-runner, and they looked disparagingly at the political also-rans who seemed foolish enough to run against the obvious winner.

Perhaps unwittingly, television news media contributed to the development of a consensus among many Republicans in favor of the Bush candidacy. By depicting Bush in the role of a successful political actor who could raise more money, attain higher poll standings, and garner more endorsements from his fellow Republican officeholders than any of his rivals, television news media were also depicting Bush as unusually qualified for national leadership. In their view, personal successes in accomplishing campaign tasks were the proper standards for evaluating the quality of potential leaders. Politics was clearly a game in this media world of political races, and Bush was the winner. Hence, he was qualified to be the next president. In contrast, television news media depicted the remaining candidates as unqualified for office. These candidates could not raise enough money, or attain favorable poll standings, or garner the requisite endorsements needed for challenging Bush. News coverage of this nature helped Bush expand his already significant lead among his own partisans and contributed to the relatively early conclusion of the primary election season.

There was more to the story, of course. Bush faced what proved to be a temporary setback when he lost the New Hampshire primary to McCain. He quickly overcame this, however, with victories in South Carolina, Virginia, and seven of the primaries of March 7. Perhaps like his father in 1988, George W. Bush may have been helped in 2000 by the actions of Democrats. Many southern Democratic leaders had created "Super Tuesday" in 1988 in the hope of enhancing the nomination prospects of a candidate from their region. They wanted such a candidate to win most of the seventeen primaries scheduled for the second Tuesday in March and in doing so, build an insurmountable delegate lead for the nomination. Much to their dismay, these primaries produced no clear Democratic winner but did resolve the Republican battle. George Bush won every primary and clinched the role of Republican standard bearer.

In the current election cycle, the DNC had forced states other than Iowa and New Hampshire to schedule their primaries or caucuses at a date no earlier than the first Tuesday in March. This decision led to the creation of the equivalent of a national primary on March 7 that resolved the nominations for both parties. It also brought the McCain challenge to an abrupt end and may well have prevented the Republicans from destroying their general election prospects. Fortunately for Bush and the Republicans, the DNC efforts to prevent votes before the first Tuesday in March had the unintended political effect of encouraging several states to schedule their events for that particular day. The decisions of California and New York to hold their votes on March 7 virtually guaranteed a "national primary." Bush now had an opportunity—and he certainly used it—to bring a rapid conclusion to a contest that under other scheduling rules might have been a months-long struggle between two candidates that could have lasted until the national convention and compromised the party's electoral prospects. The DNC rule also aided Bush because it helped bring about the existence of several Republican primaries with no Democratic counterparts during February and contributed to a political and media context in which the battle between Bush and McCain was the only political story available. In response, television news media aided Bush once again by depicting him as a front-runner acquiring most of his support from Republicans while describing McCain as a party outsider appealing to Independents and Democrats in an attempted hostile takeover of the party. This context gave Bush an opportunity to unite his partisans and project imagery in which he appeared as Clinton's likely successor.

GORE'S DILEMMA

Neither candidate appears to have overcome the dilemma unique to his strategic position, however. Although the outcome of the popular vote suggests Gore might have won the election were it not for the Florida controversy, there is also ample evidence attributing his loss to an inability to master the dilemma of escaping from the limitations of incumbency without forgoing its advantages. Gore had occupied a supporting actor role between Clinton and Bush for nearly the entire campaign prior to the onset of the Democratic convention. He seems to have escaped from this dilemma through his forceful actions at the convention, but he may have forfeited his strongest advantage while doing so.

Gore was trapped in the supporting actor role for a considerably longer time than earlier vice presidents had been. Hubert Humphrey emerged as a major contender for the Democratic nomination in April 1968 after Lyndon Johnson announced his retirement. Although the divisiveness of the Democratic race was a significant factor in Humphrey's eventual loss to Nixon, the fact that there was a race helped him during the months preceding the fateful Democratic convention in August. The Republican campaign was virtually over and the nomination of Nixon apparent to nearly everyone when Humphrey announced his candidacy. As a consequence, Humphrey rapidly emerged as a major actor in the televised succession battle and frequently appeared in contrast to rivals Eugene McCarthy and Robert Kennedy.

In 1988, Vice President George Bush initially faced a strong challenge for the Republican nomination from five rivals, including Robert Dole; the Democrats had seven little known aspirants competing for their nomination. Television news media found the Republican race far more interesting than the Democratic and therefore focused much of their attention on it. As the front-runner, Bush was the most televised candidate during the initial months of the year and particularly when he vanquished his competition on Super Tuesday. No Democrat had emerged as the front-runner by the time Bush had clinched the Republican nomination.

The extensive televised coverage of the 2000 Democratic convention provided Gore with an excellent opportunity to break from his supporting actor role. He succeeded while emphasizing in his acceptance speech that he was his own man. Gore rapidly eliminated Bush's lead in the polls and even seized first place in early September. Television news media responded to these changed circumstances by depicting Gore as the probable winner. They frequently illustrated his speaking in an upbeat manner to his supporters while focusing far more of their attention on Bush's troubles. Viewers of televised politics could now see more of Bush's off-color remarks, his mispronunciations of key words, and his verbal gaffes relating to the costs of some proposals. Despite these indications of success, Gore's campaign soon stalled and his lead in the polls disappeared. He trailed Bush through much of October, although mostly within the polls' margin of error, and finally closed the gap just in time to lose in one of the closest elections in American history.

Gore's emphasis on being his own man initially helped his effort, but it may also have contributed to his eventual defeat. Although there were strong signs of public dislike of Clinton's personal behavior, a substantial majority of voters approved of the direction in which the nation was moving and of Clinton's stewardship over foreign and domestic policy. Unfortunately for his own campaign efforts, Gore tried to distance himself from Clinton in a number of ways while rarely seeking to embrace any aspect of the incumbent's persona. Perhaps the most significant features of media interest in Gore's selection of Lieberman as his running mate were the Connecticut senator's denunciation of Clinton's behavior and the reputation Lieberman had among his congressional colleagues for moral rectitude. Gore appears to have encouraged this interest in an attempt to distance himself from Clinton. Gore was also reluctant to let Clinton assume any significant role in influencing undecided voters in key states.

Any president, even a retiring incumbent, can generate significant news interest and aid a campaign. Clinton had kept the Bush campaign off target for several days before the Republican convention with his remarks about the Texas governor's lack of qualifications at a time when television news media were ignoring Gore. Moreover, Gore had not wanted media attention focused on Clinton during the latter stages of the campaign in October but was unable to prevent it. Reagan had generated considerable news attention during the final days of the 1988 election by visiting undecided states on behalf of his vice president; Clinton generated news simply by his absence from his vice president's effort. Gore needed Clinton to speak on his behalf in locales such as the I-4 corridor in Florida, and in undecided states such as Ohio, New Hampshire, Arkansas, and West Virginia.

Gore had used the Democratic convention as a forum to reassure voters he would prevent Clinton-like scandals, and most voters seemed convinced. He did not need to continue avoiding Clinton, however. Gore needed to link his promises for the prosperous future with the successful policy record of an administration of which he had been an integral part. Instead, he all too often spoke as if he were simply another Democratic congressman running for president. He emphasized the range of issues that most congressional candidates of his party often favored, but he failed to demonstrate that he possessed important experience that would distinguish him from any other candidates, including even Bush. This was particularly apparent during the second debate when the two candidates agreed with one another on sixteen issues relating to foreign affairs and national defense. Rather than emphasize the value of his policies, Gore attempted to frighten voters into believing that serious disasters would befall the nation if Bush were to win. Unfortunately, he failed to indicate just how a Gore administration would differ from one led by Bush. His assertion in late October that "Prosperity was on the ballot" paled in comparison to the Reagan mantra "It's morning in America."

While speaking about how he might spend a future budget surplus, Gore indicated that he believed that an important period of American history had just ended and then suggested that he wanted to lead the nation into the next one. The Clinton administration had solved a great problem of the past: it had placed the federal government's financial house in order after decades of deficit spending. Instead of attempting to make an abrupt break with the immediate past, Gore needed to convince voters that his agenda was linked to, was actually a continuation of, a fiscal policy that had reduced deficits without cutting popular middle-class entitlements. Gore tried to create a future that did not seem much different from the one advanced by Bush, however. As a consequence, voters could cast their ballot for Bush and be secure in the belief that little, if anything, would likely change. By failing to link his agenda with an immediate past that most saw as successful, Gore undermined his own case and offered voters few convincing reasons to support him.

Finally there is the Nader question. At the outset of the election, Nader did not appear to be a particularly strong threat to Gore or anyone else. In fact, it was not even a certainty that he would finish any better than fourth with Reform candidate Buchanan taking third. The collapse of the Reform Party transformed Nader into the only minor party candidate likely to attract any significant percentage of the vote. The Gore campaign, and much of the television news media, believed that many of those potential Nader votes would be at Gore's expense and might thereby deprive the vice president of the electoral votes of several key states. A variety of national polls indicated that about half of the Nader supporters might have voted for Gore if Nader had not been a candidate and about 20 percent might have preferred Bush. The remainder suggested that they might have abstained from voting for president. Both Gore and television news media focused attention on this feature of the Nader candidacy, and Gore and some of his supporters attacked the consumer advocate as a threat to liberal causes. Network correspondents directed their attention to campaign activities in states where they thought Nader might deprive Gore of victory. Although Nader's candidacy may have been threatening to Gore in some states, the vice president and many of the network correspondents failed to comprehend the main problem posed by the existence of the Green Party. There were important differences between Nader's efforts and those of other recent minor party candidates such as George Wallace (1968), John Anderson (1980), and Ross Perot (1992, 1996), and these differences required responses other than those that only raised fears about the consequences of a Bush presidency.

These earlier efforts were mostly personal crusades by solitary individuals who started and then used minor parties as vehicles for attaining access to state ballots. The parties disappeared shortly after their founders stopped running for president. This was not the case with Nader and the Greens. The Green Party was already in existence when it persuaded Nader to serve as its standard bearer in 1996. This party would certainly have nominated another candidate had Nader refused. American Greens are a component of a social and political movement in industrial democracies from Germany to Australia embedded in what has come to be known in this nation as the *counterculture*. Attempts to personalize the Green movement in the identity of Nader or any other single political actor would be comparable to personalization of the antiwar movement of the 1960s in the name of only one individual, such as Eugene McCarthy, George McGovern, Wayne Morse, or William Fulbright. Unlike Wallace, Anderson, and Perot, Nader was far less significant than his party to the movement he represented. Gore needed to address the concerns of activists like those who protested at the World Trade Organization (WTO) meeting in Seattle in 2000 rather than limiting his attacks to the alleged threat that Nader might pose to his electoral prospects. Greens viewed the Clinton administration and its spokesman Al Gore as unresponsive to the threats they believed multinational corporations and globalization posed to workers, consumers, and the environment. It was necessary for Gore to address these voters in a manner comparable to Hubert Humphrey's response to opponents of the Vietnam War. Speaking in Salt Lake City in September 1968, Humphrey said he would stop the bombing of North Vietnam; he began reducing Nixon's lead in the polls shortly after his address. Gore had no comparable response and therefore failed to distinguish himself from Bush to a key bloc of voters over a number of interrelated issues that may become even more salient in the immediate future. Nader does not appear to have cost Gore thousands of votes; Gore simply failed to win them.

Gore failed to master the dilemma that threatens all vice presidents who attempt to succeed retiring incumbents. To his advantage, he used the institutional and rhetorical advantages of incumbency to convince his partisans that he was the deserving successor of the president they had twice elected to office. To his disadvantage, he failed to expand upon those advantages and convince a significant portion of the general electorate that he was his own man, who could bring about desired personnel changes in public life within the context of policy continuity. Gore was trapped by incumbency at the onset of the campaign but then transformed into a candidate who seemed unleashed from it entirely. He changed his status from that of a supporting actor in the televised world of national politics to a coequal player with Bush in a campaign to which incumbency seemed irrelevant. He did not project imagery to allow voters to see him as a vice president of a successful administration attempting to link the better features of the immediate past with the uncertainty of the undefined future. Instead, he appeared as merely another government official striving to rally his own partisans behind the promises of congressional Democrats. Television news media responded accordingly and treated him as coequal with Bush and downplayed or even ignored his incumbency other than to introduce him as the vice president. Exit polls indicated that approximately 20 percent of the electorate approved of the policy directions of the Clinton administration but disapproved of the person Bill Clinton. The polls also indicated that about one third of these people voted for Bush. Gore's inability to master the vice presidential dilemma cost him the votes of many of these people and ultimately deprived him of the nation's highest office.

BUSH'S DILEMMA

As Gore needed to convince voters he was more than a surrogate, Bush needed to persuade them that he had the personal and political qualities they expected of a president. These qualities involved the personal features of intelligence, integrity, and communicative style that define a president's public persona and the ideological direction, administrative competence, and bargaining skills a president employs while advancing his political agenda. Bush's successful nomination quest encouraged widespread perceptions that he enjoyed these qualities. Relying on both his family name and landslide reelection to a second term as Texas governor, Bush quickly attained a national poll lead among Republican presidential aspirants. He then translated this lead into an insurmountable fund-raising and endorsement advantage that encouraged television news media to depict him as the front-runner for the nomination and to focus more attention on him than on another candidate. This attention in turn helped Bush generate a consensus among Republicans in support of his candidacy and contributed to his victories in the presidential primaries. By March 2000 Bush had become the new and unifying leader of a rejuvenated opposition party holding out the promise of electoral victory. Except for a few days at the end of the primary election season in March, Bush led Gore in national surveys by double-digit margins from the beginning of the campaign in early 1999 until the onset of the Democratic convention in August 2000.

The nomination of Gore changed the political equation. The vice president emerged as a significant actor in his own right as television news media expanded its coverage of the campaign and began depicting the race as a personal struggle between two equally matched aspirants. Bush lost his long-time advantage: television news media stopped illustrating him as the central political actor in the succession battle. For the remainder of the campaign, he would have to share that role with Gore. Bush now faced the dilemma that all nominees of the opposition party encounter in elections with surrogate incumbents. He would have to demonstrate that the electoral success imagery he had projected earlier in the year was not merely the euphoria of a previously disunited party suddenly united behind a new leader who held out the promise of victory but a probable outcome. Although he advocated many of the same policy positions that his father had emphasized in 1988, Bush faced a dilemma far more akin to that of his father's rival, Michael Dukakis. Dukakis had also assumed a double-digit lead by midsummer of that earlier election while his opponent, the vice president, was trapped in the role of supporting actor in an administration dominated by Ronald Reagan. The Massachusetts governor had developed his lead by employing imagery of electoral victory and vague promises of new national leadership. He started losing support when voters began seeing the race as a battle between an untested governor who might bring about the wrong kind of change and an experienced vice president who offered continuity with the success of the immediate past.

Bush faced the same dilemma in 2000. His experience in public office was limited to the six years he had spent as governor of Texas. In addition, the Democrats were claiming that his proposals favored wealthy corporations or Christian conservatives and not most middle-class Americans. The polls soon reflected Gore's emergence as a revitalized candidate and the public's increasingly skeptical view of Bush. Gore seized the lead in most polls during the final days of August and appeared headed to a certain victory. Television news media changed the tone of their political coverage and became far more critical of Bush. The Texas governor needed to overcome this change, and do so quickly, or he would meet the same fate Dukakis had.

Since Bush won the election, one might suspect that he overcame this dilemma. The answer appears to be quite the contrary, however. Bush's triumph would not have occurred without the twenty-five disputed electoral votes from Florida. If no such controversy had existed, Bush might well have lost the electoral vote to Gore by a margin of 292 to 246. He seems to have failed to overcome the dilemma that was unique to his position as the nominee of the opposition party.

Bush lost his lead in the days immediately after the Democratic convention after Gore and Lieberman began a series of attacks about the effects the Texas governor's policy proposals might have on middle-class families. Bush trailed through much of September while facing a series of problems ranging from verbal gaffes to subliminal messages. He eventually reduced Gore's lead during the latter part of the month after an appearance on Oprah Winfrey's show, when network correspondents had a growing interest in some of the vice president's factual misrepresentations. Nonetheless, Bush did not take the lead; he merely caught Gore in the polls and then lost his lead once again during the initial days of October. The dynamics of the campaign throughout September indicated that Gore would win a close election. Bush's support appeared consistent, his daily percentages of the vote as recorded by the Gallup-CNN-*USA Today* daily tracking poll between Labor Day and the first debate ranged between 41 percent and 47 percent with an average of about 44 percent. Gore maintained a daily average of approximately 47 percent during this same time and also seemed to have a consistent level of support. This was to change in the aftermath of the first debate, although there is some question about the extent of Bush's contributions. He was responsible for some of the poll changes but received significant help from Gore.

Bush gained few new supporters through the debates, but he accomplished the most important political tasks demanded by the event. He retained his present backing and with a little help from Gore became a more attractive candidate to the remaining undecided voters. Network polls conducted shortly after the first debate indicated that viewers saw Gore as the winner, although the results were close. Bush demonstrated that he was a fairly equal match with Gore, however, in a performance superior to those of other rivals the vice president had vanquished in previous elections. Gore had dominated the vice presidential 1992 and 1996 debates with Dan Quayle and Jack Kemp and was the clear winner of a 1993 debate with Ross Perot on *Larry King Live*. He also overpowered Bill Bradley in the Harlem debate of February 2000. Bush competed with Gore for the middle ground on a number of issues often identified as Democratic, including education and Social Security, and by doing so muted charges that he would implement many of the unpopular proposals of congressional Republicans. With overtones of the 1960 debate between John F. Kennedy and Richard Nixon, the visual features of the first debate may have outweighed the verbal. Many critics believed Nixon won the debate with the stronger answers. Others gave the debate to Kennedy because of the ease and confidence the Massachusetts senator demonstrated compared to Nixon's sickly appearance and nervous demeanor. Gore often had stronger answers but repelled many viewers with his aggressive personal style, attempts at extending his speaking time, and eye movements. Viewers seemed more comfortable with Bush's relaxed style. Whereas the initial polls had indicated a Gore victory in the first debate, subsequent polls demonstrated that voters were changing their opinion and increasingly viewing Bush as the winner.

Cheney's effective performance in the vice presidential debate helped Bush answer the competence question and set the stage for one of the most significant of Gore's missed opportunities, the foreign policy component of the second debate. Network polls indicated viewers saw Bush as the winner of the second debate in the wake of Gore's anemic performance. The numerous agreements of the two candidates on issues of international significance and the realization by many voters that Cheney and Colin Powell would be major actors in a Bush administration diluted the advantages Gore might have attained from incumbency. This debate gave Bush an invaluable opportunity for demonstrating competence on an important aspect of the presidency, and he seized it. Finally, most polls indicated that viewers saw Gore as the winner of the third and last debate, but this was of little consequence in light of the outcomes of the earlier ones.

Bush took the lead in the Gallup-CNN-*USA Today* tracking poll after the first debate and held it until the final days before the election. His daily average during the final month of the campaign was 47.8 percent, which was very close to his actual vote tally of 47.9 percent. Bush seemed to have mastered the dilemma of the opposition party nominee by convincing enough of the people who had favored him during the summer months that he was qualified for the presidency. He nearly lost the election, however. Two of the three previous opposition party nominees, Kennedy in 1960 and Nixon in 1968, had seen their leads decline during the final hours before election day as undecided voters began moving in the direction of the vice president. The same pattern seemed to be occurring again in 2000 as

Gore began rising in the polls during the concluding weekend. Gore had averaged about 43 percent in the tracking polls for nearly one month but gained with every poll during these closing days. The final polls of CBS and NBC had Gore ahead and those of ABC and CNN showed Bush with a small lead. State polls showed Gore as taking the lead in a number of key states, including Pennsylvania, Michigan, Wisconsin, Washington, and Florida. Other than Florida, Gore won them all. Unlike Kennedy and Nixon, Bush does not seem to have held off the late surge of undecided voters to his rival. With the Florida electoral vote, however, he became the third opposition party nominee in the television age to win the presidency at the expense of a sitting vice president.

The presidential election of 2000 ended with a split decision and without a clear winner, thus setting up a legal and constitutional process that ended with a five to four Supreme Court ruling in which partisanship was a significant factor. George W. Bush owes part of his victory to the outcomes of elections of the immediate past. These included Florida elections that produced a Republican secretary of state who could rule on recounts and certification in ways favorable to Bush. It also included other Florida elections that chose a Republican legislature that might have aided Bush by demanding that its alternative slate of electors be seated had Gore triumphed in the recounts. Finally, Bush reaped the benefits of previous Republican presidential victories because the winners of those elections—Richard Nixon, Ronald Reagan, and George Bush—had appointed five Supreme Court justices who ruled in his favor in what proved to be the final event of election 2000.

Despite these unusual features, the 2000 election was remarkably consistent with other tallies of the television age. It clearly falls into a category that includes 1960, 1968, and 1988, which this writer calls "elections with surrogate incumbents." This election was similar to the previous ones in several significant ways that demonstrate the existence of a pattern that is likely to be repeated in future years. The modern presidency's institutional and rhetorical powers and the pervasiveness of television as a medium of political communication have helped transform national elections into referendums on the performance and personality of the incumbent. Mediated incumbency, the strength of incumbency and the manner in which television news media interpret and transmit it to their viewing audiences, is now the leading determinant of the outcomes of television age presidential elections. Although most elections involve an actual incumbent's seeking another term, occasional elections do not. The power of the presidency has become so vast that even these occasional elections can now be explained by mediated incumbency. Elections with surrogate incumbents exhibit three recurring features, all of which were present in 2000. One is the nomination of the vice president as the standard bearer of the presidential party; a second is the ability of the opposition party to unite behind the vague but unifying appeals of a candidate who holds out the promise of victory. Last—and the factor that eventually decides the outcome—is the ability of the two major party nominees to overcome a dilemma that is unique to their position of incumbent or challenger. This last feature places the outcome squarely in the realm of the personal skills of the participants, a feature that virtually guarantees a close election.

Three of the four vice presidents who sought to succeed the retiring incumbent fell short in their quest, although all lost exceptionally close elections. The elections of 1960, 2000, and 1968, in that order, were the three closest elections of the past one hundred years. The fact that each involved a vice president is no accident but resulted from the ambiguous nature of elections in which a surrogate who has been overshadowed by the president for many years seeks to succeed that same president. The surrogate must convince voters that he is more than an understudy: he must convince them that he is a leader in his own right. He must do this in a way that separates him from the incumbent but does not dilute the advantages of incumbency. He must defend the record of the administration of which he is an integral part, but he cannot use the institutional and rhetorical powers of the modern presidency to make his case to the American people. This is a difficult task, as illustrated by the fact that three of the four vice presidents who have attempted it have ultimately failed. The fact that their losses were so close, and that Gore might have succeeded had it not been for the troubles in Florida, indicates that possession of the vice presidency is not a political albatross with a guarantee of failure as demonstrated by the outcome of 1988. Perhaps ironically, the only vice president to win a surrogate incumbent election during the television age also helped advance the political career of the next opposition party nominee who would defeat a vice president, a governor who also happened to be his son.

SELECTED BIBLIOGRAPHY

ABC World News Tonight.

Abramson, Paul R., Aldrich, John H., and David W. Rohde. *Change and Continuity in the 1980 Elections*. Washington D.C.: Congressional Quarterly Press, 1982.

Abramson, Paul R., Aldrich, John H., and David W. Rohde. *Change and Continuity in the 1984 Elections*. Washington D.C.: Congressional Quarterly Press, 1986.

Abramson, Paul R., Aldrich, John H., and David W. Rohde. *Change and Continuity in the 1988 Elections*. Washington D.C.: Congressional Quarterly Press, 1990.

Aldrich, John H. *Why Parties?* Chicago: University of Chicago Press, 1995.

Ansolabehere, Stephen, and Shanto Iyengar. *Going Negative: How Political Advertisements Shrink and Polarize the Electorate*. New York: Free Press, 1995.

Ansolabehere, Stephen, Behr, Roy L., and Shanto Iyengar. *The Media Game: American Politics in the Television Age*. Boston: Allyn & Bacon, 1993.

Asher, Herbert B. *Presidential Elections and American Politics: Voters, Candidates, and Campaigns since 1952, 5th ed.* Pacific Grove, CA: Brooks/Cole, 1992.

Atherton, F. Christopher. *Media Politics: The News Strategies of Presidential Campaigns*. Lexington, MA: Lexington Books, 1984.

Barilleaux, Ryan J. *The Post-Modern Presidency*. New York: Praeger Press, 1988.

Barone, Michael, and Grant Ujifusa. *The Almanac of American Politics, 2000*. Washington, D.C.: National Journal, 1999.

Bartels, Larry M. *Presidential Primaries and the Dynamics of Public Choice*. Princeton, NJ: Princeton University Press, 1988.

Barzman, Sol. *Madmen and Geniuses: The Vice President of the United States*. Chicago: Follett, 1974.

Bennett, W. Lance. *The Governing Crisis: Media, Money, and Marketing in American Elections*. New York: St. Martin's Press, 1992.

Black, Earl, and Merle Black. *The Vital South: How Presidents Are Elected*. Cambridge, MA: Harvard University Press, 1992.

Brace, Paul, and Barbara Hinckley. *Follow the Leader: Opinion Polls and the Modern Presidency*. New York: Basic Books, 1992.

Buell, Emmete H., Jr., and Lee Sigelman. *Nominating the President*. Knoxville: University of Tennessee Press, 1991.

Burke, John P. *The Institutional Presidency*. Baltimore: Johns Hopkins University Press, 1992.

Busch, Andrew E. *Outsiders and Openness in the Presidential Nominating System*. Pittsburgh: University of Pittsburgh Press, 1997.

Campbell, Colin, and Bert Rockman, eds. *The Clinton Presidency: First Appraisals*. Chatham, NJ: Chatham House, 1995.

CBS Evening News.

Ceaser, James W. *Reforming the Reforms*. Cambridge, MA: Ballinger, 1992.

Ceaser, James W., and Andrew Busch. *Upside Down and Inside Out: The 1992 Elections and American Politics*. Lanham, MD: Rowman & Littlefield, 1993.

Ceaser, James W., and Andrew Busch. *Losing to Win: The 1996 Elections and American Politics*. Lanham, MD: Rowman & Littlefield, 1997.

Ceaser, James W. and Andrew E. Busch. *The Perfect Tie: The True Story of the 2000 Presidential Election*. Lanham, MD: Rowman & Littlefield, 2001.

Ceaser, James W., et al. "The Rise of the Rhetorical Presidency." *Presidential Studies Quarterly* 11 (Spring 1981), pp. 158–171.

Cogan, John. *The Budget Puzzle*. Stanford, CA: Stanford University Press, 1994.

Corrado, Anthony J. *Creative Campaigning: PAC's and the Presidential Selection Process*. Boulder, CO: Westview Press, 1992.

Cronin, Thomas, ed. *Inventing the American Presidency*. Lawrence, University of Kansas Press, 1989.

Cronin, Thomas. *The State of the Presidency*. 2nd ed. Boston: Little, Brown, 1980.

Cronin, Thomas E., and Michael A Genovese. *The Paradoxes of the American Presidency*. New York: Oxford University Press, 1998.

Crotty, William J., ed. *America's Choice: The Election of 1992*. Guilford, CT: Dushkin Publishing Group, 1992.

DeGregorio, William A. *The Complete Book of U.S. Presidents, 4th ed.* New York: Barricade Books, 1993.

Delli Carpini, Michael X. and Scott Keeter. *What Americans Know About Politics and Why It Matters*. New Haven, CT: Yale University Press, 1996.

Denton, Robert. *The Primetime Presidency of Ronald Reagan*. New York: Praeger, 1988.

Denton, Robert E., ed. *The 1992 Presidential Campaign: A Communication Perspective*. Westport, CT: Praeger, 1994.

Denton, Robert E. *The 1996 Presidential Campaign: A Communication Perspective*. Westport, CT: Praeger, 1998.

Denton, Robert E., and Rachel L. Holloway. *The Clinton Presidency: Images, Issues, and Communication Strategies*. Westport, CT: Praeger, 1996.

Dionne, E. J. *Why Americans Hate Politics*. New York: Simon & Schuster, 1991.

Dionne, E. J. *They Only Look Dead: Why Progressives Will Dominate the Next Political Era*. New York: Simon & Schuster, 1996.

DiSalle, Michael. *Second Choice*. New York: Hawthorn Books, 1966.

Dorman, Michael. *The Second Man: The Changing Role of the Vice Presidency*. New York: Delacorte Press, 1968.

Dover, E. D. *Presidential Elections in the Television Age: 1960–1992*. Westport, CT: Praeger, 1994.

Dover, E. D. *The Presidential Election of 1996: Clinton's Incumbency and Television*. Westport, CT: Praeger, 1998.

Duncan, Dayton. *Grass Roots: One Year in the Life of the New Hampshire Presidential Primary*. New York: Viking, 1991.

Edwards, George C., III. *The Public Presidency: The Pursuit of Popular Support*. New York: St. Martin's Press, 1983.

Edwards, George C., III and Wayne, Stephen J. *Presidential Leadership: Politics and Policy Making*. New York: St. Martin's Press, 1990.

Entman, Robert M. *Democracy Without Citizens: Media and the Decay of American Politics*. New York: Oxford University Press, 1989.

Fallows, James. *Breaking the News: How the Media Undermine American Democracy*. New York: Vintage Books, 1997.

Feerick, John D. *From Failing Hands: The Story of Presidential Succession*. New York: Fordham University Press, 1965.

Fiorina, Morris. *Retrospective Voting in American National Elections*. New Haven, CT: Yale University Press, 1981.

Fisher, Louis. *The Politics of Shared Power: Congress and the Executive*. 4th ed. College Station: Texas A&M University Press, 1993.

Foote, Joe. *Television Access and Political Power: The Networks, the Presidency, and the "Loyal Opposition."* New York: Praeger, 1990.

Gais, Thomas L. *Improper Influence: Campaign Finance Law, Political Interest Groups, and the Problem of Equality*. Ann Arbor: University of Michigan Press, 1996.

Gallup-CNN-*USA Today* Polls.

Gans, Herbert J. *Deciding What's News*. New York: Vintage, 1980.

Geer, John G. *Nominating Presidents: An Evaluation of Voters and Primaries*. Westport, CT: Greenwood, 1989.

Germond, Jack W. and Jules Witcover. *Blue Smoke and Mirrors: How Reagan Won and Why Carter Lost the Election of 1980*. New York: Viking Press, 1981.

Germond, Jack W. and Jules Witcover. *Wake Us When It's Over: Presidential Politics of 1984*. New York: Macmillan, 1985.

Germond, Jack W., and Jules Witcover. *Whose Broad Stripes and Bright Stars: The Trivial Pursuit of the Presidency 1988*. New York: Warner Books, 1989.

Germond, Jack W., and Jules Witcover. *Mad as Hell: Revolt at the Ballot Box, 1992*. New York: Warner Books, 1993.

Ginsberg, Benjamin. *The Captive Public: How Mass Opinion Promotes State Power*. New York: Basic Books, 1986.

Goldstein, Joel. *The Modern American Vice Presidency: The Transformation of a Political Institution*. Princeton, NJ: Princeton University Press, 1982.

Graber, Doris, McQuail, Denis, and Pippa Norris. *The Politics of News: The News of Politics*. Washington, D.C.: CQ Press, 1998.

Hadley, Arthur T. *The Invisible Primary*. Englewood Cliffs, NJ: Prentice Hall, 1973.

Hansen, Richard. *The Year We Had No President*. Lincoln: University of Nebraska Press, 1962.

Hart, John. *The Presidential Branch: From Washington to Clinton*, 2nd ed. Chatham, NJ: Chatham Hall, 1995.

Hart, Roderick P. *The Sound of Leadership: Presidential Communication in the Modern Age*. Chicago: University of Chicago Press, 1987.

Harwood, Michael. *In the Shadow of Presidents: The American Vice Presidency and Succession System*. Philadelphia: Lippincott, 1966.

Hatfield, Mark. *Vice Presidents of the United States: 1788–1993*. Washington, D.C.: U.S. Government Printing Office, 1997.

Healy, Diana Dixon. *American's Vice Presidents: Our First Forty-Three Vice Presidents and How They Got to Be Number Two*. New York: Atheneum, 1984.

Heard, Alexander. *Made in America: The Nomination and Election of Presidents*. New York: HarperCollins, 1991.

Hertsgaard, Mark. *On Bended Knee: The Press and the Reagan Presidency*. New York: Farrer, Straus, & Giroux, 1988.

Hinckley, Barbara. *The Symbolic Presidency: How Presidents Portray Themselves*. London: Routledge, 1990.

Hoffstetter, Richard. *Bias in the News: Network Television Coverage of the 1972 Election Campaign*. Columbus: Ohio State University Press, 1976.

Ippolito, Daniel. *Uncertain Legacies: Federal Budget Policy from Roosevelt through Reagan*. Charlottesville: University Press of Virginia, 1990.

Iyengar, Shanto. *Is Anyone Responsible? How Television Frames Political Issues*. Chicago: University of Chicago Press, 1991.

Iyengar, Shanto and Donald R. Kinder. *News That Matters: Television and American Public Opinion*. Chicago: University of Chicago Press, 1987.

Jackson, John S., III, and William Crotty. *The Politics of Presidential Selection*. New York: HarperCollins, 1996.

Jacobson, Gary C., and Samuel Kernell. *The 2000 Elections and Beyond*. Washington, D.C.: CQ Press, 2000.

Jamison, Kathleen Hall. *Eloquence in the Electronic Age: The Transformation of Political Speechmaking*. New York: Oxford University Press, 1988.

Jamison, Kathleen Hall. *Packaging the Presidency: A History and Criticism of Presidential Campaign Advertising*. Oxford: Oxford University Press, 1996.

Jamieson, Kathleen Hall. *Everything You Think You Know about Politics . . . and Why You're Wrong*. New York: Basic Books, 2000.

Jones, Charles O. *The Presidency in a Separated System*. Washington, D.C.: Brookings Institution, 1994.

Just, Marion R., et al. *Crosstalk: Citizens, Candidates, and the Media in a Presidential Campaign*. Chicago: University of Chicago Press, 1996.

Keeter, Scott, and Cliff Zukin. *Uninformed Choice: The Failure of the New Presidential Nominating System*. New York: Praeger, 1983.

Keith, Bruce, et al. *The Myth of the Independent Voter*. Berkeley: University of California Press, 1992.

Kellerman, Barbara. *The Political Presidency*. New York: Oxford University Press, 1984.

Kerbel, Matthew Robert. *Edited for Television: CNN, ABC, and the 1992 Presidential Campaign*. Boulder, CO: Westview Press, 1994.

Kernall, Samual. *Going Public: New Strategies of Presidential Leadership*, 2nd ed. Washington, D.C.: Congressional Quarterly Press, 1993.

Kettl, Donald. *Deficit Politics*. New York: Macmillan, 1992.

Ladd, Everett Carll, Jr. *Where Have All the Voters Gone? The Fracturing of America's Political Parties*, 2nd ed. New York: Norton, 1982.

Lavrekas, Paul J., and Jack K. Holley, eds. *Polling and Presidential Election Coverage*. Newbury Park, CA: Sage, 1991.

Lichter, S. Robert, Amundson, Daniel, and Richard Noyes. *The Video Campaign: Network Coverage of the 1988 Primaries*. Washington, D.C.: American Enterprise Institute for Public Policy Research, 1988.

Lichter, S. Robert, and Richard Noyes. *Campaign '96: The Media and the Candidates*. Washington, D.C.: Center for Media and Public Affairs, 1996.

Lichter, S. Robert, and Richard Noyes. *Media Monitor*. Washington, D.C.: Center for Media and Public Affairs, 1996.

Lichtman, Allan J. *The Keys to the White House*. Lanham, MD: Lexington Books, 2000.

Light, Paul C. *Vice Presidential Power: Advice and Influence in the White House*. Baltimore: Johns Hopkins University Press, 1984.

Light, Paul C. *The President's Agenda: Domestic Policy Choice from Kennedy to Reagan*. Baltimore: Johns Hopkins University Press, 1991.

Lowi, Theodore J. *The Personal President: Power Invested, Promise Unfulfilled*. Ithaca, NY: Cornell University Press, 1985.

Lowi, Theordore J. *The End of the Republican Era*. Norman: University of Oklahoma Press, 1995.

Maranto, Robert. *Politics and Bureaucracy in the Modern Presidency*. Westport, CT: Greenwood Press, 1993.

Mayer, William G. *The Divided Democrats: Ideological Unity, Party Reform, and Presidential Elections*. Boulder, CO: Westview Press, 1996.

Mayer, William G. *In Pursuit of the White House 2000: How We Choose Our Presidential Nominees*. New York: Chatham House Publishers, 2000.

McCubbins, Mathew D. *Under the Watchful Eye: Managing Presidential Campaigns in the Television Era*. Washington, D.C.: Congressional Quarterly Press, 1992.

Milkis, Sidney M. *The President and the Parties: The Transformation of the American Party System since the New Deal*. New York: Oxford University Press, 1993.

Milkis, Sidney M. and Nelson, Michael. *The American Presidency: Origins and Development, 1776–1993*. Washington, D.C.: Congressional Quarterly Press, 1994.

Nathan, Richard. *The Administrative Presidency*. New York: Macmillan Publishing, 1983.

Natoli, Marie. *American Prince, American Pauper: The Contemporary Vice Presidency in Perspective*. Westport, CT: Greenwood Press, 1985.

NBC Nightly News.

Nelson, Michael. *The Elections of 1984*. Washington, D.C.: Congressional Quarterly Press, 1985.

Nelson, Michael. *A Heartbeat Away: Report of the Twentieth Century Fund Task Force on the Vice Presidency*. New York: Priority Press Publications. 1988.

Nelson, Michael. *The Elections of 1988*. Washington, D.C.: Congressional Quarterly Press, 1989.

Nelson, Michael. *The Elections of 1992*. Washington, D.C.: Congressional Quarterly Press, 1993.

Nelson, Michael. *The Election of 1996*. Washington, D.C.: Congressional Quarterly Press, 1997.

Nelson, Michael. *The Elections of 2000*. Washington, D.C.: Congressional Quarterly Press, 2001.

Nelson, Michael, and Sidney M. Milkis. *The American Presidency: Origins and Development 1776–1993*, 2nd ed. Washington, D.C.: CQ Press, 1994.

Neustadt, Richard. *Presidential Power and the Modern Presidents: The Politics of Leadership from Roosevelt to Reagan*. New York: Free Press, 1990.

Orren, Gary R. and Polsby, Nelson W. *Media and Momentum: The New Hampshire Primary and Nomination Politics*. Chatham, NJ: Chatham House, 1987.

Owen, Diana. *Media Messages in American Presidential Elections*. Westport, CT: Greenwood Press, 1991.

Palmer, Niall A. *The New Hampshire Primary and the American Electoral Process*. Westport, CT: Praeger, 1997.

Parenti, Michael. *Make-Believe Media: The Politics of Entertainment*. New York: St. Martin's Press, 1992.

Patterson, Thomas E. *The Mass Media Election: How Americans Choose Their President*. New York: Praeger Press, 1980.

Patterson, Thomas E. *Out of Order*. New York: Knopf, 1993.

Peterson, Mark. Legislating Together. Cambridge, MA: Harvard University Press, 1990.

Pfiffner, James P. *The Modern Presidency*. New York: St. Martin's Press, 1994.

Phillips, Kevin P. *Mediacracy: American Parties and Politics in the Communications Age*. New York: Doubleday & Company, 1975.

Phillips, Kevin P. *The Politics of Rich and Poor: Wealth and the American Electorate in the Reagan Aftermath*. New York: Random House, 1990.

Pomper, Gerald M. *The Election of 1980: Reports and Interpretations*. Chatham, NJ: Chatham House Publishers, 1981.

Pomper, Gerald M. *The Election of 1984: Reports and Interpretations*. Chatham, NJ: Chatham House Publishers, 1985.

Pomper, Gerald M. *The Election of 1988: Reports and Interpretations*. Chatham, NJ: Chatham House Publishers, 1989.

Pomper, Gerald M. *The Election of 1992: Reports and Interpretations*. Chatham, NJ: Chatham House Publishers, 1993.

Pomper, Gerald M. *The Elections of 1996: Reports and Interpretations*. Chatham, NJ: Chatham House Publishers, 1997.

Pomper, Gerald M. *The Election of 2000: Reports and Interpretations*. New York: Chatham House Publishers, 2001.

Popkin, Samuel L. *The Reasoning Voter: Communication and Persuasion in Presidential Campaign*. Chicago: University of Chicago Press, 1991.

Riccards, Michael P. *The Ferocious Engine of Democracy: A History of the American Presidency*. New York: Madison Books, 1995.

Robinson, Michael J. and Margaret A. Sheehan. *Over the Wire and on TV: CBS and UPI in Campaign '80*. New York: Russell Sage, 1983.

Sabato, Larry J. *Feeding Frenzy: How Attack Journalism Has Transformed American Politics*. New York: Free Press, 1991.

Sabato, Larry J. *Toward the Millennium: The Elections of 1996*. Boston: Allyn & Bacon, 1997.

Salmore, Stephen A., and Barbara G. Salmore. *Candidates, Parties, and Campaigns*. Washington, D.C.: Congressional Quarterly Press, 1985.

Savage, James D. *Balanced Budgets and American Politics*. Ithaca, NY: Cornell University Press, 1988.

Schick, Allan. *The Federal Budget: Politics, Policy, Process*. Washington, D.C.: Brookings Institution, 1994.

Schramm, Martin. *The Great American Video Game: Presidential Politics in the Television Age*. New York: Morrow, 1987.

Seligman, Lester G., and Cary R. Covington. *The Coalitional Presidency*. Chicago: The Dorsey Press, 1989.

Shull, Steven. *The Two Presidencies*. Chicago: Nelson-Hall, 1991.

Sindler, Allan. *Unchosen Presidents: The Vice-President and Other Frustrations of Presidential Succession*. Berkeley: University of California Press, 1976.

Skowronek, Stephen. *The Politics Presidents Make*. Cambridge, MA: Harvard University Press, 1993.

Smith, Larry David, and Dan Nimmo. *Cordial Concurrence: Orchestrating National Conventions in the Telepolitical Age*. New York: Praeger, 1991.

Smoller, Fred. The Six O'Clock Presidency: "Patterns of Network News Coverage of the President." *Presidential Studies Quarterly* XVI (1986), pp. 31–49.

Sorauf, Frank. *Inside Campaign Finance: Myths and Realities*. New Haven, CT: Yale University Press, 1992.

Southwick, Leslie. *Presidential Also-Rans and Running Mates: 1988 through 1996*, 2nd ed. Jefferson, NC: McFarland, 1998.

Spitzer, Robert. *President and Congress: Executive Hegemony at the Crossroads of American Government*. New York: McGraw-Hill, 1993.

Squire, Peverell. *The Iowa Caucuses and the Presidential Nominating Process*. Boulder, CO: Westview Press, 1989.

Tally, Steve. *Bland Ambition: From Adams to Quayle—the Cranks, Crooks, Tax Cheats, and Golfers Who Made It to Vice President*. San Diego: Harcourt Brace Jovanovich, 1992.

Taylor, Paul. *See How They Run: Electing the President in an Age of Mediaocracy*. New York: Knopf, 1990.

Teixeira, Ruy A. *The Disappearing American Voter*. Washington, D.C.: Brookings Institution, 1992.

Teixeria, Ruy A. and Joel Rogers. *America's Forgotten Majority: Why the White Working Class Still Matters*. New York: Basic Books, 2000.

Troy, Gil. *See How They Run: The Changing Role of the Presidential Candidate*. New York: Free Press, 1991.

Tulis, Jeffrey. *The Rhetorical Presidency*. Princeton, NJ: Princeton University Press, 1988.

Turner, Michael. *The Vice President as a Policy-Maker: Rockefeller in the Ford White House*. Westport, CT: Greenwood Press, 1982.

Walch, Timothy. *At the President's Side: The Vice Presidency in the Twentieth Century*. Columbia: University of Missouri Press, 1997.

Waldrup, Carole Chandler. *The Vice Presidents: Biographies of the 45 Men Who Held the Second Highest Office in the United States*. Jefferson, NC: McFarland, 1996.

Waterman, Richard. *Presidential Influence and the Administrative State*. Knoxville: University of Tennessee Press, 1989.

Wattenberg, Martin P. *The Decline of American Political Parties: 1952–1980*. Cambridge, MA: Harvard University Press, 1990.

Wattenberg, Martin P. *The Rise of Candidate-Centered Politics: Presidential Elections in the 1980's*. Cambridge, MA: Harvard University Press, 1991.

Waugh, Edgar. *Second Consul: The Vice Presidency, Our Greatest Political Problem*. Indianapolis: Bobbs-Merrill, 1956.

Wayne, Stephen J. *The Road to the White House 2000: The Politics of Presidential Elections*. New York: St. Martin's Press, 2000.

Wekon, Thomas J. *The Politicizing Presidency*. Lawrence: University of Kansas Press, 1995.

West, Darrell M. *Air Wars: Television Advertising in Election Campaigns, 1952–1996*, 2nd ed. Washington, D.C.: CQ Press, 1997.

White, Theodore H. *The Making of the President 1960*. New York: Atheneum, 1961.

White, Theodore H. *The Making of the President 1964*. New York: Atheneum, 1965.

White, Theodore H. *The Making of the President 1968*. New York: Atheneum, 1969.

White, Theodore H. *The Making of the President 1972*. New York: Atheneum, 1973.

White, Theodore H. *America in Search of Itself: The Making of the President 1956–1980*. New York: Harper & Row, 1981.

Wildavsky, Aaron, *The Beleaguered Presidency*. Lawrence: University of Kansas Press, 1991.

Wildavsky, Aaron, and Naomi Caiden. *The New Politics of the Budgetary Process*, 4th ed. New York: Longman, 2001.

Williams, Irving. *The American Vice Presidency: New Look*. Garden City, NY: Doubleday, 1954.

Williams, Irving. *The Rise of the Vice Presidency*. Washington, D.C.: Public Affairs Press, 1956.

Winebrenner, Hugh. *The Iowa Precinct Caucuses: The Making of a Media Event*, 2nd ed. Ames: Iowa State University Press, 1998.

Witcover, Jules. *Marathon: The Pursuit of the Presidency 1972–1976*. New York: Viking Press, 1977.

Witcover, Jules. *Crapshoot: Rolling the Dice on the Vice Presidency from Adams and Jefferson to Truman and Quayle*. New York: Crown Publishers, 1992.

Witcover, Jules. *No Way to Pick a President*. New York: Farrar, Straus & Giroux, 1999.

Young, Donald. *American Roulette: The History and Dilemma of the Vice Presidency*. New York: Viking Press, 1974.

INDEX

About the Author

E. D. DOVER is Professor of Political Science, Public Policy and Administration at Western Oregon University. He is the author of *Presidential Elections in the Television Age* (Praeger, 1994) and *The Presidential Election of 1996* (Praeger, 1998).